BEYOND THE WELFARE STATE
Economic Planning and Its
International Implications

Storrs Lectures on Jurisprudence
Yale Law School, 1958

BEYOND THE
WELFARE STATE

Economic Planning and Its
International Implications

by GUNNAR MYRDAL

New Haven, Connecticut
YALE UNIVERSITY PRESS
1960

PREFACE

The World Perspective

This little book is concerned with the trend towards economic planning in the rich and progressive Western countries and with the international implications of this trend. In Part One an attempt is made to throw some light on the interplay of social forces which have resulted in this trend, and on the type of national community which is emerging. Part Two is devoted to the effects of national economic planning in these countries on their economic relations with each other and with the rest of the world, in particular with the underdeveloped countries in the non-Soviet world.

National economic planning is, of course, an even more prominent feature of economic policies in the countries of the Soviet orbit. In the underdeveloped countries outside the Soviet orbit, national economic planning is almost everywhere a commonly acclaimed ideal, even if its implementation is usually, as yet, haphazard or absent. But, in the broadest world perspective, it is true to say that economic planning is becoming increasingly the common experience of people who live together in organized society.

Indeed, the rapid spread to all countries, rich and poor, of an urge for economic development, and the increasing concern of all governments, democratic and autocratic, to initiate and to coordinate public policies in order to bring about economic development, are among the indications that we are now witnessing a fundamental convergence in

v

our thoughts and aims. The differences in circumstances are immense, it is true: differences in modes and levels of living, and in the shape of the communities—national, local, and sectional—by which the destinies of the individuals are intertwined. In some respects, these differences are increasing; in all respects, our awareness of them is increasing. The ideological clashes are mounting and we see apocalyptic perils of world cataclysm. The rising awareness of differences and inequalities, as well as the ideological and political clashes, are themselves largely the result of speedier and better communications, which have also allowed the more intensive interplay of thoughts and aspirations—of which the worldwide trend towards economic planning is itself one of the manifestations. It is also evident that the intense and universal realization of international competition and conflict provides a further spur towards economic planning in all countries.

Pursuing such very broad considerations, it would not, of course, be without interest to inquire what can be ascertained about economic planning in general, wherever in the world and under whatever conditions it takes place. The economist is bound to stress, however, that as things are today there are crucial differences in methods of economic planning, both between the Soviet and the non-Soviet world and between the rich and the poor non-Soviet countries. These differences cannot be overlooked in any discussion that proceeds beyond generalities of little practical consequence.

The three orbits have entirely different types of planning. Each is now developing in a different historical, material, cultural, ideological, institutional, and political setting. Economic planning is facing widely different problems for establishing goals, choosing means, fixing targets, and implementing policies. Decisions on the public policies implied in planning are arrived at in very different ways, and the sanctions applied in order to carry them into effect are also different.

The borderline separating the communist countries from the rest of the world is clearly drawn by the governments of those countries themselves, and does not need any elaboration.

The division between rich and poor non-Soviet countries is a matter of statistical gradation, but is hardly less clear-cut. Any grouping of the non-Soviet countries according to real national income per head reveals that there are two fairly distinct economic classes of nations: one small upper-class group of nations which is comparatively very well off, and one much larger lower-class group which is very poor. Between the individual nations in both groups there are differences in levels of average income, though not so large as to invalidate the distinction made; there is also a smaller middle-class group of nations. "Income" stands here as an approximate indicator of economic well-being. As between the two main groups, there is a pronounced inequality in nutrition, housing, education, health, and all other levels of living. The poor countries generally show greater internal economic inequalities, and their social stratification is usually more inegalitarian and rigid.

In the first group, which I will refer to as the "rich" or the "Western" countries, belong the countries in North America, Australasia, and Northwestern and Central Europe; their total populations comprise little more than one-sixth of the total world population outside the Soviet orbit. All the rest are here reckoned to be the "poor" countries, except for the few scattered middle-class countries: a few in Latin America, in Asia only Japan and, perhaps soon, Israel, and those regions in Southern Europe which are not plainly underdeveloped. When I use the term "underdeveloped," it is to be understood as a synonym of "poor."

These differences in economic status between two main classes of nations in the non-Soviet world, as they exist today, are a result of the fact that the upper-class group of nations have enjoyed rapid development for several generations. In spite of occasional depressions and wars, the trend of production and income has been rapidly and steadily ascending in these nations; levels of living have been rising, and at the same time greater equality of opportunity for the individual has gradually ensued, though with different speed in the several nations of this group. Meanwhile the poor nations have on the whole been developing much more slowly, if at all. Even now their development is largely lagging, and some of them are stagnating or declining. The capital formation and industrialization which are taking place in the non-Soviet world are mainly a continued increase of productive capacity of the already rich and industrialized countries. The international class gap has been widening all the time, and it is widening today.

The division of the world into two distinct economic classes of nations is thus of long standing. Those few nations which today form the exclusive upper-class of world society were already at the top at the beginning of this century and still earlier, though they were not as much richer as they are now. The countries in the Soviet orbit then mostly belonged to the orbit of underdeveloped countries, while a few of them had attained, or were attaining, a precarious middle-class position. In the non-Soviet world, there have been hardly any decisive movements across the class line, though, of course, very significant shifts of relative position within the groups have taken place. In the upper-class group, the United States has been steadily climbing in wealth and welfare, not only absolutely but also relative to the other countries in the group. Following closely are the white dominions, particularly Canada, and also the Scandinavian countries, while Britain and France have lost in relative class status. During the last decade, Western Germany has been surging ahead, after her total collapse in World War II, so that she is regaining, and will perhaps soon exceed, her earlier relative class position. But all of these nations are by now very much better off and enjoy average real incomes which are double or more than double the figures reached at the beginning of the century, when they were already far ahead of the underdeveloped world. And they are steadily and rapidly progressing still further. From a world point of view, the important thing to stress is that they are all relatively very rich and getting richer all the time.

It is only since the last war that the problems of economic development and planning for development in the poor countries have come to the fore, and this has been the result of the huge political changes which have taken place. More particularly, this new direction of economic discussion can be traced to the disintegration of the colonial power system and to the Great Awakening in the underdeveloped countries themselves. These peoples were, of course, just about as poor and in need of development twenty or fifty years ago as they are today, but the power situation at that time did not give practical political significance to their development problems. Today, however, a very large and ever-increasing part of the work of economists and other social scientists is directed to these problems.

Within the stream of this big reorientation of the social sciences, the author is engaged in studying the development problems in one large region of the underdeveloped world, South Asia. When I had the honor of being invited

to give the Storrs Lectures for 1958 at Yale University, my
first inclination was to use this occasion to try to characterize the differences between planning in the three main
orbits of the world. I ended, however, by falling back on
my old knowledge of what has happened and is happening
in the Western countries, sharpened somewhat, I hope,
by my more recently acquired acquaintance with countries
in a very different situation.

In these lectures I am thus mainly restricting myself to
an attempt to analyze the trend towards planning in the
rich countries, and the international implications of this
trend, with nothing more than very general hints about
how different conditions and policies are in the other two
orbits. For one thing, the larger subject turned out to be
too unwieldy to be satisfactorily handled in four lectures.
I also felt that I did not want to commit myself to too
definite formulations on specific issues of planning in the
underdeveloped countries while still struggling with those
problems, as this might not be conducive to keeping subjectively as free in further explorations as I should wish.

I have felt a need, however, to preface this little book on
the trend towards planning in the rich and progressive
Western countries by stressing the fundamental differences,
not only between the non-Soviet and the Soviet orbits
but also between the two main classes of nations outside
the Soviet orbit. For doing this, and also for including some
sections and short chapters in the text carrying this thought
a few stages further, I have several reasons. One is that the
existence of these differences and their tendency to increase
as a result of the continual and rapid development in the
rich countries are tremendously important elements in the
world setting which should always be borne in mind, even
when studying only one part of the non-Soviet world.
Another reason is that, because these differences are so big,
analogies drawn from one type of country are apt to be

misleading if they are applied to another type. In this
connection, even if I am not in a position to make my
point in the most specific terms, I want to warn against
such analogies and against the utilization of a more general
conception of economic growth and of planning for
economic development than is warranted by the facts,
and to give at least the general reasons for these warnings.
My third reason is the need for an excuse and explanation
when treating the problems of planning in the Western
countries in such a very general way as I have attempted.
The differences in planning among the several countries
within this group are small indeed when compared with
those between all of them taken together and the rest of
the world. This gives sense and, I believe, importance to
trying to find, and set in high relief, what all the rich
countries have in common.

Lastly, I should mention that in preparing the manu-
script for publication, I have permitted myself to enlarge
considerably upon some parts of the four lectures as they
were originally delivered. In this connection I have drawn
also on some earlier papers: The Ludwig Mond Lecture,
1950, "The Trend Towards Economic Planning," *The
Manchester School of Economic and Social Studies*, Jan-
uary 1951; The Kurt Lewin Memorial Award Lecture,
1952, "Psychological Impediments to Effective International Co-operation," *The Journal of Social Issues*, Sup-
plement Series, No. 6, 1952; the Foundation Day Address
at the Delhi School of Economics, 1956, "Problems of Economic Integration," unpublished; The Dyson Lectures,
1957, "Economic Nationalism and Internationalism," *The
Australian Outlook*, December 1957; a lecture at The New
School for Social Research 1956, "Aid and Trade," *The
American Scholar*, Spring 1957; two radio talks over the
Australian ABC on the "International Organisations in the
Economic Field," published in Swedish in *Svenska Dag-*

bladet, 1957; and my opening address on "Social Needs and the Resources to Meet Them in Under-developed Countries" at the meeting in Tokyo of the *International Association for Social Work,* 1958. For the permission to use this material I am grateful to the editors of the journals mentioned. In various stages of preparing the text for publication I have benefited much from the criticism of colleagues and friends including, Mr. Michael Lipton, who has also prepared the text for printing.

G.M.

Contents

Preface: The World Perspective   v

INTRODUCTION

  1. *A Stale and Confused Controversy*   3

PART ONE: THE TREND TOWARDS PLANNING

  2. *The Impact of the International Crises*   19
  3. *Internal Forces*   30
  4. *The Organizational State*   43
  5. *Planning in the Welfare State*   62
  6. *The State and the Individual*   84
  7. *Planning and Democracy*   103
  8. *Economic Planning in the Two Other Orbits*   119

PART TWO: INTERNATIONAL IMPLICATIONS OF NATIONAL PLANNING

  9. *International Disintegration*   139
  10. *Economic Nationalism in the Western World*   159
  11. *The Institutional and Psychological Levels*   177
  12. *Economic Nationalism in the Underdeveloped Countries*   200
  13. *Towards a New World Stability*   226
  14. *The Growth of Inter-Governmental Economic Organizations*   265

Introduction

1

A Stale and Confused Controversy

In the Western countries, one of the least informed and least intelligent controversies of our time has concerned the question whether we should have a "free" or a "planned" economy. This controversy has always been unrealistic and is becoming ever more so. Life in our national communities and our actual practical problems cannot be dealt with adequately and relevantly in these antithetical terms.

A Tautology

The very words used in this protracted public debate remind us of its origin in intellectually unclean philosophies of bygone times. The term "planned economy" contains, of course, a plain tautology, since the word "economy" by itself implies a disposal of available means towards reaching an end or a goal. To add "planned" in order to indicate that this coordination of activities has a purpose, does not make sense; at lease it cannot be good usage. Language, as we know, is full of illogicalities. But seldom do they derive, as in this particular case, directly from the learned idiom.

The reason why this particular tautology became necessary to express the thought lies in the meaning of the term "economy" as it was used in liberal economic theory from its inception more than two hundred years ago. In that theory it expressed the teleological conception of the

non-purposive achievement of a purpose, and was thereby
deprived of its original and common meaning as a planning
or household activity.

This conception of an automatic direction of economic
life towards an inherent goal, i.e. of a "non-planned planning," was the fundamental metaphysical value notion
underlying that theory, as it had developed within the
framework of the philosophies of natural law and utilitarianism. It flourished particularly in those branches of
economic speculation which we group under the collective
term *laissez-faire*. To express the contrary political attitude, *viz.,* that the economic process should be intentionally directed, the tautological expression "economic
planning" was then invented.

The Innocence of Marx

This idea of economic planning has commonly been
related to Marx and Marxism. This is a factual mistake.
I do not even believe that the term "economic planning"
or "planned economy," *Planwirtschaft,* can be found in
Marx's works. Marx was not a planner but an analyst and
a forecaster. In the former capacity, he has had an immense
influence on the fundamental approaches to the study of
history and sociology; in economics his influence has been
particularly strong on theories of business fluctuations
and development. As I have pointed out in an earlier
connection, Marx's influence has been especially strong
in the American social sciences, and strongest in sociology,
though it has often been unconscious and seldom suffi-
ciently acknowledged.

As a forecaster, Marx shared the common destiny of
all prophets: to be belied by events. And while we continuously enjoy pointing out that Marx's prophecies,
made more than a hundred years ago, did not come true,

we are apt to forget that it is a sign of his genius as an analyst that he foresaw so many relatively important things as accurately as he did.

What is remembered above all is Marx's grandiose vision that, as industrialization proceeded, natural forces —aided by those far-sighted propagandists and organizers who, in a Hegelian fashion, anticipated and fell in line with the natural development or, rather, acted as its spearhead—would cause a violent revolution when the time was ripe for the impoverished masses to "expropriate the expropriators." The proletariat in temporary possession of dictatorial power would then destroy the state as being the institutional form of exploitative class society.

To this main forecast Marx made many qualifications and reservations which need not bother us in this connection. More important is the fact that Marx left in great vagueness what would happen next. There is a strand in his thoughts, it is true, that claims that the state would "wither away," as Engels put it, and be followed by a situation which Marx occasionally referred to as the "realm of freedom." Focusing our attention on these often-quoted expressions, and simplifying the ideas of a writer who was anything but uncomplicated in his thinking, it would be tempting to characterize Marx not only as a fatalist but even, basically, as an anarchist.

But there are clear indications that the "state," which Marx expected to disappear after the revolution, was the particular social order which was biased by the domination of the rich, rather than the social order of the state as such. Moreover, Marx certainly thought of that other state, which would come to succeed the class state, as an organized one, based on those new social relations that would unfold under conditions of abundance and economic equality. When I nevertheless stress that Marx was not a planner, my sole intention is to point to the fact that Marx never developed these latter ideas beyond the most general, abstract, and vague formulations, which can even escape the reader altogether if he is not looking for them. By his empiricism as much as by his conception of history, Marx was constrained from becoming more specific about a future state and state policies, which were on the other side of such enormous changes as the revolution and its immediate aftermath.

There is thus, throughout Marx's writings, very little thought given to the actual organization of that end product of the natural development of capitalist society, the free and classless communist society where the rule is: "from each according to his ability, to each according to his need." Neither was he interested in clarifying the techniques of policy which the temporary dictatorial government in power after the revolution would employ to transform the old class state into the new egalitarian one. And the very idea of introducing, in the capitalist state, peacefully and without revolution—in fact, as a substitute for the revolution—coordinated public policies of such a far-reaching consequence that they could gradually bring the economy of a country to function in accordance with the majority interests of all the citizens, which today constitutes the essential idea of economic planning in the democratic Welfare States of the Western world, is what the Germans would call *systemfremd,* that is, entirely foreign to Marx's way of thinking.

To deny that the free and classless society was the implicit value premise for Marx's intellectual exertions is, of course, a hopeless attempt. It was from this point of view that he carried out the merciless vivisection of early capitalist society which takes up the bulk of his writings. But it should be noted that the same radical vision is at the basis of all liberalistic speculation from John Locke on, though the economists in the classical liberal line, by straining the logic, managed to make conservative compromises with their main value notion. This notion, however, remained ultra-radical, and these economists, despite their compromises, never retracted it in principle. Moreover, the non-purposive achievement of a purpose through a natural development, moving towards an end which is inherent in, and predetermined by, the facts as they already exist is the teleological conception underlying not only Marx's thinking but also the liberal economic doctrines in the classical line. Like everybody else in our long spiritual history—including, I am sure, the present writer and his present reader—Marx was conditioned by the dominant ideas of his age, even in his heresy, and was thus encompassed by the same fundamental metaphysical preconceptions, as was the whole school of economic liberalism.

Indeed, Marx, and even more emphatically Engels, condemned as "unscientific" the free-wheeling schemes of economic planning embraced by earlier French and English socialists. Marx's refusal to follow in their steps was not only due to the fact that their planning was carried out with too little consideration for economic, social, and political forces. There is in all planning, even if it were ever so earthily rooted in comprehensive studies of facts, an element of belief in reason as an independent force in history and in the freedom of choice by which man can change reality according to his design and so turn the course of future development. In essence, planning is an exercise in a non-deterministic conception of history, though it recognizes the limitations put up by existing conditions and forces and their causal interrelations.

Again, it is wrong to tie Marx to a simple doctrine of historical determinism. He was much too sophisticated a thinker to be kept within any of the doctrinal boxes which have been constructed for him by simplifying and vulgarizing his thoughts. But it is safe to say that Marx was enough of a determinist to prevent him from ever having become a planner. He was little disposed to consider planning, because he regarded capitalist society as incapable of reforming itself fundamentally; he also declined to indulge in drawing blueprints for a future and very different socialist society, emerging after the collapse of capitalism.

The Analogies from the Soviet Union

My thesis about Marx's complete innocence in regard to the modern idea of economic planning is not contradicted by what later happened in Russia. The revolution that broke out in that industrially retarded country towards the end of World War I was an historical event contrary to Marx's own predictions, for he had concluded that it was the maturing capitalism in advanced countries that would first run into political explosion. Nor did Marx foresee that, in Russia, the "dictatorship of the proletariat" that followed the revolution would not be a passing phase, but would be consolidating itself into a permanent and absolute state power. Yet this is what has happened in Russia; and despite Marx's vision this new state, maintained and strengthened its absolute power, and later on inaugurated a system of economic planning.

I shall have more to say later about the fact—already mentioned in the Preface—that there is a major difference between, on the one hand, the type of economic planning imposed by the totalitarian and monolithic Soviet government upon Russia in order to bring about a rapid industrialization of that initially backward country and, on the other hand, the type of coordinated economic policy which has gradually evolved in the Western countries. The difference between the two types of economic planning is so fundamental that analogies become false.

Nevertheless, such analogies have continually been made, and they have played a considerable role in the public controversy in the Western world concerning a "free" *versus* a "planned" economy. In the beginning they were sometimes invoked by the propagandists of a "planned" economy. Later on, as the political tension between the Western countries and the Soviet Union grew, they were often found useful as brickbats by those who stood for a "free" economy. In both cases they represented an irrational and confusing element in the discussion.

The Communists never make such analogies but maintain that there is a basic difference between the two types of economic policy. On this particular point I am inclined to agree with the Communists.

The Disparity Between Ideologies and Facts

In the United States, and to an only slightly lesser degree in all the other rich and economically progressive Western countries, public debate has at all times been dominated by the adherents of a "free" economy. As a quantitative measurement would show, the great bulk of speeches, popular pamphlets, articles in newspapers and periodicals and books on the issue, and the public pronounciamentos by political personalities in power or seeking power, have, even in recent generations, been directed against state control of economic life.

Interest groups and political parties that fought, often successfully, for protectionism or other large-scale state intervention were usually very careful not to argue their case in terms of a planned economy and state control of economic life. In their programs, socialist parties de-

manded nationalization of the means of production—the
most comprehensive system of planned economy; but they
often also requested free trade, without ever clarifying
very well how that mixture would work. In any case, as
soon as they even approached positions of power, they made
the tactical adjustment—presumably to popular opinion
—of playing down the former issue and presenting themselves as ordinary progressive political parties with the
emphasis on social reforms.

In more recent times the Great Depression, and, in
Europe, a short period towards the end of the last war
and a few years afterwards, formed interludes when the
idea of the usefulness of comprehensive state economic
planning tended to gain popular ground and became somewhat more respectable. But even the New Deal and similar
political movements in the other rich countries, particularly the social-democratic labour parties, did not come
out very definitely and clearly for a state-directed economy,
except in limited fields. In most circles, the idea of economic planning has been in disrepute most of the time
and, particularly in America, has almost carried connotations of intellectual and moral perversion and even political subversion. It has been a little like the stand on
virtue and sin in a Christian community, where of course,
in principle, the side taken by responsible persons cannot
be in doubt.

Several things have contributed to this ideological
situation: the consistent strength of the liberal heritage,
which I exemplified by pointing out how the idea of
planning had even to seek a tautological expression in
order to get out in the open; the mistaken assimilation of
economic planning to Marx and Marxism, with respect to
both of which Western societies had good reason to feel
uncomfortable; and the false analogies to economic planning in the Soviet Union, which was viewed with antipathy

from the beginning and which—except for a few years during the last war, when the Soviet Union was a cherished and widely idealized ally in the war against the fascist powers—became increasingly disliked as time went on and the cold war got under way.

The irony is, however, that meanwhile our national economies have become increasingly regulated, organized, and coordinated, i.e., "planned," to an extent nobody would have dreamt of a century, or even half a century, ago. As I shall later demonstrate, this has all happened in a piecemeal and almost offhand way. With us, governments, parliaments, and the citizenry at large have never made up their minds that this type of society was what they wanted. On the contrary, its gradual emergence through induced changes, all working in the direction of more and more social controls requiring an ever-increasing degree of planned coordination, has mostly proceeded to the accompaniment of loud proclamations from almost all sides that it was not to happen and that ours was a "free" economy. In all countries, these formulae have been the gospel for businessmen and politicians whose daily labor it was to regulate markets and frame new public interventions and also, in more recent times, to participate in the efforts to improve the coordination of all those acts of intervention with one another and with the general goals of national development.

The whole discussion of a "free" versus a "planned" economy has thus become strangely unrelated to reality and to the interests people feel and pursue in their daily lives. It should thus, perhaps, not be astonishing when we discover that in the Western countries people generally tend to keep themselves unaware of how far they have proceeded from a "free" economy: how very much regulatory intervention by organized society there actually is in their countries, and how important national economic planning of a pragmatic, non-comprehensive type has in fact become.

This situation of opportunistic unawareness, however, is unstable. Anybody who makes a plea for the ideals of a "free" economy and who then chooses to point out—as I just did—how we are leaving those ideals behind us, and who from there goes on to characterize what we are indulging in as "creeping socialism" and warns that we might be on the "road to serfdom," can be sure of a sympathetic audience, particularly if he does not become too specific. This reaction has its parallel in people's attitude to taxation—to which it is also closely related, as I will come to point out. There is probably, in all Western countries, a majority holding the view that taxation is out of hand and has become much too high and oppressive. But there is apparently nowhere a workable majority in the representative assemblies for making the specific cuts in expenditure which could bring down the taxes, and in election after election the people vote into power representatives who are as unable as they are unwilling to do anything about it.

I would not suggest that the ideological situation I am describing is entirely without its practical consequences. In all Western countries, we are probably keeping down our expenditures for public consumption in the fields of health, education, roads, and many other things below the level which our relative values would warrant. In the United States a stereotype like "socialized medicine" can, because of its association with this controversy between a "free" and a "planned" economy, provide, at least for a while, an emotional block to clear thinking on the social distribution of costs for health and to progress in health reform. Indeed, it can be used to cover up an occasional fumbling by the administration, say, in making polio vaccine available to the people in an efficient manner. The "free enterprise" formula—which has its emotional appeal because we all have a sincere attachment to liberty and to elbow room for the individual to seek his opportunity—can be thrown at persons and institutions who, in what they conceive to be the public interest, would want to reveal, say, the monopolistic pricing policies of the big and impersonal international oil monopolies, though certainly they are not much akin to the ideal type of free enterprise invoked in defense of their secretiveness.

I may now sound grossly partisan, as I am illustrating the irrational associations to the sacred words of only one side in this popular controversy. But however sincerely I search my memory, I cannot find striking parallels where in our countries a policy line has been made more attractive to people by lining it up in an emotional way with the idea of economic planning. I do not suggest that this is so because the propagandists of a "planned" economy are more considerate of truth and logic. The explanation is instead the remarkable fact, which I stressed, that while the actual development in our countries has continually been towards more and more planning, the anti-planning attitudes have remained the respectable and popular ones —and the more so when the discussion has moved on that general level where specific issues and individual and group interests are not in the foreground.

The Underdeveloped Countries

But such examples, where something that is not really intellectually respectable can be successfully expounded to a credulous public by assimilating it to "planned" economy, can be found in plenty of discussions in many of the underdeveloped countries. For there the situation is mostly the opposite one: there the advantage in public discussion instead belongs to those who want a "planned" economy. Planning has social prestige, while the pleaders for a "free" economy are suspect.

Also as opposed to the situation in the rich countries of the Western world, there are still, in fact, usually relatively few planned and effective measures of state intervention in the economic life of underdeveloped countries. From the colonial regimes, under which many of them were kept until recently, they have inherited much of the regimentation, red tape, and petty bureaucracy with which the metropolitan powers ruled foreign peoples of inferior status. Also, they have all used their short period of independence to add considerably to such administrative fetters. But in more fundamental respects the social controls are utterly weak. To a businessman from the Western countries with their allegedly "free enterprise" economies, economic life in some of these countries, with or without a plan, must resemble the jungle. People in the underdeveloped countries succeed in keeping themselves largely unaware of this fact. For, as economic planning in these countries has the stamp of public approval, so a general tendency is often prevalent there to overestimate its actual importance, just as in the Western countries people cling to the idea that they have a "free" economy, even when planning and controls have developed very far.

Economists now generally endorse the opinion that the underdeveloped countries need much more planning and state intervention if, under very much more difficult conditions than the now-developed countries ever faced, they are to have any chance of engendering economic development. Statesmen and officials from the rich and progressive Western countries have also been led to take the same stand on those other countries' behalf, when the matter has been up for discussion and resolution-making in international organizations—although it is very apparent that they often had their fingers crossed when swearing on that strange bible.

A Declaration of Non-Participation

To the social scientist, this popular controversy in the Western world, as it has evolved through the decades and generations, concerning a "free" *versus* a "planned" economy, and the relation between this discussion and the actual political and economic conditions and developments there, are, of course, interesting as a topic for study. But he should not be expected to step down and become a participant in such a discussion. I am always astonished when some of my colleagues do this.

In any case this book is not a tract in defense of a "free" economy; neither is it a plea for a "planned" economy. Experience proves that so firmly have people got their minds fixed in this shallow, unrealistic, sterile, and antithetical way of looking at things, inherited from ages long back in a very different type of society, that any new book on economic planning will be expected by most readers to be another contribution to the old, stale controversy between two unworldly abstract conceptions. A firm declaration of non-participation therefore needs to be made.

And having given this bare sketch of a matter which would be worthy of a book of its own, I now leave the doctrinal issue. This book will deal with factual matters: how economic planning has actually developed in the Western world, what it now is, what its effects are for international relations, and what the prospects are for the future.

To define my approach, I need only add that my value premises are the long-inherited ones of liberty, equality, and brotherhood. So far as relations within the individual nations are concerned, the trend towards economic planning has broadly implied an ever fuller realization of these ideals. I will, therefore, in the course of my study, also be in a position to give an interpretation of the ideology of the rapidly developing modern democratic Welfare State, which, because of people's preoccupation with the stale and barren controversy referred to in this Introduction, is a conspicuously unclarified topic.

As regards international relations, national economic planning has not had effects in line with those ideals. The Welfare State is nationalistic. Internationally the ideals of liberty, equality, and brotherhood can be attained only by a political development towards a Welfare World, which would imply rather fundamental changes in the trend towards economic planning in the individual countries.

In Part One I shall be discussing merely the national problems, leaving the international ones to Part Two.

PART ONE

The Trend towards Planning

2

The Impact of the International Crises

Planning An Unplanned Development

No development has been more unplanned than the gradual emergence and increasing importance of planning in all the Western countries. Ideas and ideologies, theories and propaganda, political programs and political action directed consciously towards promoting planning, have played an altogether insignificant role.

As I have already pointed out, in public discussion in these countries, particularly in the United States, there has been, since the breakthrough of economic liberalism many generations ago, an overwhelming body of opinion against state intervention in general, more particularly against state planning. The steady growth of state intervention has been sponsored and administered by political leaders who were constantly proclaiming the virtues of a "free" economy. While admittedly the state and the citizen, step by step, have been taking over more and more responsibility for the direction and control of economic life, they have been led by events, not by conscious choice.

The Liberal Interlude

To begin far back, the industrial revolution in the Western countries was the result not of state planning for economic development towards higher economic levels for

19

the masses—which is now the formula in underdeveloped countries, as it had previously been proclaimed in the Soviet Union—but of the undirected and dispersed enterprise of individual entrepreneurs seeking to exploit new inventions for their own profit. Its impact on the old system of guild and state regulations was to break them down, gradually and one at a time.

The extent and completeness of this, and its relation to the industrialization movement, varied considerably in the different countries of the group. In the end, the liquidation of the old regulations can be seen to have been carried further in Britain and Scandinavia than in the countries on the Continent of Europe, while in the New World there had been less of them from the beginning. I will return to the heritage from the pre-liberal era at the end of Chapter 4.

State intervention in economic life remained, however, frequent and important everywhere, though it now tended to become different in type and direction as it was increasingly steered by the new dynamic forces of industrialization and the many other changes concomitant with that movement. These changes tended to be dispersed and even less subject to planned coordination than in the pre-industrial era. Indeed, they were not meant to be planned. This is related to the fact that, while the earlier regulations were supported by interventionist theories—different in important respects, but together known conventionally as Mercantilism, itself a development of various forms of Cameralism—the theory of the liberal era, as it dawned in the Western countries, was one version or another of non-interventionism. The less complete liquidation of the old regulations on the European continent had its ideological parallel in a less complete victory there of this liberal theory.

State Intervention Precedes State Planning

Taking the broad view—and leaving out of the picture the differences between the several countries and, in particular, the longer or shorter periods of retardation that occurred in some of them in some fields—the total volume of state intervention has been steadily increasing and at an increasing rate. All the time, new measures have been introduced *ad hoc*, to serve limited and temporary purposes, to safeguard special interests, and often to meet an immediate emergency of one sort or another. Policies to promote the construction of new railroads, to open up new lands for settlement, to establish the conditions under which mineral resources and water power were to be exploited, or to protect industries and agriculture—all, in one country or another, at some time or another, have been part of a perspective of development. But even then there was not much overall economic planning in the modern sense.

Indeed, in response to popular animosity against state direction of economic life, the politicians could usually be relied upon to do their best to avoid incorporating acts of state intervention into a planned and coordinated economic policy. New intervention was usually not only motivated by special circumstances—a particular need, an emergency, or a pending crisis—but also designed accordingly, as limited and often temporary measures. I do not need to stress the difference between this historical development and the introduction of programmatic, comprehensive, and systematic state economic planning by political fiat in the Soviet Union, or the present attempts at planning for development in the underdeveloped countries. As a matter of plain historical fact, state intervention in Western countries has not been the outcome of a conscious decision to plan, but has generally preceded planning. The regular sequence has been that intervention caused planning. And planning, when it developed, thus became a very different thing.

What happened was that, as measures of state intervention in a particular field grew in volume and in complexity, attempts to coordinate them more rationally had from time to time to be thrown into this development—"putting the yeast in the oven after the bread," as the peasant's expressive metaphor runs. Such attempts at coordination were forced upon the state: when it turned out to have been an illusion that the need for a particular intervention was only temporary; when the acts of intervention proved to have disturbing effects, often far outside the field where they were applied, effects which had not been taken into account at the time the measures had been decided upon; when their lack of compatibility with each other and with other aims and policies of the national community stood out as irrational and damaging; and when they created serious administrative difficulties.

The development towards economic planning, in all the Western countries, has had its course demarcated by such intermittent attempts to bring more order and rationality to those measures of state intervention which had already grown up in a particular field. For a long time, these attempts at coordination were often—as they often still are —limited in scope. As a rule, they did not go far towards a permanent solution. New acts of state intervention, again usually assumed to be of only a temporary nature, were continually added, and soon diminished even the attained modicum of coordination.

Everybody acquainted with the internal history of the Western countries knows that this is the road we have travelled towards economic planning. In situations where the withdrawal of acts of intervention was out of the question for practical and political reasons, the politician and public servant with serious liberal inclinations, seeking to keep down state intervention to the minimum, often found himself the proponent of central state planning in one field after another. It has been part of the irony of history during the last decades that planning was often the more "liberal" alternative to the veritable chaos created by uncoordinated and disorganized state interventions.

When in this inquiry I discuss the trend towards planning in the Western countries, I understand by the term "planning" conscious attempts by the government of a country—usually with the participation of other collective bodies—to coordinate public policies more rationally in order to reach more fully and rapidly the desirable ends for future development which are determined by the political process as it evolves. As a result of the historical origin of these attempts at planning, and of the institutional and political conditions under which they have operated in these countries, planning becomes pragmatic and piecemeal and never comprehensive and complete. As a rule, planning in these countries has the nature of compromise solutions of pressing practical issues. It has been gradually growing, and will in all probability continue to grow, in scope and in relative importance. A major force propelling this trend towards planning has been, and continues to be, the steady growth of the volume of state intervention requiring coordination. My first task thus becomes to explain that latter trend.

The Sequence of International Crises

This growth of the volume of state intervention in economic life has been tremendously accelerated by the unending upheavals in international relations, beginning with World War I. Since then all nations have continually experienced the effects of the onslaught of successive and cumulative waves of violent economic crises, each one piling up on the crest of the last.

To protect the national interest in internal stability, the employment of the workers, the welfare of the farmers, and, in general, the undisturbed continuation of production and consumption, all states have felt themselves compelled to undertake new, radical intervention, not only in the sphere of their foreign trade and exchange relations, but also in other sectors of the national economy. When one crisis abated, the removal in the several countries of the protective policy measures taken in defense against its effects was seldom complete and never instantaneous. One reason why they could not be simply removed was that the crisis often left in its wake a number of more durable changes in conditions at home and abroad. This again was partly a result of the protective measures themselves, taken in all countries, and their tendency to persist. Moreover, a partial explanation why the defensive policy measures tended to be retained was that vested interests had been built up in the normal fashion behind all of them, some of those having a perfectly legitimate case, and all representing political pressure in one degree or another.

For the moment I am interested only in the effects of the sequence of international crises since World War I in spurring the secular trend towards the growth of the volume of state intervention in each country. Looking towards the future, we have to reckon with a continuation of this influence from international relations having the same effect upon national policies. There is, indeed, no rational ground for hoping that we shall ever see the reestablishment of stable international economic relations of the old quasi-automatic type.

I shall make some comments in Part Two in support of this judgment, when I come to discuss the international implications of the trend towards national economic planning which is my present concern. A better-integrated world economy would now have to be an organized one; and this holds good even if we confine ourselves to relations within the partial world community of the rich countries. It would imply international planning and coordination of national economies, which then, of course, would need to be planned individually even more than they are now. At this stage of the argument my point is only that, as a matter of fact, for half a century international crises have been important among the forces making for an increase in the volume of state intervention in all countries, and that, so far as the future is concerned, we cannot now see any end to the sequence of such crises.

Effects on the Structure of Our Values

Living in a crisis-ridden world has consequences for people's attitudes towards society which deserve much more serious study than they have as yet received. For our particular problem they are important, as they tend to accustom people not only to huge adverse changes coming over them from outside, but also to the idea that something should be done to mitigate their effects. More generally, people become less inhibited from wanting to change social and economic conditions in a radical fashion according to their own interests, and from being prepared to think of state intervention in ever wider spheres as possible and useful for this purpose.

All sudden and violent changes, whatever their causes or character, must tend to decrease the respect for *status quo* as a natural order of things. In particular, the important property and contract taboos, so basic for a stable liberal society, were forcibly weakened when large alterations were permitted to occur in the real value of currencies and, consequently, of incomes and costs, individual fortunes, debts, and obligations.

Furthermore, the large-scale regulations and state undertakings, which in time of war or severe crisis simply had to be resorted to in the national interest, and sometimes in order to safeguard survival, made people familiar with the thought that such intervention is possible, and must be coordinated in order to be successful. People "learn by doing."

The central state economic planning which had to be improvised during World War I turned out to be technically not too unsuccessful—at least far less so than could have been expected, and actually was expected, by the liberal economists of that time. State planning during World War II was technically far superior to that earlier experience.

The Crumbling of the Gold Standard

A reference to what happened to the monetary system may illustrate how the cumulation over a period of short-term effects of such shocks from the international sphere affected people's attitudes, which in their turn had effects back upon international relations, and so on, in a pattern of circular causation.

The old gold standard, which, even if it was never universal and never functioned so perfectly as in the textbooks, nevertheless secured, for a considerable period, a measure of international stability for the main trading nations, resting in the last instance on certain given and known, unchallenged commonly observed ways of thought and patterns of behavior in the banking community and, further, on certain respected taboos on the part of the politicians. Thanks also to some "gold superstition"—which the better-versed could always justify to their intellectual conscience by its wholesome effects—monetary policy was in principle no policy at all. It was in any case kept out of politics.

The central banks reacted to recurring changes according to a prescribed set of rules. A tendency to deterioration in the balance of payments of a country—due, for instance, to a crop failure or to the undertaking of a big investment scheme—was followed by certain movements in the international capital market and, eventually, some changes in the gold holdings. To this, the central banks answered by certain adjustments in credit conditions, at that time mainly the discount rate, which, according to another set of rules, were reflected in the behavior of the private banks. This, in turn, had several effects on the business situation, on the volume of stocks, and on production, employment, and prices, which then, in their turn, had a new set of effects on imports, exports, and short-term foreign lending and borrowing, all tending to restore international exchange equilibrium.

It was accepted that nothing very much could be done about it: things would have to take their natural course. The whole system was rocking beautifully between certain extreme limits, of which two were the so-called upper and lower gold points, signifying the rates of exchange where it became profitable to move gold from one bank vault to another. Short-term credit, activated by the prospects of tiny speculative gains, flowed as water between connected vessels, making it more possible for equilibrium to be maintained without too violent, non-synchronized reactions within the individual countries.

This is a textbook idealization of a reality which was much less than perfect. The important thing is that it is now utterly inapplicable. The international pre-conditions for the functioning of such an automatic monetary system do not exist any more after the violent crises the world has gone through. International trade is dislocated. And there no longer exists a long-term international capital market. The short-term international capital market is shrunken and erratic, and cannot be relied upon to cushion the effects of tendencies to disequilibrium in the balance of payments. Rather, it is an irrational force which has to be watched carefully and neutralized by intentional policies.

I do not exclude the possibility of creating an organized international monetary system. But it could not be the old automatic system under the gold standard. And we might just note in passing that the International Monetary Fund, which was indeed set up to provide this organized system to replace the defunct gold standard, has hardly even begun to function in this role, though it is useful in furnishing a forum for discussion and in managing stopgap credits.

But this is not the whole story. The old system depended upon the belief, shared by people in all countries, in its continuance, and on the equally prevalent absence in all countries of any preparedness to interfere with its automatic operation. The downfall of the gold standard cannot be explained simply as due to the international disequilibrium in trade and payments and the insufficiency of forces acting to restore equilibrium. The national pre-conditions for a proper functioning of the automatic system are also now absent.

No country today—and certainly not the United States—is willing any longer to accept a level of economic activity and employment determined by the automatic repercussions, through the banking system, of changes in its international payment situation. To put it another way: no country is prepared to abstain from interfering in the "free" economy. No country is now in a position to allow monetary matters to remain outside economic policy—or even outside politics.

And everybody now knows that monetary matters can be influenced by national policy measures, and also how it can be done. A fundamental social taboo is broken. And once broken it cannot be built up again, even if we ever so sincerely wanted to do so. Indeed, social taboos can never be established by decisions, founded upon reflection and discussion. They never come into existence except in an absent-minded way: events happen to arrange themselves within a particular pattern of behavior, in this case on the part of politicians, certain government officials, bankers, and businessmen; this pattern happens to avoid public criticism and discussion and, in the ideal case, even conscious apperception and reflection; its observance then becomes "natural," "sound," and respectable, and aberrations from the pattern seem hazardous, unwise, and bad. Social taboos are shy like virtue; once lost, there is no remedy.

This is indeed a reason why so many social changes are as irreversible as the reaction when sodium is thrown into water. And this particular chain of events, which has led us away from the relatively high degree of automatism which in the nineteenth century ruled monetary matters, definitely has such a character. One of the great economists of the old school, my teacher and friend, the late Professor Gustav Cassel, when he was expressing his nostalgic thoughts on the gold standard of bygone times, sadly summarized the wisdom of that remarkable chapter in Genesis about Adam and Eve falling into sin: "When man has tasted the fruits of the tree of knowledge about good and evil, he will never be innocent again."

3
Internal Forces

Changing Structure and Role of the Market

There is no doubt that in many ways the unbroken succession of international crises during the last half-century bears a major responsibility for the steady increase in the volume of state intervention in the economic life of the Western countries, which, in turn, I am positing as a main driving force behind the trend towards economic planning. In recent years, the cold war, in all of them, has been a very potent cause of new and massive state intervention, not only by siphoning off very considerable productive efforts into state expenditures for armaments, but also by providing reasons for redirecting investment, production, and, indeed, the whole life and work of each national community into line with the governments' pursuance of the cold war and the safeguarding of state security interests.

These international crises would, however, not have had such large and lasting effects upon the volume and structure of economic policies in the several Western countries, had they not been pushing in the same direction as a whole array of interrelated, and cumulatively very powerful, internal forces. Even in the absence of world crises, these internal forces would anyhow have led to an increase in state intervention, though the historical process would have evolved much more slowly.

One of these forces has been the tendency towards organization of markets. To focus our attention on what this has implied as a steady cause of increasing state intervention, I might be permitted to revert for a moment to an economic model which—for good reasons—is not playing the same role in academic teaching today as it did in my youth: the liberal economic theory of perfect competition.

We are rightly accustomed to characterize this theory as being, on the one hand, static and, on the other hand, atomistic. The society of which this theory was a very idealized rationalization, had a basic assumption without which it could not function, namely a specific combination of immobility and mobility. The social frame had to remain stubbornly unchanged. It was possible to conceive of such a rigid frame under the atomistic assumption of instantaneous movements of all the elements contained within this frame towards full adjustment.

The main thesis of the theory of perfect competition was, as I will be allowed to recall, that *if* the economic units are infinitesimally small in relation to the size of the market, and if they do not act together, then no unit can by its own actions have any influence in the market. If anybody should decide to change his behavior—i.e. his demand or supply—it would have no perceptible effect on the total demand and supply for the product, nor, consequently, on the price.

The markets and the prices were, therefore, to the individual, whether he acted as a buyer or a seller, independent variables, a set of objective and given conditions for his behavior. They were as entirely outside his control as the seasons and the weather, to which he had to adjust in order not to perish. Under the assumptions implicit in the model, the price formation in the market performed continuously and smoothly the "function" of restoring equilibrium after every change of the primary conditions.

This perfect market was understood, of course, never to have existed. A more important thing, however, of which we are also all aware, is that for a long time reality has been moving steadily further and further away from this liberal idealization. Technological and organizational developments have in many fields been increasing the size of the units in relation to the markets. At the same time, in all other fields the individual units have found the means by which to combine.

They have thereby come into a position where they can influence the markets and manipulate the prices. The markets and the prices have more and more lost their character of being given and objective conditions, outside the influence of the individual units, which merely have to adjust to them. The markets have become consciously "regulated" by the participants.

And when the atomism has gone, then the assumed static institutional frame is no longer protected, but can be influenced, as can the price formation taking place within that frame. Instead of obediently adjusting themselves to a given framework of society and accepting the burdens and rewards as they come out from the working of the forces within this framework, the individuals begin to cooperate in order to influence this process and, going even further, to adjust the framework itself according to their own interests.

When this happens on a large enough scale, a fundamental institutional change has occurred in the position of the human beings in relation to each other and to the community. I do not need to recall to what extent practically all markets are manipulated at the present time. Many markets are dominated by one or a few sellers or buyers. But, apart from these cases, almost every individual person in any one of the Western countries who has something to sell or who earns an income or seeks a profit, is associating himself with his compeers with the intention of influencing the conditions under which he is acting.

This development compels the state to large-scale measures of intervention. They become necessary simply to prevent the actual disorganization of society, which would result from the organization of the individual markets, if this development were not controlled and coordinated. And they are needed in order to prevent those who have acquired a stronger bargaining power from exploiting the others.

Changed Outlook

But before I proceed, in the next chapter, to analyze the effects of the organization of markets on the relations between the individuals and between them and the state, I need to make some comments on the deeper changes in people's attitudes to the economic processes in which they are participating. As usual, these psychological changes are partly effects, partly causes of the institutional changes.

They are, in addition, causally related to industrialization, to increased geographical and social mobility, to intensified intellectual communication, to secularization, and to many other social changes, which have quietly but steadily been going on in our civilization while levels of living have been rising. Meanwhile "folkways and mores" have been gradually breaking down in this process. The more instinctive, less questioned norms for behavior of the old society generally lost their hold upon the mass of the people, and a reflective weighing of rational interests was increasingly substituted for them. People became less inhibited by existing social taboos and traditions, as I have just illustrated with regard to the monetary system. They were thus becoming more enterprising, more experimental, more sophisticated, more hedonistic, more "economically rational."

All this has, indeed, application far beyond economic behavior in relation to demand and supply, prices, wages, and profits. It has, for instance, been studied rather intensively in the field of family morality. The pattern of birth control did not, as is often popularly assumed, reach out to ever broader social strata, so beautifully revealed in vital statistics, from the diffusion of knowledge about birth control or the availability of technical contraceptives. The still most widely used means of contraception are not technical at all and have always been known to everybody. Birth control is, as a matter of fact, directly caused by more rationalistic attitudes to the family institution under changing economic conditions.

"Planned parenthood" in the social history of the Western countries is, indeed, a phenomenon intrinsically related to those very changes in people's attitudes which, on the political plane, have been causing the trend towards economic planning. I have used this parallel of birth control, not as an intellectual pleasantry, but most seriously. I want to bring home the depth of the social and psychological causes of the destruction of liberal economic society which I am analyzing.

Economic liberalism was certainly part of a rationalistic philosophy. It was paralleled in the science of psychology by shallow hedonism and by the theory of intellectual association. In economics the rationalistic principles of this philosophy were elaborated in the marginal theory of value and in the utilitarian deduction of social welfare out of the enlightened self-interest of individuals. But as rational hedonism actually began to spread, and as people in general really started to think and act a little more like the theoretical "economic man," the bottom fell out of liberal economic society.

The explanation of this paradox is that, contrary to all the theorizing about man of this intellectualistic and rationalistic liberal philosophy inherited from the era of Enlightenment, its basic assumptions—atomism and a static frame of society—implied the prevalence in society of human beings who were the very opposite to the rationalistic "economic man" of its economic theory. They had to be traditionalistic, strongly inhibited by existing taboos, non-questioning, non-experimenting, non-reflecting conventionalists. Otherwise the theory would not work. It is no accident that the Victorian age, the hey-day of conventionalism, was the cultural bloom of economic liberalism. Seldom in the history of mankind has a social philosophy been so naive about its own psychological foundations as this one, whose honest pretension it was to be so enlightened and so rational.

Here again we can observe a fundamental difference between the ways in which economic planning has come to the Western and to the Soviet world. In Russia the psychological and social development which I have just sketched had barely started. Economic planning was clamped down upon a largely illiterate, pre-industrial folk society. And after some insignificant intermezzi, during which Westernized intellectuals attempted to rationalize social attitudes—as, for instance, in family matters—all the forces of the state were directed strongly towards stabilizing and conventionalizing people's behavior patterns in accordance with the proclaimed aims and values of the Soviet state. As every visitor to Russia has been able to observe—usually to his pleasant surprise—the personality type which then developed is in many fundamental respects the cherished one of our grandparents or their parents.

It is interesting to note that the communist state, while forcibly lifting the population out of the inhibited and impoverished stationary life of folk society, is fostering a kind of human being who would—with slight modifications of stereotyped and often not too deeply rooted ideologies much more than of fundamental attitudes—make even liberal society function, while liberal society was destroyed because people in general started to behave as rationally as its theory had always wrongly assumed that they did.

The reason why it is important to stress the deeper changes of people's attitudes as a causal factor underlying the trend towards intervention and planning in the Western world is that these psychological changes, related to the whole development of our modern society, make the process non-reversible. If it were only a question of changes in human institutions and nothing more, those changes could be reversed and probably would be reversed. But once people have adjusted their minds to new situations, this is no longer so.

It is true that these changes of attitude have been partly caused by the shocks of events and by the policies instigated to cope with these events. Those shocks and those policies, however, have then tended to break up established norms and to release the inhibitions of the *status quo*. But, even initially, inherent in the whole development of Western civilization, was a tendency for the minds of the people to change, and to change in that same direction. This is a typical cumulative process of circular causation. As a result, the whole social system and the human beings within it are made to move, and to move much further than anybody could have foreseen originally.

There is obviously no way back. We cannot make people less rational and sophisticated. Who would do it? In our democracy rationalistic education is our faith. Should we attempt to de-educate people?

Democratization and Equalization

One important trend in all Western countries, which is closely related not only to this general rationalization of attitudes but also to the rising levels of living and to the altered position of the individual in the markets where he sells and buys, is the democratization of the political process by which the public will of the state is becoming established. This was a gradual development. In particular, we need to remind ourselves that in most Western countries universal suffrage is a fairly recent accomplishment.

It was easy to foresee that, as ever larger strata of the population were given their full share of political power and became ever more aware of having this power and the possibilities to use it in their own interest, they would press for redistributional state intervention on a large scale. Aristotle had already foretold this development.

The whole setting for such intervention was also changing. The institutional structure of the national communities was being loosened up by large-scale state intervention, necessitated by international crises. The property taboos, as I have pointed out, had been damaged and weakened by the large and perilous changes in people's fortunes brought about by inflation, deflation and many other processes. The markets in which the individuals moved were losing their institutional aura of given and objective norms with which one could not tamper. The rising social mobility, the increasing and variegated social contacts between all sorts of persons in a society which was becoming industrialized, and the general rationalization of attitudes were all influential in taking away from the existing economic inequalities much of their unquestioned appearance of being natural.

When, a little more than a hundred years ago, John Stuart Mill made his compromise with socialism and formulated what was then called the "new liberalism," his main thesis was that legislators should feel free to change the distribution as they wished, although the economic laws in the field of production had to be obeyed and should not be interfered with. Faced with the concrete issue of a progressive income tax, he hesitated, however. I wonder

what Mill would have thought if he had had a revelation
of the dominant attitudes towards income taxes and death
duties in his homeland and in other western countries a
century later. If he then should go a little deeper into the
study of the tax laws, he would find that as yet the steep
progressivity of taxation is more an illusory appearance
than a stern reality; I shall return to this question in Chapter 7.

The Egalitarian Motive for State Action

The urge for economic equalization is everywhere present,
and it is commonly proclaimed as a principle. Its sphere of
operation is not limited to taxation and to redistributional
expenditure schemes like those for various forms of social
insurance. It enters into, and determines, the scope of all
other state intervention.

The important thing is that it then becomes one of the
main driving forces behind the general trend towards increasing the volume of state intervention, which is our
present concern. Generally speaking, the less privileged
groups in democratic society, as they become aware of their
interests and their political power, will be found to press
for ever more state intervention in practically all fields.
Their interest clearly lies in having individual contracts
subordinated as much as possible to general norms laid
down in laws, regulations, administrative dispositions, and
semi-voluntary agreements between apparently private
but, in reality, quasi-public organizations.

The rational basis for this general interest of people in
the lower income brackets in intervention is that, when
private relations become public relations in the Western
countries, now so firmly dedicated to equality, there is a
better chance that the poor man's concerns will be looked
after. Income distribution has the form of a pyramid with

a broad basis and a narrowing top. In a democracy with effective universal suffrage, this is one of the explanations why we are steadily proceeding in the direction of government control and direction. Even the conservative and liberal parties will have to become the vehicles for this development, or else disappear from the political scene.

When the state becomes involved in regulations of the building industry and the business of real estate, such intervention takes on, by political necessity, the character of social housing policy. Likewise, when the profitability of farming becomes a matter of public price fixing, the interest of the small farmer, or, indeed, of any farmer living on or near the margin of profitable production, must be taken care of. When wages are becoming regulated by ever more inclusive national settlements between the organizations in the labor market, one general effect is a tendency to diminish the wage differentials between different occupations. When commodities have to be rationed, the principle is again equality—and it might happen, as during the war in England and Sweden, that families in the lowest income groups were actually placed in a situation where they could increase their consumption of a rationed commodity.

All this can easily be demonstrated from the recent history of all Western countries. Whenever new measures of state intervention or semi-public regulation are introduced, even if their purpose is quite a different one, they will tend to be utilized as a means of equalization as well. That they can be so used is therefore a general reason why state intervention is seen to be in the interest of the lower income groups and, in general, actually is so, and why the drive for equality of opportunity becomes a pressure or support for state intervention, even outside the sphere of redistributional reform proper.

Again, it is a different story, which for the moment—

when I am only analyzing the causes for the trend towards an increasing volume of intervention—I pass over, that often enough the poor are given more an appearance of advantage than a real one. Their appetite for intervention is bound to grow, as they get more of it. With the greater rationality of attitudes and increasing knowledge, they will also press forward with more effectiveness. I shall return to this question in Chapter 7.

Planning for Development

My account of the internal forces behind the trend towards state intervention in the Western countries would be incomplete if I did not conclude by pointing specifically to the urge there for continually rising levels of investment and production, incomes, and well-being. In this particular respect people today in the Western world are not different from those in the other two orbits. In the very first paragraphs of the Preface, I referred to what I believe is a fact, namely that, in spite of the chasms of ideologies and the wide gaps as between the three orbits in levels and modes of living and working, we are all existing in the same era of civilization, with a considerable and growing unity of basic ideas and ideals. One such congruity of thoughts and strivings is the dynamic conception implicit in our thinking about the national economy. In all countries we are now striving for "development."

This is most emphatically the case as far as the poor nations are concerned, as they become aware of their low economic levels and form the ambition of raising them. When they insist upon being given the designation of "underdeveloped" countries—instead of the static one, more commonly used in earlier times: "backward regions"— they want to characterize themselves as needing development, and being bent upon achieving it.

In the Soviet Union of the Five-Year and Seven-Year

plans, and in all the other countries within the Soviet orbit, people have been living, and are now living more intensely than ever, in an orgy of climbing percentages, symbolizing the rise of every level in the economy. The development targets are spelled out in individual production plans splashed at the entrance of every factory and on the walls in the meeting room of every collective farm. Within the country, within every region and, indeed, within every enterprise, "socialist competition" makes the fulfilment—and preferably the over-fulfilment—of the targets a concern to every manager and every worker. In relation to the outside world, the targets represent a constant race with the capitalist world, a race of momentous, fateful, and almost religious import.

But all the rich countries of the Western world, whose road to planning I am here reviewing, and not least the richest of them all, the United States of America, demonstrate a similar preoccupation with economic development to a degree that we would feel astonishing, were we not ourselves so conditioned by our milieu and our time. Indeed, we have geared the stability of our entire economy to constantly rising investment and an increasing volume of production, pressed foreward by rising demand. I once met an elderly English gentleman who confided to me that he did not understand all this craze for development when we could be so well satisfied with the levels we had reached. But the reason why I remember him is, of course, that such an attitude is so exceedingly rare.

It is not unlikely that this insatiable craving for development in the Western countries is to some extent simply a reaction to the valiant exertions in the Soviet countries. Under the conditions of the mounting political tension in the cold war, the steeply ascending development curves in the countries under communist rule are in the Western world very generally felt to be a challenge to their way of life and their security. Admitting that, in the prevailing international situation, the very evident accomplishments in the Soviet world must have tended to raise the development interest in the Western countries as well, I believe that our bustle for development here has its main cause on the deeper level of our entire cultural orientation.

At least when acting as participants of organized communities, we seem all bent upon continued and limitless expansion. Whatever the levels already reached, every national, provincial, or municipal assembly of citizens' representatives, every private organization for a cause or an interest of whatever type, regularly finds itself being put under severe restraint by the purse strings from undertaking, within its field of action, a great number of improvements which are all felt to be important and urgent. Similarly the normal individual himself, notwithstanding the station in life he has reached, can be seen continuously and eagerly striving upwards economically. Apparently, both collectively and personally, we all know any number of useful things we would want to spend money on, had we only more of it. We are, in any case, behaving as if we did. And the whole communications industry is pressing us in this direction.

The underdeveloped nations, in their great poverty and their dire need, should certainly have much stronger rational motives to exert themselves in order to attain higher economic levels. But the very type of civilization that goes together with accomplished wealth and welfare in the industrially advanced nations seems to condition people there to strive equally and, in fact, even more diligently for still higher levels than those they have already attained. Sometimes it looks as if, the better off they become, the bigger do they conceive the gap between what is actually their lot and what would be desirable, while in the poor countries large masses of people seem to be satisfied by merely surviving.

4

The Organizational State

The Organization of the Markets

Among the main internal causes of the development towards an increased volume of state intervention in the Western countries I have mentioned the gradual breakdown of the competitive markets, resulting from the technological and organizational developments and the sophistication of people's attitudes in regard to the economic processes in which they were participating as buyers and sellers of services and goods. The price in the market, and the market itself as an institutional frame for the interplay of demand and supply, were no longer placidly accepted as given, objective norms, but were manipulated.

Society, faced with this illiberal trend, would become disorganized, if it stayed liberal and declined to intervene. And if left unchecked, the clever and strong would exploit the others. The existence of monopolistic combines as such was always recognized as implying the usurpation of the state's power of taxation, which could not be permitted.

One line of reaction on the part of the state would obviously be to use its might to suppress the trend to market organization and restore free competition. To some extent, this has been attempted in all the Western countries. To a considerably smaller extent, those attempts have been successful. The main and important reaction by the state, however, has been instead to accept the trend, but to take such measures to regulate its course that the public interest in both order and equity would be protected. And thus a powerful but state-controlled infra-structure of collective organizations has come into being, beneath the constitutional frame of the state.

In the Western countries, this development represents, on the one hand, an extension, and probably the most important one, of state interference in economic life. On the other hand, it has left an even bigger scope for interference by the organizations. The interest of equity in particular, as determined by the increasingly democratic political process, has led the state to take measures to strengthen the bargaining power of the weaker groups, sometimes by aiding them to become organized when necessary, but more generally by improving the conditions under which they are bargaining.

Collective Bargaining Instead of
Free Market Economy

All these measures imply a change in the framework of the markets according to dominant social ideals and the strength of social forces. The inherited liberal ideal of fair play has more and more generally and definitely been translated into a demand that wages, prices, incomes, and profits should be settled by various sorts of collective bargaining. It has become the responsibility of the state to provide such conditions by legislation and administration, and by an umpire service of such a kind that just and equitable agreements will be reached.

The workers in all the Western countries have succeeded in getting the state to lay down a great number of rules and create institutions which very much strengthen their bargaining position in the labor market against the employers: legislation concerning hours of work, paid vacations, provident funds, factory inspection, various forms of social insurance when no regular income is earned, including unemployment insurance, and sometimes minimum wages. Gradually, the state has been moved to enter the labor market more directly, by undertaking to increase the demand for labor in times of rising unemployment by means of public works and in other ways.

The logical end of this development towards the reshaping of the labor market in the workers' interest was taken after World War II when in all Western countries the state committed itself to preserve "full employment" by means of a planned readjustment of all economic policies. As periods of large under-utilization of labor and other productive resources represent gross waste from a national point of view, and a slowing down of economic development, such protection of the workers' interest, by stimulating a brisk demand capable of absorbing the total labor supply in the market, could be advocated from a wider point of view than that of the special interest of the workers. But in the labor market it greatly strengthened the workers' bargaining power as against that of the employers.

Similar developments of state policies have taken place in other markets. The principle has always been to improve the bargaining position of a group of the people that might otherwise not fare so well. In most Western countries the farmers, next to the workers, have been drawing the greatest immediate advantages from this type of state interference in the markets.

Once these rectifying conditions for the operation of the organized markets have been created by the state, we witness how nationwide organizations of buyers and sellers in a market, through elected officers and through appointed and salaried officials, make binding agreements for all their members. These relate to wages, prices, and many other things as, for instance, the conditions under which entrance is permitted to a profession, or the location, number, and proprietorship of new shops of a particular type. If it sometimes looks as if the state had left it to the powerful organizations themselves to fight it out and come to an agreement—as, for example, in the labor market—this is so only because it is felt that a balance of strength between the buyers and the sellers in the market has been established by state intervention. These organizations then actually function as organs for public policy. The applicability of this conception is indicated by the state's growing interest in guaranteeing that the organizations are constituted on open and democratic principles, and that they function under the restraints of financial auditing and of adequate publicity, like other public organs.

Many of the most important policy decisions, then, are taken outside parliament, and put into effect by other organs than those of state administration. This can be permitted as long as the organizations succeed in settling their differences peacefully and efficiently, and are felt to carry into effect the public will—and as long as a reasonable degree of national coordination is preserved. As national economic planning proceeds, we witness more and more frequently integration at the still higher level of market regulations through combines. In such cases, general price and income agreements, covering many different markets in a nation and, perhaps, almost the whole economy, are made after multilateral collective bargaining, in which the organizations of workers and other employees, farmers, industrial employers, and perhaps bankers and consumers participate under government leadership.

This pattern is particularly noticeable in Scandinavia. I believe that, as years pass by, such forms of general income settlements among the main organized interest groups in a national community will gradually become the rule. All prices and wages and, in fact, all demand and supply

curves, are then in a sense "political." We are as far away
as possible from the "free market" of liberal economic
theory. The government and the administration, representing the point of view of central economic planning and
backed by a parliament with sovereign powers to legislate,
will then gradually find it as important to lead the negotiations and to control the compromises between the nationwide organized power groups, as it is to lead parliament
itself.

The Infrastructure of Organized Society

As a result of this development the whole character of our
national communities is changing. What in reality—constitutional forms aside—constitutes public policy is now
decided upon and executed in many different sectors and
on different levels: not only directly by the central state
authorities and by provincial and municipal authorities,
which in this process are taking over more and more responsibilities, but also increasingly by a whole array of
"private" power groups organized to promote group interests and common causes. Even individual business concerns, if they become so big that—contrary to the assumption of liberal economic theory—they can by their own
actions determine or decisively influence the market, and
if they are left holding this power, have to be included in
this institutional infrastructure of modern organized society in the Western countries, in charge of what in effect is
public policy.

I made the point that it was the very growth of the
amount of state intervention—most of the time entered
upon *ad hoc* and often thought to be temporary in nature
—which from time to time pressed upon the growing state
the necessity for coordination, i.e. planning as I have defined the term. To the measures of state intervention we

must now add those taken, not only by the provincial and municipal authorities which are within the formal structure of the state, but also by all the other organizations outside this structure. The development towards an increasing volume of interference in the markets by these organizations has raised the need for new state intervention and thus, not only directly, but also indirectly, immensely increased the total volume of interference in the markets and, consequently, the need for coordination.

This development, then, must also have increased the importance of the state, which is the central organ for coordination of public policies in a national community. Only the state could meet the ever more pressing need for coordination—not merely of its own acts of interference in social and economic life, which were already, and for other reasons, increasing in volume, and of the similarly sprouting activity of all the public authorities of a local or sectional character below the state level, but of the new and mushrooming growth of all those private organizations for collective action on behalf of various citizen groups which are outside the formal constitutional arrangements. In the Western countries, the strong and effective state was the accomplishment of political liberalism at a time, more than a hundred years ago, when the total volume of public policies was kept at a minimum. In the end, the modern and very different state has acquired a position where it has retained and increased that strength.

The state had to assert itself as the final arbiter. It had to lay down rules for what went on within the organizational infrastructure. It had to change the conditions for collective bargaining among the organizations and to control them so as to make the results conform to the public will. It is only on the instigation of the state or with its acquiescence and within the framework of its legislation and administration, that these other manifestations of

organized society are given play—that they are allowed to
function, to plan, and to regulate.

This, however, is not the whole truth. Within the framework of state controls the organizations have gained and
not lost in influence, and they have continuously increased
their scope of action. They hold more and more real power
in their fields of activity. Even the regulatory coordination,
undertaken by the state authorities, is ordinarily carried
out only after consultation and actually in cooperation
with the organizations.

In the advanced Welfare State, the increasing strength,
number, and activity of these organizations, as well as
of the authorities for provincial and municipal self-
government, has meant a spreading out of participation,
initiative, and influence over what is, in reality, legislation
and administration to ever larger sections of the people
themselves in their various localities and occupations. It
represents a decentralization of the making and implementation of public policies. Our democracies would be very
much poorer in substance, and the developing Welfare
State would have much less reality, were the participation of the individual citizens in the conduct of public
affairs restricted to giving their votes at intermittent elections of a national parliament. In fact, those elections
themselves become, in the advanced Welfare State, much
more important, and more clearly understood by the citizens in terms of real and concrete interests, as a result of
all the activities through which they increasingly participate in the collective instruments of public policy beneath
the state level.

The Quest for Democratic Participation

This development is not without its very serious problems,
however. At bottom they are all concerned with whether

and to what extent the individual citizens care to avail themselves of their right to participate actively in directing the organizations which are being provided to defend their various interests.

If popular participation lapses, then the organizations easily become merely the basis for a widespread complex of oligarchies of officials and officers, functioning beneath the state level, uncontrolled by their memberships. At best, they will then act as enlightened and autocratic business managers for the collective interests of which they are in charge. They may, however, easily fall prey to various practices which are not to the best advantage of the members. Collusion with other pressure groups, individual profiteering, or even plain corruption is not excluded. In any case, lack of popular participation will, as a rule, diminish an organization's drive and momentum in its activities as a living organ of the national community.

In so far as the organizations are not effectively controlled by their own members, a situation is created where the state will feel itself impelled to exert more checks and controls through its legislation and administration, which tends once more to decrease the spontaneity of life in the national community. Indeed, under such conditions more direct state controls may even be necessary in order to safeguard at least some honesty and efficiency within the organizational infrastructure of the state. The crux of the matter is, however, that when people are apathetic in their organizations, perhaps not even becoming members, they are often also apathetic as citizens of the state. As nonparticipation in both respects is more common in the lower income brackets, this will easily lead to a situation where the organizational structure becomes badly balanced in favor of big business and generally the interests of the higher income brackets. This runs contrary to the implicit political mores of democracy.

Very much the same observations hold good for provincial and municipal self-government. There are differences among the Western countries in regard to the degree to which responsibility of government is actually delegated to smaller units of civic action than the state. But, primarily and in the longer run, these differences are largely a function of the interest the citizens themselves take in finding communal solutions for their own problems. And if the smaller units of government become inefficient, boss-ridden, or corrupt, this is in the last instance due to the lack of participation in responsibility by the citizens. If such a situation prevails, it may even be a rational solution to lessen the scope of local self-government and to increase the central state controls.

It is fair to say that this problem of building up responsible participation by the individual citizens in directing their organizations, their local communities, and, ultimately, their state is shared by all the Western nations. The tremendous complication of all issues in modern life as a result of the process of social change which I am reviewing in this book—and not least as a result of the growth of the organizational structure itself—must tend to make those issues very much more difficult to grasp for ordinary people who do not specialize in handling them. Moreover, as the scope of collective activity increases, resort must more often be had to participation through election and appointed representatives. Active and informed participation was a much simpler matter in the local cooperative store, loosely joined with others in a national federation, than it is in the present huge national cooperative enterprise handling a very large wholesale and retail business, often running big industries and import businesses, and establishing international relations of many and varied types.

It should be added that, paradoxically enough, the very

success of the modern democratic Welfare State in attaining a high degree of "created harmony" of interests, on which I will comment towards the end of the next chapter, may also decrease some of the stimulants to participation. When cooperatives and trade unions were still in their fighting stage, this provided an emotional appeal which is now largely lost, as they have acquired powerful positions in the national establishments of which they have become parts. And when the danger of mass unemployment is no longer a psychological reality to the generation of workers who are now growing up in our Welfare States, the organizations and political parties built up to defend the workers' interests tend to lose in subjective importance to them.

This danger of forfeiting active participation, particularly in the broader strata, is, of course, realized by all organizations and political parties. The Welfare State has to devote continual vigilance to the building up and preservation of its human basis in democratic participation on the part of the people. In the countries where this problem has been tackled most seriously, and which also, on the whole, have been most successful in their strivings to keep up and widen active popular participation, a widely diversified educational campaign is continually carried on by the organizations and the political parties. They equip themselves with research facilities, they have specialized organizations for young people and for women, they run publishing houses, they issue papers and periodicals, print pamphlets and books, they have set up training schools of their own and organize local study groups and discussion circles, etc. They correspond intensively with their members and are sometimes prepared to make considerable sacrifices in managerial efficiency by putting up important decisions to membership referendum.

The Special Case of the United States

As regards active participation, the situation varies considerably as between the several Western countries. Generally speaking, it is still rather low in the United States. The explanations usually offered for this deficiency in the American national community are not very convincing. One such popular explanation is the size of the country. That the country is big does not explain, however, why the percentage of the electorate voting in elections, national or local, is relatively so small. Neither does it explain why such a large proportion of counties and towns are inefficiently governed, nor why they have sometimes lapsed into corrupted boss rule.

Another popular explanation is that the country is still so young. This is a statement of doubtful validity in the present context. The United States, in fact, is the oldest modern democracy; and its trade union movement, for example, is several generations older than that of the Scandinavian countries, where it has reached so much higher levels of efficiency and democratic control. A scrutiny of the facts in the United States itself, as well as a comparison of the facts in the several Western countries, does not reveal any positive correlation between the age of an institutional pattern of cooperation and bargaining and the degree of effective popular participation and control. If anything, we observe rather that the malaise of non-participation is particularly prevalent in many of the organizations in America which carry their records furthest back, and in some of the national communities in the rest of the Western world—as in England and Australia—which were once pioneers in building up the organizational state.

The observation that people in America move around

more frequently and over a wider area does not by itself explain the lower level of popular participation and the consequent failings in efficiency and honesty in local and sectional self-rule. Historically, among many other concomitant social changes accounted for in Chapter 3, it was, in Northwestern Europe, precisely the intensified internal migrations following industrialization that ultimately resulted in the coming into being of the closely integrated national communities, dramatized by an ever more intensified civic activity also in the organizations for provincial and municipal self-government—though this development occasionally led through periods of maladjustment related to the migrations. On balance and in the longer run, the high mobility in America is the surest basis of hope for a more closely-knit national community with more intensive popular participation in civic life on all levels. And, as a matter of fact, deficiencies in these respects have consistently been most glaring in those pockets of the American national communities which have been relatively isolated and stagnant and where mobility has been low.

As neither size and youth, nor mobility, by themselves, afford a satisfactory explanation for the relative imperfections in democratic participation on all levels in the United States, I believe that instead we must relate them to the fact that the country, until comparatively recently, has had much immigration which in its later stages brought in people from national cultures rather different from the older stock. In spite of the very rapid advances made towards national integration, heterogeneous elements still linger everywhere in the population, and with them remnants of separatistic allegiances.

This line of explanation should make us optimistic in regard to the future development of the democratic organizational state in the United States. As national integration proceeds, it should be fairly safe to assume that the intensity of active participation by the Americans in their organizations and their other communities, from sectional and local to national level, will rise. No one who has watched America over a couple of decades can remain unaware of the tremendous improvement in this respect, and of the consequent rise in efficiency, democratic control, and honesty, particularly in the private power groups and the authorities for provincial and municipal self-government, where the deficiencies were biggest and are still rather considerable.

This problem of citizens' participation is of the utmost importance, not only in America but everywhere in the Western countries, and should be made the subject of intensive study. I am aware that, to a varying degree in the several countries, the Welfare State is, as yet, more of a hope and an appearance than a reality. In some countries and in some fields it is indeed very imperfect; I shall return to the failings of the Welfare State in Chapter 7. Many will find that I have given my analysis of the operating forces behind the organizational state a too optimistic slant, and that I have been describing more what is possible than what is the actual reality. And they can point to some rather awkward facts in support for this judgment.

Nevertheless, I persist in my optimism which in this case I believe is realistic. What is possible—what is accomplished here and there, and what we see glimmering everywhere—has reality as a goal which can be reached and, indeed, must be reached, if democracy shall not lose its chance. I trust that, once people are free to organize for cooperation and bargaining, and once they also have got equal say in determining state policy which sets the conditions for this cooperation and bargaining, they will not for long tolerate such deficiencies. I cannot believe that, when the people have become sovereign, they will choose to leave their Welfare State as that rather shallow, bureaucratic, strongly centralized, institutional machinery, manipulated by crafty organizational entrepreneurs and vested interests, which it is doomed to become, if it is not vitalized by citizens' participation to an ever higher degree. I shall come back to the problem of the lessening of bureaucracy in the Welfare State in Chapter 6.

An Historical Note

My observations in this and the foregoing chapters are made in terms of huge generalizations. They raise a number of questions concerning constitutional law and administrative and political science. They cover and conceal great individual differences amongst the several countries in the Western world. In order to bring out the main argument more clearly, I have simplified the course of history considerably.

As I mentioned in Chapter 2, the liberal epoch was never so void of state interventions and of regulations of markets by organizations as its theory assumed in its more abstract formulations. In some countries the theory of economic liberalism never became so absolute and never reigned so supreme. And the liberal epoch was nowhere more than a short interlude in history.

Before this epoch there were in all countries plenty of organizations for cooperation and mutual assistance, for sharing of markets while excluding outsiders, for fixing of prices and wages, and so on. And the state was an authoritarian and regulatory one. Some of the old interferences in the markets administered by those organizations and by the authoritarian state withstood the onslaught of the liberal era. In some countries, many such interferences were retained. And even when the organizations and the

state regulations from pre-liberal times were largely suppressed and abolished, something of their spirit was often
preserved as a tradition, which could soon sprout freely
again when the liberal impulses faded out.

The tenacity of institutions and traditions has a historical basis, which explains some important differences
among countries in the Western group. Where the trade
unions, when they grew up, were more directly taking over
the traditions from the aristocracy of craft workers, who
had been organized under the guilds in pre-liberal times,
and where they were sticking more firmly to these traditions as, for instance, in Britain or Denmark, they have
to a large part remained craft unions until this day. There
they are still generally animated more by that spirit of
solidarity which is centered upon inherited skills, traditional modes of doing things, and a feeling of exclusive
rights to their particular kind of work as established
privileges than is the case in countries like Sweden, where
the unions early became open industrial unions. In the
United States where, as I have already pointed out, the
trade unions have a far longer history than is generally
realized, and in Canada, this demarcation split the movement along a line which broadly corresponded to the
difference between the two main organizations in the labor
market, the A.F. of L. and the CIO.

On the level of the entrepreneurs, America was from the
beginning more independent of the old pre-liberal heritage, and I feel that there is truth in the common notion
that in business there is now generally less of a competitive
spirit in Europe than in America. In a country like Switzerland, where the organizations on all levels are particularly
monopolistic in spirit as well as in their actual practices,
and are not disturbed much by the state, it is apparent
that the institutional infrastructure has retained strong
roots in pre-liberal traditions. It is, incidentally, a rather

extreme example of that disparity between facts and ideologies on which I commented in the Introduction, that
Switzerland has in a particularly high degree succeeded in
convincing itself and the world that it, even more than
other Western countries, has a "free economy."

The "corporative" institutions, set up by the fascists in
Italy and to an extent copied and amended by the national-
socialists in Germany, were conscious attempts at finding
a new non-liberal compromise between the old European
traditions and the needs of modern business. These attempts were built on the re-establishment of an authoritarian state, and this explains why for a time the fascists
and nazis could get such astonishingly strong support
from industrialists and persons in other higher social strata
who trusted that they themselves would hold the positions
of authority in such a state. The earlier system of "chambers" in Austria was another, though more euphemistic,
type of corporatism, which has even been preserved after
the collapse of fascism in World War II—having been
cleansed from authoritarianism and become more democratically based and balanced. In the original, authoritarian form, the chambers had been planted in Northern
Italy in pre-liberal times, when it was under Austria; they
had lent many traits to Mussolini's constructions and
indirectly to Hitler's.

The authoritarian corporative ideas were, as we might
recall, taken over by Vichy France—at the same time as
"liberté, égalité, et fraternité" were changed into *"patrie,
famille, et travail"*—and now the world is wondering
whether France, after de Gaulle, will make a similar adjustment backwards again. The queer constellation in France
of extreme individualism and extreme centralism, which
has been preserved through the successive waves of revolutions and through eras of bonapartism, bourbonism, and
parliamentary democracy, has there effectively prevented

the growth both of provincial and municipal self-government—of which there is practically nothing—and of an
infrastructure of democratically balanced interest organizations. There are laws in France biased against the creation
of independent interest organizations, and by local self-
government a Frenchman is apt to mean the authority
awarded to the Prefecture. And it is much more than a
joke that a French Minister of Education can look at his
watch and proudly inform the visitor what the students in
a particular grade of a particular type of school are doing
all over France.

The centralization of government in France, and the
concomitant weakness of democratic provincial and municipal authorities, and her lack of balanced private
power groups, render France very different from the other
Western countries and less resistant to radical movements,
whether of the Left or the Right. Spain and Portugal
have never really had a liberal era, and they do not belong
to the economic upper-class group of countries discussed
in this book. There the state policies and the organizational
structure are much more of the old, unreformed order.

A Fundamental Difference

But when all this is said—and particularly if we place a
parenthesis around the outbreaks of fascism and nazism in
recent decades, and if we also agree to deal with France as
a very special case—there is a world of difference between
the preliberal state and the modern organizational one.
To characterize the latter as a Neo-Mercantilist state is only
a half-truth, if even that.

To begin with, the old order was much more geared to
a static conception of national economy. However much
the Mercantilist state was bent upon improvements in
particular sectors of the economy, it was hardly imbued

with the spirit of general progress, expansion, and development which is now ours. And even more significantly, the organizations in pre-liberal times were much more built up to defend vested interests and privileged positions, and therefore tended to be more exclusive, restrictive, and monopolistic than they are today. That there is a big difference is this regard between then and now holds good generally to a considerable extent, even if we take into account the lingering traditions, operating even today; indeed, it is the differences in the strength of these traditions which, as I noted, have caused differences between the organizations in different fields and different countries.

Connected with all this is the fact that the state in those earlier times was upper-class authoritarian and apt to side with those who were better situated. They were also the only ones who were effectively organized in defense of their interests. From a modern democratic point of view, the organizations in pre-liberal time were very badly balanced. Broadly speaking, the Mercantilist organizations, as inherited from the Middle Ages, consisted of collusive city burghers, seeking to prevent the poor country folk from intruding upon their monopolistic privileges to trade and to manufacture goods for the market. And in the cities the rich merchants and manufacturers were organized to defend their monopolistic positions against the poor people there, and particularly against the workers. Almost nowhere did the peasants, whether serfs or, as in Sweden, free farmers, succeed in organizing themselves effectively and on a permanent basis for defense of their interests. Amongst the workers, only the skilled ones in the crafts, where the enterprises were modest in size, managed to become organized, and even then they were most often kept in a dependent position.

The policies of the state usually reflected and fortified this power situation. Strikes were usually illegal. The regulation of the market by state authorities as well as by provincial and municipal interference was ordinarily directed towards keeping labor abundant, cheap, and docile. The farmers were kept in their place.

The state was not democratic; suffrage was severely limited by income and other class restrictions. The organizational system was equally inegalitarian, loaded heavily in favor of the rich against the poor. The mode of functioning of these organizations was not collective bargaining between parties of comparable bargaining strength, but dictation by the stronger party, backed by the state which was very much only an institutional tool in the hands of the rich.

Quite generally, with all differences between the several Western countries, the situation is now an entirely new one. As suffrage has been extended, the state has become democratic. It has increasingly been induced to use its power to help the weaker economic strata to build up their own organizations; by legislation and administration it has given them support by changing the conditions under which they can bargain. In the Western countries, it is now almost impossible to comprehend a situation where the farmers had no effective organizations and where defenseless masses of workers were treated as they used to be by their employers and by the authorities.

5

Planning in the Welfare State

The Historical And Causal Order

In the last half century, the state, in all the rich countries in the Western world, has become a democratic "Welfare State," with fairly explicit commitments to the broad goals of economic development, full employment, equality of opportunity for the young, social security, and protected minimum standards as regards not only income, but nutrition, housing, health, and education for people of all regions and social groups. The Welfare State is nowhere, as yet, an accomplishment; it is continually in the process of coming into being. In no country was it originally planned in advance—certainly not as a structure of its present imposing ramifications and importance for the individual citizens. In all countries, even in those where the building of the Welfare State is most advanced, the architects are continually laboring with the tasks of simplification, coordination, rationalization and achievement of efficiency. Indeed, this planning becomes pressing as the edifice of the Welfare State rises.

That this must be so, should be clear from the analysis I have given of the forces behind the trend towards planning in the Western countries. The historical and causal order has been that acts of intervention in the play of market forces came first, and that planning then became a necessity. In a process of cumulative causation, the secular increase in the volume of intervention has been spurred on by the sequence of violent international crises since World War I, the increasing rationality of people's attitudes, the democratization of political power, and the growth of provincial and municipal self-government and of large-scale enterprises and interest organizations in all markets. Thus, as public and private intervention became more frequent and more far-reaching and closely related to the other constituents of this mighty process of social change, so there arose situations of growing complexity, contradiction, and confusion. With ever greater impact, the need for a rationalizing coordination of them all was pressed upon the state as the central organ for the public will.

Coordination leads to planning or, rather, it *is* planning, as this term has come to be understood in the Western world. Coordination of measures of intervention implies a reconsideration of them all from the point of view of how they combine to serve the development goals of the entire national community, as these goals become determined by the political process that provides the basis for power. The need for this coordination arose because the individual acts of intervention, the total volume of which was growing, had not been considered in this way when they were initiated originally.

As the state is increasingly involved in coordinating and regulating the national economy, it becomes compelled to make short-term and long-term forecasts, and to try to modify its policies for commerce, finance, development, and social reform in the light of what these forecasts show. A very much improved basis of statistical and other information is also becoming available to the governments. This coordination of policies, and their continued modification in order to remain appropriate in the setting of factual trends revealed by the forecasts, does not take the shape of a rigid, all-embracing plan. Nevertheless, it constitutes a steadily developing approach to planning, which tends to become firmer and more embracing as present tendencies work themselves out.

From Intervention to Planning

As regards the activities of the big enterprises and the organizations in the infrastructure beneath the formal constitutional structure, it is, of course, clear at the outset that they were not from the beginning part of a rationally coordinated national plan. They regularly represented special interests, not the general and common interests of the nation. But, as a matter of fact, the lack of coordination is equally apparent in public policies as they were initially motivated and decided upon. The history of economic policies in every country, as regards, for instance, tariffs and taxes, gives abundant proof of this thesis.

There is further proof in the records of how the huge structures for primary and higher education and for public health were built up, and also in the big redistributional reforms, such as the social security schemes and other measures for the care of the sick, the disabled, the unemployed, the aged, and the children. All these complexes of economic and social intervention, as they now exist, have been the end product of a long process of piecemeal, gradually induced changes, which in the different fields have been pressed forward, at first as independent and unrelated policy measures, motivated on their own merits or undertaken in response to group pressures.

It is, for instance, remarkable that the social security schemes, which are becoming increasingly expensive, were initially supported only by arguments of social justice and welfare for specific groups of people in need; and such arguments remained predominant for a long time. When the opponents of these schemes, who argued all the time that they would ruin the economy of the country, were again and again proved wrong, this was largely the result of the effect of these reforms in raising the productivity of the mass of the people—an effect which had never played an important part in their motivation. As considerations of these wider effects and interrelations gradually come to the fore in public discussion, the explanation is mainly that these policy measures have by now become so numerous and important, and that they re-direct the distribution of such a very large portion of the national product, that they simply must be coordinated with one another, and with the development of the entire national economy. Thus we arrive at planning in the modern sense.

Public intervention in the field of housing and construction of new houses, affords another example. Since the scanty and diffuse beginnings of a few decades ago, it has been increasing tremendously in all Western countries. The state now finds itself responsible for influencing decisively—directly through its legislation and administration and that of the provincial and municipal authorities, or indirectly through the organizations in the infrastructure that operate under the state's indulgence and sanction—the conditions under which people can find houses to live in, and under which some people can make it a business to provide homes. This involved complex of intervention concerns the level of rents, the availability and price of building and mortgage credits, the conditions on the several labor markets and the markets for building materials, and, indeed, every aspect of the entire economic process by which houses are built, owned or rented, and inhabited. The future number and the age composition of families and other factors determining both human need and effective demand for housing, must be predicted and allowed for, as must the effects of building activity upon trends of general business activity, in the short and long run. The latter effects are so important that the level of building activity has to be watched carefully, even from the point of view of general economic policy. As the cities grow, and as more public investment becomes involved in preparing for such growth, town planning becomes ever more necessary, as does the general public preoccupation with planning and directing the location of industry.

In the same way, the rapid development of higher and professional education now absorbs so much money, and concerns so many young people in all these countries, that it is gradually becoming realized that this activity cannot continue as an independent process of dispersed public policies. Instead, it has to be planned carefully on the basis of calculations of future demand for, and supply of, labor trained in different ways. This necessarily involves a forecast and a plan for the whole national economy. Again, the converse also applies; no long-range forecast or plan for the national economy can any longer be made without including policies for education and training.

Sweden is now inaugurating, as a final effort to complete the edifice of social security, a compulsory provident and pension scheme, aimed at eradicating what are almost the last remnants of class distinction between manual workers and other employees of public and private enterprises. It is probably taking the lead in a reform movement which other Western countries will soon join. All old people will, by legislation, be guaranteed an income corresponding to two-thirds of their earnings during the best fifteen years of their working life. It is clear that a redistributional reform of this huge magnitude must be founded on the most careful forecast of the development of the entire national economy for a long period ahead, and must be integrated into the whole system of public policies influencing this development. Otherwise it would represent the most reckless gambling with the future economy of the country, risking the frustration of national efforts in all fields. This is more evidently the case as the social security payments to the old are being guaranteed in real terms. It is characteristic of the situation Western countries have now reached in regard to planning that a main criticism raised in Sweden against this reform is that the calculations of its effects on the total economic development of the country are not complete and tight enough. This preoccupation with planning is not least prominent in the minds of the conservatives, who oppose the reform.

"Full Employment"

In a sense, the biggest commitment to economic planning in the Welfare State of the Western countries is that they are all now pledged to preserving "full employment," though the definition, as well as the form, of the commitment varies. The political process by which governments have gradually reached this situation illuminates this trend towards planning.

Not many decades ago the periodic appearance of mass unemployment was accepted as a more or less natural consequence of necessary market adjustments to changing business conditions, about which not much could be done. As, however, the political power of the workers increased in the process of democratization, to which I have referred, and as the social conscience became more alert to the sufferings of the unemployed and their families—two changes which, of course, are closely related—measures of financial aid to the unemployed were instituted in one country after another.

At first, these policy measures were all of a compensatory nature, aimed merely at providing the unemployed workers with some of the incomes they had lost by becoming unemployed. It was the sympton, not the cause, of unemployment that was being dealt with. Unemployment insurance, which now forms an integral part of the social security system in all Western countries, represents the consummation of this line of social policy. But soon the demand was raised that the state should take positive measures in order to create additional work opportunities for the unemployed. In the twenties, and still more during the Great Depression, public works policies spread in all Western countries. At the same time, the workers began to press for full wages even in these public works.

These developments represented only steps towards demanding that the state should so direct all its financial and economic policies as to create demand for labor sufficient to liquidate mass unemployment and to keep the national economy uninterruptedly in high gear. Economic theory now responded to the ideological needs of the time by placing the responsibility for economic depressions and unemployment on an imbalance between aggregate demand and supply, opening up a rational way for the state to raise investment and production and to create employment simply by raising its expenditure while keeping down taxation. In Sweden, which amongst the Western countries was the first, both theoretically and practically, to adopt this policy, "pump priming" worked fairly well even in the early years of the Great Depression, as it happened to be supplemented by other simultaneous changes in general business conditions which were favorable to a recovery but not part of intentional policy. Similar policies in the United States and many other countries were less successful, the main explanation being that the over-spending was too small to have much effect.

After World War II we have all become accustomed to much bigger budgets and also to taking huge budget deficits less seriously. The expansionist theory of spending one's way out of a depression is now on the way to becoming orthodox, even in the more conservative sections of the business world. It has, as yet, not been put to much of a test, however, as first the urgent reconstruction needs and the pent-up demands immediately after the war, and later the immense armament expenditures and other financial consequences of the cold war, have contributed in mighty fashion to sustain total demand. Inflation and not deflation has been the continuous worry. But, whatever the explanation, it is in any case a fact that on the whole all the Western countries have enjoyed full employment, not only during but also after the war. Now only a dwindling minority of workers in these countries have any personal experience of mass unemployment or any recollection of the situation some few decades ago, when even in boom years the fear of unemployment was a sinister cloud on the horizon for every working-class family. It is safe to predict that in none of the Western countries will a period of severe unemployment ever again be tolerated by the people.

In a sense, this determination to preserve full employment is the crowning accomplishment of the democratic Welfare State. It is generally understood and accepted that this implies a preparedness to use even radical policy measures, when needed, in order to keep the entire labor force employed, and also that this assumes a most careful watch on the entire economic development and a planned coordination of all economic policies.

The Fiscal Budgets

All these developments towards planning in the Western world have, of course, had their consequences for the fiscal budgets, which integrate a certain type of public intervention and, in one way or another, reflect others. A steady rise in the size of these budgets and an increased level of taxation were secular trends in Western countries even before World War I. These trends would have continued their course upwards, even without the push of the crises and the world wars, although they would have risen much less steeply. A convenient way of illustrating what has happened to fiscal policy may be to focus our attention on the science of public finance.

Public finance remained for centuries primarily a study of the rational conduct of the households of the states, the provinces, and the municipalities. Modern science took over directly from the Cameralists. Taxes were studied from the point of view of their ultimate incidence and their just distribution among the citizens. The relation between the public finances and the total economy of a country was dealt with in the same way as is natural and appropriate for an individual person or a business concern: exclusively as a one-way relation, from economy to taxation and public spending. The problem was how the development of the total economy reflected itself in changes in the need for public expenditure and in the yield of taxes and other public incomes at given rates.

For, before World War I, the public finances were not a large enough part of the total economy of a country to have any very significant influence in the other direction, i.e., on the business situation. And during this era, people, including the economists, were not interested enough anyhow in directing the national economy in a planned way to give much importance to this other problem. It lacked political actuality. This is the science of public finance we still find in our old textbooks.

This characterization of the science of public finance before 1914 is broadly correct. However, it must be borne in mind that even before the eighteenth century there had been plenty of speculation and discussion as to the role of fiscal policy, and especially of the effects of state borrowing on the general business situation. That interest, though, was usually centered upon one particular practical issue; it never determined the structure of fiscal theory as a whole. National budgeting was never approached with a view to its general effect upon the trade cycle or economic growth.

World War I had vast fiscal consequences, in many ways, and these were widely discussed. But such discussion never mentioned the possible use of the budget as a tool in social or economic engineering.

When the Great Depression set in during the thirties, public finances had already, because of the growth of public intervention in economic life, come to absorb so large a proportion of the national product that a variation of public incomes and expenditures could have a substantial influence on the development of the economy as a whole. And the interventionist spirit was rising. The science of public finance during the thirties became, therefore, focused on the problem of how to manipulate the fiscal budgets in such a way as to counteract business variations downwards.

This second stage turned out to be very short. Now, after World War II we are in the third stage. Often something around a third of the national income passes through treasury accounts and the trend is still rising. It thus becomes impossible to distinguish a separate public finance problem any longer. Both the old textbooks and our discussion during the thirties of a planned, counter-cyclical budgetary policy appear outmoded.

The problems of public finance are now inseparably merged with problems of international trade and payments, wages and incomes, money and credit. The theoretical organizing device is the national budget, conceived as the central bookkeeping control in the service of an over-

all state economic forecasting and planning network. The
national budget accounts for the composition of the entire
national income and its disposal for investment and consumption by private as well as public agents. In this national budget, the fiscal budget appears only as a set of
items to be analyzed as part of the whole.

The problems of the two earlier stages of the development of the science of public finance still exist and are
important: the incidence and the equitable distribution of
taxes and the influence of public finances on the general
business situation. But they are now integrated inextricably
with all other problems of economic policy and are subordinated to the one dominating question of the direction
of the whole national economy. In the short span of a
lifetime, the science of public finance has had its scope
and content radically changed, not once but twice. This
illustrates the impact of the growth of public policies and
points to the final result of this trend towards overall
state economic planning, even if this planning is as yet of
a compromise character and anything but comprehensive,
programmatic or politically ostentatious.

Converging Political Attitudes

One interesting aspect of this gradual perfection of the
modern democratic Welfare State is that many divisions
of opinion, once of burning importance, now tend to fade
away, or to change character and thereby to become much
less important.

This is, for instance, to a large extent true of the discussion of redistributional reform. Nobody nowadays gets
very excited about the issue of whether or not there should
be progressive taxation. The disagreement between participants in public debate, and between political parties, no
longer concerns this issue of principle, but to what extent

and by what devices taxation should be used to influence the distribution of wealth and income. Similarly, the discussion about whether there should be a system of social security has ended. The practical problem is now only how much money should be devoted to this purpose, who should pay it, and how it should be used. Reforms that have been carried through in a country generally win quick and sincere acceptance from the whole population. Even the continuation of this policy is accepted, and more redistributional reforms are becoming an almost automatic consequence of economic progress. We tend to arrive at a situation where there is a large measure of agreement among all the political parties. They sometimes even compete in propagating new and constantly more sweeping redistributional reforms as levels of income rise. In any case, we have seen very few examples, if any, where the coming into power of a more conservative political party has meant a substantial retraction of reforms previously carried through by a party which was further left.

This implies a gradual retreat from their earlier positions by the conservatives. In the opposite direction, we can also witness a coolness on the left towards many ideas of radical reform which were propounded by the Social Democrats when they were a small minority party without influence. Their demand for public ownership of banks, insurance companies, and industries, for instance, did not begin to take hold, and thus never built up any cumulative force. I have already referred in the Introduction to the inherited aversion, in the Western countries, to a "planned economy," of which large-scale nationalization, of course, is an extreme variant. That this aversion was supported and exploited by the business interests—whose power over the communications industry is everywhere strong—is obvious. It is apparent that, as the Social Democrats gradually won popular support and achieved political influence, they

generally tended to play down the nationalization issue
—with a longer or shorter ideological lag in the different
countries. It now plays an ever decreasing role in all
Western countries, and may be on the way to disappearing
altogether from the political scene.

There was, however, a more logical reason for this adjustment on the part of the Social Democrats. Nationalization could only be a means to reaching the basic aims of
their policy. As the Welfare State developed, these were,
however, largely attained by other means, and nationalization was no longer necessary, or even very desirable.

Private banks and insurance companies, for instance,
are now closely regulated by legislative and administrative
controls, initiated primarily to safeguard the interests of
the depositors and policy-holders, but increasingly used to
serve wider social ends. In the advanced Welfare State,
these enterprises become increasingly involved in regular
cooperation, both among themselves and with the central
bank and the treasury, in order to preserve the balance in
the money and capital markets. This cooperation can be
made more efficient, and the leadership of the state authorities, as the guardians of the public interest, can be
asserted, by an extension of such controls—without nationalization. Moreover, state and cooperative enterprises
enter as competitors, establishing standards in their markets. Last but not least, the enterprises are legally bound
to subject more and more of their activities to public
scrutiny. They are followed in detail by an increasingly
vigilant public and in particular by a whole array of private
power groups, each with its own facilities for research.
When all these things have happened, these enterprises
are not very private any more. Usually nothing much
could be attained by their being taken over by the state.

Or consider even the private industrial concern. Its
activities in the market are as a participant in industrial

associations. For most of its labor relations, it has to abide by agreements reached between the employers' association, of which it is a member, and the trade union system. It is legally bound to disclose periodically its complete accounts and also to discuss these and all major policy decisions with representatives of the workers. All profits from it are heavily taxed, as a matter of fact twice, according to steeply graduated rates, when they are distributed as incomes to the shareholders. Its decisions on the disposal of profits and internal consolidation are becoming increasingly regulated by law, and are open to state intervention when considerations of general economic policy make this desirable. In all these respects public control can be tightened, without resort to nationalization.

The industrial firm is a participant in a national community which is developing rapidly in the direction of the democratic Welfare State of equity and solidarity. Whether it is a family affair or a more impersonal concern, it is already, in essential respects, "socialized." Moreover, all its operations are constantly influenced by the knowledge, on the part of its owners as well as its managers, that each year it has to justify its existence as a private undertaking on pain of becoming more closely controlled and, perhaps, nationalized.

I may be exaggerating slightly. It is anyhow a fact that during the time, over a quarter of a century, that Sweden has been ruled by the Social-Democratic Labor Party—in fact longer, i.e., since that party in the 'twenties started to become a rising political force—while in all respects the development towards the Welfare State has been exceedingly rapid, there has, in that country, been no major move towards nationalization, although the party is committed to such a line by its formal program, which it has conservatively left unaltered. I would expect that sooner or later nationalization will disappear from the program, too.

In judging this development, it should, of course, be remembered that the Swedish state, as a legacy from long ago—and usually very long ago, in many cases from the era preceding even the liberal one—disposes of large domains of land, forests, and ore deposits, and, together with the municipalities, most water power; and that the state runs the railways and, together with the municipalities, has always owned almost all other public utility industries. That the nationalization issue, at least until recently, has played a more important role in English politics is very much due, I believe, to a difference in the initial situation, as well as to the lag in rationalization and efficiency in many private enterprises and to the relative lack of effective social control of private business, particularly through taxation.

It is possible that, in the Welfare State of the future, public ownership and public management will come to play a somewhat larger role, perhaps in the very long run a much larger one. But the change will in any case not come suddenly over the whole field. Whether or not to nationalize a particular industry will stand out less and less as a question of political principle and will be more and more a matter of practical expediency.

And in the individual case the change will not usually be of great importance. New state enterprises cannot now be run very differently from any other enterprise, state or private. They will not be "freer" towards other partners in the markets where they sell their products. In the labor markets they will have to negotiate the wages of their workers with the trade unions, as other enterprises do. The profits will go to the state, but through taxation some, and in some countries most, profits of private enterprises are going that way already, and the taxation screw can be further tightened, if that is desirable. The power relations in the national community will be changed by nationalization. But these are being changed anyway, by all the other changes in this process I have been analyzing, which has not nearly reached its end in any country and which in some countries is still far from the democratic ideal. As a matter of fact, all private enterprises in the advanced Welfare State are already in essential respects publicly controlled or are becoming so—without any nationalization of formal ownership.

A "Created Harmony"

The examples I have given of a trend towards convergence of attitudes and ideologies—in regard to the now largely undisputed, and consequently almost automatic, progress of further redistributional reforms, to which could be added educational and health reforms, etc., and the virtual disappearance of the nationalization issue—point to the increasing political harmony that has come to exist much more generally between all the citizen groups in the advanced Welfare State. The internal political debate in those countries is becoming increasingly technical in character, ever more concerned with detailed arrangements, and less involved with broad issues, since those are slowly disappearing.

To some extent, this harmony of interests and opinions is often spirited away and concealed by the professionals in the political parties and in the interest organizations. They have all a vested interest of self-preservation in making their flocks so much dissatisfied with existing conditions and trends that they can keep up active participation and retain momentum in their organizations. When they then occasionally mobilize the old armory of slogans from the time when people were still basically divided on broad issues of principle—liberalism, socialism, and capitalism; free enterprise and planned economy; private property and nationalization; individualism and collectivism, etc. —it can add emotional stimulus to a public debate otherwise tending to become colorless and bickering, because it arouses the associations still lingering in the old battle cries from a time when there were wider divisions of interest and wider disagreements on major issues as to how the national community should be organized. To the simpleminded it can almost give a feeling of intellectual elevation.

But these slogans are actually becoming rather shallow, and are generally felt to be so, when applied to the practical problems of the day in a functioning Welfare State. When instead the professionals restrict themselves merely to bickering in order to stimulate popular backing for their strivings on behalf of political parties and interest organizations, they are more in tune with how people really feel in a Welfare State—or can easily be brought to feel by propaganda.

The professionals' interests are divided, however. They seek, at the same time, to give the people to whom they appeal a feeling of satisfaction, and to associate this with an appreciation of what they have attained through participation in the organizations. When, in the advanced Welfare States, complete participation in the ordinary interest organizations, like the trade unions, is becoming the established pattern, this more positive interest in keeping people satisfied is becoming the stronger one. Even in such a state, political parties naturally still mostly have to take up a fighting position—at least at election times when they have to stimulate the lazy and undecided voters to vote, and to vote for them. All professionals, including the politicians, have, however, an interest in preserving favorable conditions for the normal day-to-day cooperation and collective bargaining among them all.

All things considered, it is my feeling that in the most

advanced Welfare States the professionals, except for special occasions such as elections or strikes, tend to do their best to keep people happy and tone down their dissatisfactions. There are, of course, always plenty of frustrated querulants, and they play a not altogether insignificant role in every Western country. But the general mood of the ordinary citizens in the advanced Welfare State can be observed to be one of quiet satisfaction—although combined with a ubiquitous urge, but also a reasonable hope, to get more and more of the good things of life.

Behind this attitude is the reality that in the Welfare State a higher degree of harmony of interests actually becomes attained through cooperation and collective bargaining. When in recent years the Social Democrats in Sweden sponsored, and had a decisive influence in inaugurating, social security legislation affording insurance payments rising with a person's income up to a very high level—in unemployment, sickness, and old age insurance —this was an indication, among many others, that the present income distribution, including the expectation of how it is going to change, is widely accepted in that country as just and fair, even by those who are in the relatively lower income brackets.

Not the Liberal Harmony

This gradually accomplished harmony of interests is not the old liberalistic one, which was supposed to emerge out of the unhampered working of free forces in the market. Quite the contrary: it has, as a matter of fact, resulted from a long historical process, during which the market forces have been ever more intensely and effectively regulated by acts of public and private intervention, so that these, as they became more numerous and important, had to become coordinated and planned in an ever more

comprehensive way. The harmony which is being realized
is therefore a "created harmony," created by intervention
and by planned coordination of interventions. It is the
opposite of the natural harmony of the old liberal philosophers and theoreticians.

But this process towards "created harmony" was, especially at first, not anybody's intention. The development towards planning, as I have pointed out, was not
itself planned. It evolved into the relatively very high
degree of social harmony attained, not because this was
ever clearly perceived by a majority of those who held
power as a political ideal to be accomplished by a purposive
reorganization of the national community to that end. It
happened in a very much more accidental, less direct and
less purposive way: by an unending sequence of acts of
intervention by the state, and many other collective bodies,
in the play of market forces. These acts of intervention
were mostly motivated *ad hoc,* and regularly had the much
more limited—and often, from the point of view of the
now accomplished Welfare State, obstructionist or even
subversive—objectives, directed by special interests. Taken
individually, they can seldom, in retrospect, even be considered to have been rational steps in the direction of
greater social harmony. Quite regularly, they were, in
fact, soon found to be hurting other interests to a degree
that was intolerable to them. As interests clashed, some
sort of accommodation had to be sought, and so, from time
to time, state measures and other collective intervention
had to be revised and coordinated, though again this was
usually done only on a limited scale and in a provisional
manner.

That in the end the accumulated result of all this
intervention by public, semi-public, and private organizations, and the gradual, planned coordination which they

necessitated, came nearer and nearer the "created harmony" of the Welfare State, has to be explained by an analysis, like the one undertaken in this book, of all those non-market forces which stimulated intervention in the markets and steered the intermittent attempts at coordinating them. Importance has then to be given to the increasingly rational formation of attitudes, which was both a cause and an effect of the growth of intervention, to the gradual democratization of political power, and, not least important, to the continual economic progress which increased elbow-room and made mutual generosity less exacting. While the actual conditions of life and work in the Welfare State, as it now functions, were never during this process consciously visualized as a goal by any individual or group or political party—naturally not by the conservatives or liberals, but not by the socialists either, as can be amply demonstrated by a study of political programs and writings from earlier times—at the end of the process the gradually accomplished Welfare State can become the widely acclaimed ideal of a whole nation. And that, then, is the created harmony of interests and opinions, which we can now see coming into being.

We can, however, also see that there has been a considerable lag, seen not only in the persistence of the formulae of controversy, which once had a deep subjective relevance to people which they now mostly lack, but also in the remarkable absence of any adequate positive and realistic ideology of the Welfare State, which would correspond to people's actual feelings about their national community and their actual preparedness for action to promote further reform. That the ideological development lags is to be expected. Human society is basically conservative and tends to hold on to ideas and ideals long after they have lost any realistic moorings in actual life. In this

particular case the ideological lag is greater, because of the
unintentional, haphazard, and almost offhand way in which
a situation has been reached, or is coming within reach,
which actually is felt to be ideal by the great majority of
people or near the ideal with the potentiality of getting continually nearer by a consistent development of
present trends—though the approach to the ideal was
never by way of intentional strivings directed towards it.
In fact, the ideal is becoming accomplished *pari passu*
with, or indeed in advance of, an intellectual grasp of it
as the ideal.

In the same way as the "created harmony" of interests in
the Welfare State of the Western countries was never
planned, and thus never "created" in the strict sense of
having been purposively attained, so the actual large-scale
planning, which is today a major explanation of the high
degree of harmony that actually exists, has remained largely
unprogrammatic. I have pointed out in the introductory
chapters that the interventionist trend, which in the end
necessitated coordination and planning, was for a long
time denounced as a matter of principle by most of those
who were themselves responsible for taking the individual
steps of intervention as political leaders and voters, or
leaders and participants in the organizations. This is often
the case even today.

In some of the Western countries, and particularly in
the United States, many people are straining their minds
in order to believe, against facts and reason, that their
relative social harmony—of which they too are usually
quite proud—is not "created" at all, but just natural, and
that they have a "free economy," ruled by market forces.
It can even be seen that, to many persons, the term
"Welfare State" has negative, not positive, connotations
—not, of course, because they do not appreciate welfare,

but because they are bent upon protecting themselves against realizing that welfare has not come into being by itself, as a result of the unhampered play of market forces, but through public policies, which are all under the ultimate sanction of the state.

6

The State and the Individual

A Regulated Society

When the mesh of diversified state intervention and all other public policies of various sorts, including those of the big enterprises and the organizations within the institutional infrastructure of the democratic Welfare State, have had to be coordinated in one field after another, under central state control, into unified structures of laws, rules, regulations, and agreements, and also fitted into a forecast and a plan for the development of the entire national economy—which is what has gradually happened and is happening in all Western countries—it will, as time goes on, be less and less possible to maintain that ours is a "free" or a "free enterprise" economy, with exceptions for a certain number of acts of state intervention. The exceptions are gradually becoming the rule.

As a matter of fact, ours is a rather closely regulated society, leaving a certain amount of free enterprise to move within a frame set by a fine-spun system of controls, which are all ultimately under the authority of the democratic state. The sanctity of private property rights to do what one pleases with a piece of land; or the right to keep all, except a nominal tax charge, of one's income and wealth for private consumption or investment; the freedom to enter upon any profession one wants at one's own risk; the right of the employer to negotiate individually with his workers, to pay the smallest salary he can for the job, and to hire and fire whom he wants, when he wants; or the right of the worker to leave the shop as and when he desires; indeed, the free choice to own, acquire, and dispose, to work or to rest, to invest, to trade, to move— all these time-honored individual liberties are gradually eaten away by the controls of organized society. And even if we close our eyes, or put on blinkers, and keep to old cherished formulae, this does not alter what is, already, increasingly the case.

People Like It

One of the explanations why people in general are rather well satisfied by living and working in these regulated national communities of the Western world is undoubtedly that they do not notice the controls so much, or do not react so violently, as they are becoming accustomed to them. The present level of taxation in all Western countries, for instance, would have been unthinkable fifty or even twenty years ago. There is a deep truth in Albert Einstein's observation, that if there were beings who were flat and without thickness, and who lived on the surface of a sphere, they would have no idea of a third dimension. Like domesticated animals, people growing up in the Western type of regulated national communities have no real conception any longer of a wilder life. To the reflecting social scientist the adaptability of the human animal to new conditions will never cease to be one of this world's wonders.

But partly, and I believe more significantly, the explanation of people's satisfaction with what has happened is that regulations in the democratic Welfare State are not pressed upon them from above, by a state dictatorship. They are felt to be the outcome of a social process, in the steering of which people are themselves participating.

Also, these regulations, under this popular influence, are very broadly framed so as to give new rights to the masses of people: to increase their opportunities, open roads that were closed before by their poverty or ignorance, and to secure them against risks that in earlier times were disastrous for the individual and his family.

Most people have good reason to feel freer, not less free in the Welfare State. As the material and social limitations upon the individual's freedom to act and move are broken down, and replaced by rules laid down by legislation and collective agreements, they pass under democratic control, and can be changed by a process where nobody is without a voice. The new rules must also appear less arbitrary and more rational, as when a young person's opportunity to attend a school and enter on a career comes to be conditioned by the merits he can earn in his work, and not so much as previously by geography and the economic and social status of his parents.

And everybody also is aware, of course, of the fact that in spite of wars and other adverse events, production, incomes, and particularly the levels of living of the broader strata of our national communities have been rising more rapidly than ever, and that the prospects of the young are brighter than were those of their parents or grandparents when they started life. Economically as well as socially, the Welfare State has been a conspicuous success. Of this the history of almost every individual home is a living and articulate testimony.

The fact that so many public policies are actually taking shape within the authorities for provincial and local self-government, and by agreements after collective bargaining amongst the numerous organizations within the infrastructure of organized society, contributes to the feeling of freedom amongst people, and the feeling that they are participating themselves in making the regulations they have to obey. In an advanced Welfare State, an increasingly large portion of the adult population is participating in government through membership on various municipal boards and councils responsible for the implementation of the laws and the disposal of funds—sometimes, as in Sweden, the payment of social security benefits and assessment of taxes—and, as they are elected, they have the officials as their subordinates. Other citizens are responsible for public policy as members of the boards of trade unions, cooperative associations of various types, and other interest organizations. In the advanced Welfare State with its high level of civic education and civic responsibility, these numerous office-holders are all "of the people," and not hired professionals. Everybody meets them in the workshops, in the streets, and in daily life. Many of the popular checks on their activity are informal and continuous, and thus not restricted to meetings and elections. The regulations which flow out of this ramifying organizational life appear to the whole community more as voluntary choices, more like the individual contracts and deals people would have to enter upon in the freest economy, as, of course, they do now. By also participating, directly or indirectly in the collective settlements, they feel that they have improved the conditions under which they make their individual moves. The increasing prevalence in the Western countries of this less formal type of public policy also means that its execution becomes smoother and more effective than it would be if it were all done by the state and its proper authorities.

This latter reason for satisfaction with the regulative activity of the Welfare State becomes stronger, of course, the more intense the democratic participation is on the different levels of collective decision making, a topic upon which I touched in Chapter 4. When participation is on a low level, we should expect people to be more apt to feel that the regulations are imposed upon them from above and that they are being pushed around by "them"—the bosses, the bureaucrats, and the oligarchies in the organizations, and by the strange and distant forces in Wall Street and Washington. This might breed feelings of resentment, and will anyhow frustrate people's feelings of solidarity and identification with the purposes of the regulations.

As usual, the social mechanism works in circular cumulations of causes and effects. For such attitudes will, in their turn, inhibit the intensification of participation, the lack of which was among their causes. Viewed the other way, feelings of solidarity and identification will lead to participation, while it is only participation that can inspire such feelings. If people can come to realize a higher degree of participation, the conditions are also created for the organizations beneath the state level to gain in effectiveness and importance, which has the consequence that state regulations in many fields become less called for. The regulations can then be moved nearer to people's grasp and control.

Replacing State Interventions

In Sweden the trade unions are particularly strong. They are industrial unions, open and, under firm sanctions, democratically ruled. As hundred per cent membership on the part of the workers has become integrated in the unquestioned mores, they need not, of course, press the employers for any "closed shop" clause in order to be in the position to act with the power of the workers' full backing. There, they have certainly used their influence to get established by state legislation many general conditions in the labor market. But they have consistently been against having minimum wages fixed by law or by administrative state organs. They have been afraid that minimum wages might reflect themselves upon the fixing of actual wages. In any case they have felt themselves to be in a position where, so far as wages are concerned, they are strong enough to take care of their own interest.

For the same reasons they have joined the employers' associations in resisting any type of regulatory state interference in labor disputes and in the actual settlements of the collective agreements, by arbitration courts or in other ways. As the trade unions become entrenched, conscious of their power and settled in a routine of procedures whereby they, together with the employers' unions, regulate in a mutually satisfactory manner more and more things in the labor market, they might in time be prepared both to see the end of a lot of detailed legislation on hours of work, vacations and the like, and to take over in cooperation with the employers' unions much inspection of sanitary and other conditions, which is now still carried out by state administrative organs.

Generally, as levels of living and education rise, and as people's participation in the affairs of the national community through the regular political processes and through all the organizations within the institutional infrastructure increases, we may approach a situation where many important public policies can be put into effect without much direct state intervention in the ordinary sense, and particularly without necessitating more than a minimum of state administration, simply by activating, as a means of communal control, the pressure of enlightened public opinion, and the bargaining strength of the organizations.

I might be permitted to select still another example from Sweden, where this process has proceeded fairly far. In order to suppress restrictive and unfair business practices, we made it a law in Sweden that certain defined agreements, which might be suspected of having such purposes, whether oral or written, should be declared to, and registered by, an administrative agency. This agency was commissioned to make such agreements public by issuing a bulletin, and also empowered to make special investigations, if it felt that it would be of importance in a particular field.

The immediate effect of this law, even before the new agency had started to function, was that a number of monopolistic arrangements of the defined character were scrapped in order to avoid their being publicized. At a later stage, the industrial associations, who disliked having the state involved at all in such business matters, expressed the view that this was very much their own concern, and they set up their own agency to fight this type of business practice. It is my judgment that in an advanced Welfare State, with democratically balanced interest organizations and a vigilant citizenry, the mere decision by parliament to make the restrictive practices in business part of general knowledge is quite an effective device for public control, and that often in such a country the need for legislation, prohibiting specific practices, and administrative controls enforcing the legislation can be kept to a minimum and reserved for strategic fields.

A little more than twenty years ago, we in Sweden made a law forbidding an employer, public or private, to dismiss a woman for family reasons: because she became engaged, married, or had a child. At that time, it was a custom widely indulged in by officers of banks, insurance companies, and other large employers of female clerical workers to use such occasions as a pretext for keeping themselves surrounded by young women, who were also cheaper as they then never acquired seniority in their jobs. There were even occasional problems of that type in public service. And it was sometimes made difficult for an unmarried mother to keep her job if, for instance, she was a teacher in a rural district.

This law, which was an offshoot of the lively interest in the problems of the family in the middle 'thirties, was certainly necessary at the time it was passed in order to enforce a change of prevailing mores which the legislators deemed unwholesome. At the present time, however, when public opinion is generally more enlightened, I believe the law could be repealed without risk. An occasional attempt to dismiss a woman for one of the reasons mentioned would be censored by public opinion. And the rule would be further enforced by the sanction of the very real pressures in the possession of the women's organizations, which would now have the backing of the trade and professional unions.

I am confident, too, to take another example, that there will come a time in America, perhaps not as very far off as many believe, when there will be no practical need to retain legislation, courts, and administration to defend Negroes against discrimination in the labor market and elsewhere.

But in the immediate future I am convinced there are many fields where we should prepare ourselves for a radical diminution of state regulations. Decisions as to the hours when shops are kept open could, in good communities, be left to be settled by agreements between the interested parties, if they were well organized, including the general public of buyers and consumers. Much legislation and inspection of food and many other things could also be simplified if the general public were better educated as consumers, and if their interests were effectively protected by strong and efficient consumers' organizations. The efforts and costs necessary to reach such a situation would be small, compared, for instance, with the huge expenditure on competitive advertising.

In many cases it is undoubtedly practical, not only to lay down certain general rules by legislation, but also to sanc-

tion their enforcement not only by courts but by administration. It is my conviction, however, that it should be possible to leave much more detailed regulations to be settled
by the people themselves, in their local communities and
through bargaining between their organizations. This will
promote the coming into being of a more cooperative national community, with more identification, solidarity, and
participation on the part of the individual citizen, who
then will come to feel freer—and he actually will be more
free. As I see it, this is the inherent ideal, which the developing democratic Welfare State is reaching towards. It implies the coming into existence of a "Welfare Culture"
within the structure of the Welfare State.

The Next Phase

Let us assume that, in the next phase of growth and perfection of the Welfare State, we could achieve such a
gradual diminution of direct state intervention by activating the people to take care of their own interests within
the general rules laid down by the democratic state. The
development would then, in a sense, have completed a full
circle.

It started out from the quasi-liberal state of mass poverty,
much social rigidity, and gross inequality of opportunity.

It went through a period when the old automatism went
out of the system. Through a sequence of increasing public
and private intervention and, flowing from this, intermittent attempts at their coordination by planning, we reached
the present situation, where direct state intervention is
still continually increasing in volume, though it is now
only partially responsible for the social controls within
the bounds of which we live.

In this transitional phase of the development towards
the more perfect democratic Welfare State, while coordina-

tion and planning are becoming gradually more thorough, under the pressure of the continually growing volume of intervention, both by the state and by collective authorities and power groups beneath the state level, it often happens that people confuse planning with direct and detailed state regulations. The opposite, however, is true; there is still such a large volume of intervention because the measures are not ideally coordinated and planned. Planning should normally imply simplification and rationalization. We assume further that, as planning proceeds, it will be seen to be in line with the ideals of the Welfare State to delegate, wherever it is safe and practicable, responsibility for detailed public regulations to local and sectional collective authorities instead of having them carried out by means of direct state intervention.

The third phase could thus mean an actual decrease of state intervention. The assumption is a continued strengthening of provincial and municipal self-government and a balanced growth of the infra-structure of effective interest organizations. This would, in its turn, presume an intensified citizens' participation and control, exerted in both these fields.

I do maintain that, in those of the Western countries that have advanced farthest in the accomplishment of the democratic Welfare State, we have already seen sporadic, and sometimes more than sporadic, auguries of this third phase. If we take these omens as representing the beginning of a development that we would like to see continued, and if we extrapolate that development, implying their generalization over the whole society, we would see a quite new situation emerging. The state as such could on the whole restrict itself to doing two main things, leaving the rest for local self-government and for cooperation and bargaining between the organizations in the infra-structure.

First, the state would have to maintain and strengthen a number of established, fundamental and—in the literal sense of the word—radical policy structures of a general character in such fields as international commerce and exchange, taxation, labor legislation, social security, education, health, and, of course, defense. In addition, the state will in most countries undoubtedly continue to run the railroads and to have the exclusive responsibility for the post, the telegraph, and the telephone. In cooperation with the municipalities it will own the public utilities, or at least control them closely. The state may or may not take over the businesses of banking and insurance and perhaps even increase the number of industries it is managing under its own regime; but for reasons already given in the last chapter it does not make much difference whether it does or not. By these policies the state would be organizing the national community in accordance with the public will as determined by the people's mandate, and also changing the conditions under which local self-government operates and the bargaining amongst the organizations goes on.

Second, the state would have to establish and continually adjust rules, and provide an umpire service, for life in the local and sectional compartments of the national community, as it evolves through provincial and municipal self-government and in the interest organizations operating in the several markets, and as it is conditioned by the first type of policy as well as by the rules themselves. One important part of these rules and this general supervision will concern the public desire that the organizations within the infrastructure be democratically governed, open and under satisfactory publicity controls, like other organs for public policy.

Within the general framework provided by these two types of state policies, the public will is then realized by an enlightened and active people, without calling for much direct state intervention *in casu*. The people will do this both directly through general community pressure, establishing and sanctioning what in reality is a system of social morals, and more indirectly through their participation in local self-government and in their interest organizations. Most uncertainties about detailed norms for the carrying on of business, work, and of life in general within the national community are then settled by one form or another of organized cooperation and collective bargaining in the local and sectional communities.

On the whole the state, as such, can keep out, after it has laid down the general rules for this dispersed activity and also after it has, by its major policy schemes of the type first mentioned, induced such fundamental changes of the conditions under which cooperation and bargaining go on that the arrangements reached are just and equitable, in line with the public will as ascertained by the political process in a democracy. All the main state policies of both types would, of course, have to be carefully planned and coordinated, so that the intended result is a development of the national economy as a whole, and all social relations within it in the desired direction.

The Welfare State of tomorrow would then realize a type of society which in many fundamentals would have deeply satisfied John Stuart Mill and all the earlier liberal philosophers more than a hundred years ago, if they had had the power of imagination to envisage the final implications of a development they barely saw the beginnings of. Even that angry old philosopher-historian, Karl Marx, who gave such an uncompromising expression of the old liberal vision, held since John Locke, of a society freed from class monopolies, and who enjoyed such a sadistic dream about the painful way it was determined to be reached by a natural development, would find much of his "realm of liberty." And Thomas Jefferson would most

definitely see in the accomplished Welfare State a realization of "grass-root democracy," though in a very different,
much more complicated, world than was within his vision.
We would finally be reaching a state worthy of *consensus
sapientium*.

The Utopia and the Reality

I have intentionally meant to depict a utopia. The reality
in all our Western countries is far from realizing it. I
would nevertheless insist on the relevance of the utopian,
decentralized, and democratic state where, within the
bounds of ever more effective overall policies laid down
for the whole national community, the citizens themselves
carry more and more of the responsibility for organizing
their work and life by means of local and sectional cooperation and bargaining with only the necessary minimum of
direct state interference. This utopia is, in my belief, a real
goal. It is inherent in those ideals of liberty, equality, and
brotherhood that are the ultimate driving forces behind
the development of the modern democratic Welfare State.
If we made the ideology of the Welfare State more explicit,
i.e. if we clarified our direction and aims, this utopia would
stand out as our practical goal.

Bureaucracy, petty administrative regulations, and generally a meddlesome state should not be the signum of our
vision of a more accomplished democratic Welfare State.
To fight against regimentation from above was always a
rallying cause for the progressive elements in the Western
countries. Now, when the state has been brought more
effectively under the democratic control of the people, we
have every reason to use state legislation and administration for fundamental economic and social policies of the
two types mentioned in the last section. But we should not

make peace with bureaucracy. I view as short-sighted those would-be reformers, both in the United States and in other Western countries, who, in their urge to improve society, place an almost exclusive trust in continual extension of state regulations, thereby presenting their fellow-citizens with a sort of "etatistic liberalism."

We need to clarify in our minds two cardinal points. The first is that the purpose of planning, which in our countries has developed as a second thought, necessitated by the un-planned growth of intervention of all sorts on all levels of collective life in our national communities, should be, not only to reach more effectively our broad policy goals, but also, in accomplishing this, to simplify the interventions in a radical fashion by coordinating them. Continually in one field after another a smaller number of overall rules and regulations should be substituted for the larger number of *ad hoc* and direct interventions. The second point is that in line with all our inherited ideals, and also with the actual potentialities in our national communities, we should be intent upon reaching this simplification of state interferences by continually decentralizing the direct state controls of everyday work and life.

In fact, as levels of education and civil loyalty rise, and as we succeed in strengthening local and sectional com-munity life, the obvious direction of the efforts of progres-sive citizens should be to make more and more direct acts of state intervention superfluous. As I have pointed out, we already have, in all our countries, a great number of state laws, regulations, inspections, and controls which, even if they were once needed, are at the present time plainly unnecessary, or could easily be made so. By leaving more actual government to public and private organs be-neath the state level, we would at the same time strengthen those organizations for community control, make them more important for the individuals concerned, and give motives for more intensive popular participation in government.

The obsolete or unnecessary state regulations are partly remnants from earlier phases of the development towards the Welfare State, when the gradual steps towards central coordination of the mass of unplanned and dispersed intervention were seldom radical enough, but left a sediment of needs for direct acts of state intervention, which now remains with us as rigid and often arbitrary bureaucracy. Some of them are a legacy from still earlier history and stem from a time when our countries were less democratic, more autocratic and more rigidly stratified into classes. And, now as always, bureaucracy has its own will to survive. To give up autocratic patterns, to give up administrative controls and to dismiss personnel employed in managing them, and generally to withdraw willingly from intervening when it is no longer necessary, are steps which do not correspond to the inner urgings of a functioning bureaucracy.

But more fundamentally the "etatism" of our Welfare States in their present development phase is a reflection of the fact that no country has, as yet, brought that simplifying coordination of the mesh of proliferating intervention of all sorts, which represents the Western type of planning, to anything like perfection. And meanwhile the volume of direct state intervention is still increasing everywhere, even if the central administration's relative share of community controls is decreasing. The process by which local self-government and a balanced and effective infra-structure of open and democratically controlled organizations are coming into their own is in none of the Western countries carried to completion; in some countries it sometimes seems as if this process of decentralization of government is reversed, at least temporarily and in some fields.

To build up and preserve popular participation in government at all levels is everywhere an acute problem. Education in the operation of grass-root democracy and solidarity with the community have nowhere reached such high levels that informal community controls have acquired anything like their maximum effectiveness. It is against this background that we have to understand the tendency of the reformers everywhere to look for more direct state intervention as the means of improving the life of their national communities.

For various reasons these persistent weaknesses in the very foundation of the Welfare State are much more pronounced in the United States. There, as I mentioned in Chapter 4, popular participation is comparatively low on all levels. As a consequence of this, local and sectional cooperation and bargaining is relatively ineffective in the face of the vested interests, and sometimes infected by machine and boss rule and by corruption. The process of national integration has still a considerable distance to go before identification, solidarity, and participation reach the levels common in the other Western countries. This is so, not because the American nation is big and has so much space to live in, nor because it is young, nor because the people in America are so mobile, but because it still bears the impact of being composed of the descendants of immigrants with different cultural backgrounds who show separatistic loyalties.

Not unrelated to this, the United States has also more than its due share of a structure of social relations that is still legalistic. It depends more on rigid state regulations and has an overgrown bureaucracy with, relatively speaking, not very high standards of efficiency and economy of effort. When the Americans are ahead of all the other Western nations in productivity, it is accomplished in spite of these shortcomings in their public life, and has to be explained in terms of the rich natural resources in their spacious realm and the spectacularly efficient organization of private business: the work on the farms, in the factories, in the shops, and in the offices.

With their lingering heterogeneity and separatistic loyalties, the Americans undoubtedly need far more state legislation to lay down general rules for conduct in life and work than the more homeogeneous nations do. And as local and sectional community control is weaker and often less in line with the ideals of the national community, there are many more fields of social life in the United States where there is need for direct state control through the courts and the administration in order to enforce those general mores. This also explains why we find that in the United States further centralization of controls is so much the policy of those who seek to promote progress. It explains why the politicians and the ordinary citizens, irrespective of the political party they belong to, so regularly think of direct state intervention as the appropriate remedy for wrongs. In no other country does the thought that "there ought to be a law against" this or that so readily come up in every discussion about conditions in the national community.

It is important, however, not least in the United States, to keep in mind as a long-range goal the values in decentralizing the community controls. As I see it, the strivings towards that goal are not hopeless. Even in America the conditions are gradually being created for more efficient collective authorities on the local and sectional levels. The rapid national integration in America can also, I believe, be relied upon to gradually decrease that country's special need of laying down general rules by legislation and of having to rely upon central state controls in order to enforce their observance. And the reformers in America have reason to remember that in this process those organs beneath the state level are apt to increase more rapidly in effectiveness and active participation of the people, the more scope they are given. For this reason it is rational to take risks, and even to make temporary sacrifices, in the endeavor to spread out ever wider and deeper the roots of democracy in the national community. This is indeed the meaning of the old and cherished American saying that the remedy of what is still imperfect and wrong in society is more, and ever more, of democracy.

Another important fact is that people in America as in other Western countries dislike a meddlesome state, regimentation, and red tape. It is true, as I have stressed, that there is a growing satisfaction among ordinary people in all our countries with the relative levels of abundance, equality, and security which we are reaching. I even pointed to the emergence of a "created harmony" of interests in the Welfare State. It is also true that people become accustomed to a regulated life when that has become the set pattern. They accept that life more willingly, however, when they themselves participate in making and managing the regulations that govern them.

There is now, in all our countries, a rising tide of resentment against tinkering by the state organs, which sometimes detracts from the appreciation of the Welfare State as such. As we are still in the transitional stage, when the volume of direct state intervention is continually rising because national planning has not caught up with the need for coordination and simplification and because cooperation and bargaining in the collective organizations beneath the state level has not developed enough, such tamperings has been on the increase. The "etatistic liberals" in America and elsewhere should be aware of the danger that the reactionaries can exploit, at least partly and temporarily, the popular dislike of tampering by the state and turn it into a resistance against the Welfare State itself, and against planning. Those who stand for progress and reform in our countries may then easily be caught in a position where they defend such tampering, while the reactionaries can depict themselves as standing for freedom.

But quite apart from all tactical considerations, to de-bureaucratize the state and liberate the people from petty interferences, exerted by authorities above their heads and outside their immediate control, is a progressive cause— today as in Jefferson's time. It can be accomplished only by perfecting and strengthening the Welfare State. The essence of the argument in this book is, that though planning is continually being necessitated by the rising volume of intervention, the purpose and accomplishment of planning in the Welfare State is, in fact, constantly to simplify, and largely to liquidate, old and new intervention: to substitute a few, mostly overall state policies for a growing mesh of detailed and direct ones, and, in particular, to recondition the national community in such a way that for the most part it can be left to the cooperation and collective bargaining of the people themselves, in all sorts of communities and organizations beneath the formal state level, to settle the norms for their living together.

7
Planning and Democracy

A Strengthened Democracy

In Chapter 3 I have shown how the gradual development in the Western countries of a fully democratic system of government founded upon universal suffrage has been one of the forces that, through an involved social process, has led to the present situation which, from one point of view, is characterized by ever more planning. Logically, the fact that democracy has resulted in planning does not, of course, exclude the possibility that planning might destroy democracy. We would then be assuming a sort of satanic destiny, under which democracy would contain the germs of its own deterioration and death.

This is apparently what is assumed in much of the popular literature on the issue of a "free" versus a "planned" economy, to which I referred in the Introduction. Though, for reasons I gave there, I do not want to get mixed up in that stale controversy, which is so remote from any relation to real problems, I might point out in passing that of course the trend towards planning which I am analyzing is not endangering democracy but instead giving it wider scope and deeper roots.

In particular, the growth of local self-government, and the increasing strength of the organizations within what I have called the institutional infrastructure of the modern democratic Welfare State, imply that more means are becoming available to the citizens for taking part in the moulding of their own destinies. These agencies for collective decisions on public policy beneath the state level are, at the same time, becoming increasingly involved in determining that state planning which sets the pattern of their own activities. The political procedure of the state itself has been brought under widening popular control. Meanwhile, even in the constitutions and operations of private organizations an increasing emphasis on democratic principles of openness, publicity, and effective membership control is visible.

The degree to which these means for democratic decision-making will actually be used, and so underpin and strengthen democracy, will depend on the intensity of participation and on feelings of communal loyalty and solidarity. It is of importance, however, that even in a country where the degree of citizens' participation is not so high as could be desired, the very existence and functioning of these local and sectional agencies for cooperation and collective bargaining will tend to make people's attitudes more specific and more related to their real, even if narrow, interests. Their opinions will be more worldly and in that sense more rational: more stable on general issues and much more flexible on all practical matters. Their political choices will thus be better protected against the influence of free-wheeling phantasts and demagogues, dealing in slogans and emotionally-charged and distorted stereotypes. As this rationalization of people's attitudes is materializing —and I definitely feel it is happening in all the western countries, though with different speed and though they have arrived at different stages of progress—democracy is undoubtedly strengthened.

The Historical Perspective

In a sense this is a morphological generalization, founded upon an analysis of what is actually happening inside the machinery of the present Western democracies as the trend to planning proceeds. To it I would add that, in broad historical perspective, we have, so far as I know, never seen a democracy failing because of too much planning.

Planning did not, of course, destroy democracy in Russia, as there was none to begin with. The planning which was clamped down after the revolution on that autocratic, poor, and backward country by a totalitarian and monolithic dictatorship is of a totally different nature from the compromise coordination of public policies which has gradually developed in the rich Western countries through a social process in which political democratization, the strengthening of provincial and local self-government, and the growth of an infrastructure of voluntary organizations have been essential elements.

In the German Weimar Republic there were the beginnings of democracy. But when it collapsed in the early thirties, it was certainly not due to an overdose of planning. In part Hitlerism was caused by the heavy legacy of autocracy, junkerdom, and militarism from the time before World War I; in part it was a reaction amongst the German people to the defeat in that war. Hitlerism was also permitted to exploit the feelings of frustration amongst the German people, stemming from the deprivations and the widespread unemployment caused by the impact of the Great Depression. It is, indeed, quite probable—and I thought so at the time, too—that a little more of the type of economic planning which we already had in the Welfare States of some Western countries, by alleviating the effects of the depression in the late twenties and early thirties, would have preserved democracy in Germany and saved both the Germans and the world from great disasters. If, in the autumn of 1931, Brüning and his advisers had not adhered so passionately to the gold standard and the defunct liberalistic doctrines of monetary automatism, but permitted Germany to devalue its currency as Britain and Scandinavia did, even that modest element of "planning" might have preserved German democracy.

More recently, when democracy was eclipsed in France, again it was not an excess of planning that was the cause but, as everybody knows, quite other things. The conjunction within its tradition of a stubborn individualism with state centralism has there, as I mentioned, prevented the wholesome growth of provincial and local self-government, kept its organizational infra-structure weak and unbalanced, and even frustrated the working of its parliamentary system. In addition, more acutely, the immediate cause was France's tragic and hopeless involvement in colonial wars which were equally disastrous to the nation morally and financially.

The democratic regime in Western Germany after World War II has started to work under much better auspices, and there is little in the country's internal life to endanger its future. For reasons I have hinted at above and in Chapter 4, I am putting a parenthesis around France in my analysis. France is a very special case because of its peculiar combination of individualism and centralism. In the other countries of the Western world I see no dangers for democracy emerging from internal causes. There, democracy has had many centuries of uninterrupted growth. Long before these countries had a system of universal suffrage, they had settled down to the rule of law, regulating in a non-arbitrary fashion the relations amongst individuals and between them and the state. In all cases, the more recent trend towards the Welfare State has there strengthened and deepened the forces of democracy. Our democracy has proved that it can take violent economic crises in its stride. We have now every reason to believe that in the future we will even be able to prevent the crises from having such deep and damaging effects in the individual countries. Democracy has successfully withstood the internal pressures caused by two world wars.

Naturally, our nations could be crushed by foreign domination. In fact, all the dangers for democracy in the Western countries lie in the field of their foreign relations —as, to a crucial extent, did those in the German Weimar Republic, and as do those of present-day France—not in the working of the internal forces which I have been analyzing. Already a prolonged cold war has had deeply disconcerting effects. We have recently seen with great anxiety that even in America, which is economically so strong and so relatively secluded behind the oceans—rather more, indeed, in America than elsewhere in the Western world— the popular fear of great danger from abroad can damage the established processes of lawful democracy at home.

That is an entirely different matter, however, outside the scope of the present inquiry.

Democracy A Danger For Planning?

While in the Western countries the trend towards planning is certainly not a danger for democracy, there is more truth in the converse proposition. Democracy, which is itself amongst the forces driving forward the trend towards planning, can, in certain of its manifestations, endanger, or at least postpone, the fullest rationality of planning.

In Part II I will discuss how the democratic Welfare State tends to turn people's interests inwards and make them nationalistic. I believe that in all Western countries the Welfare State is now more narrowly nationalistic than corresponds to the ideals and the long-term interests of the citizens.

Apart from the serious international implications of planning in the Welfare State, viewing the problems entirely in their national setting, there are, in the democratic processes, dangers to the rationality of planning. This is so, as long as people are badly informed about their own interests and the facts and, therefore, gullible. They will remain the more disoriented and easily fooled, the lower their active participation is in the community life on the national, local, and sectional levels. It all boils down to this, that a more perfect democracy needs a more enlightened and vigilant people.

There is still much of sham even in our big redistributional reforms. Our taxation is advertised to be, and is commonly believed to be, steeply progressive, but by various devices the tax laws are permitting the rich to become richer while they live well, in spite of their paying most of their "incomes" in taxes. In Britain and some other countries, where there are no taxes on capital and on capital gains, and where generous means are provided for avoiding inheritance tax by giving away the wealth in advance of one's death, the situation is almost scandalous, though it is largely concealed from workers and salaried people who are really pressed by taxation and social insurance payments. In Sweden and the United States the tax system is more rigorous, but even there the real incidence of taxation is very different from what it seems to be.

The big and anonymous interests of the corporations exert in various ways an influence which is seldom democratically balanced by the power of the workers and consumers. They are highly skilled at concealment and at accepting public controls which appear to be far-reaching but which can be evaded. Their interlocking directorships, leaving little real influence to the ordinary share-holders, and the links established between top leaders in business, politics, higher education, and in all other fields, creates a virtual power oligarchy. This becomes particularly influential in countries where, as in the United States, popular participation and control in the mass organizations is often weak, so that their leaders, for instance in the trade unions, can more easily be drawn into collusion. In Britain, the surviving class hierarchy provides an elusive but firm structure to this undemocratic power concentration.

Reforms in the interest of the lower income brackets are often no more than bribes to conceal much bigger advantages given to the higher brackets. Agricultural policies in most Western countries give plenty of evidence for this. I have already pointed out that progressivity in taxation is to a large extent merely a pretense.

The rich are usually left free to "vote with the dollar" by making financial contributions to political parties that defend their interests. By a strange extension of the principle of the secret ballot, they are usually allowed to keep their contributions anonymous. They are, indeed, often in a position to deduct them from the income for which they are taxable, so that this privately directed buying of influence is actually subsidized to a large extent by the state itself. Except in Sweden, so far as I know, a person's wealth and income is not a matter for public record, but is supposed to be entirely his own private affair—with the provision only that they must be disclosed, in confidence, to the tax-assessing authorities and, perhaps, used in statistics, where the individual disappears in the group. The secrecy around one's economic status has been elevated to the dignity of an important civil liberty.

In this undemocratic and protective social system a major role is played by the formidable power of the communications industry to influence people's attitudes and choices. As freedom of communication is a basic principle in democracy, it is not possible to infringe very effectively upon its activity. But, as it is an industry, its services are available at a price, and it is conducted according to effective money demand. In so far as it influences people, this determines not only their consumption patterns but may determine their opinions on public issues and their votes. This strikes at the very basis of democracy.

As I have hinted, under the influence of propaganda for private consumption of all kinds, which is not matched by any equally powerful campaign for the consumption of services provided by organized society, the voters tend to keep public-spending below the level that would be rational. But, much more generally, reforms in the interest of the effective implementation of the voters' true inclinations, for instance in the distribution of the tax burden or the controls over business, have everywhere to overcome tremendous inhibitions created by the services of the communication industry, hired by persons and groups with a vested interest in maintaining the *status quo*.

But leaving aside the powerful vested interests of those who are in command because of their wealth and their control over the machinery of business, and also the influence over public opinion which they can buy by engaging the services of the communication industry, even in a much more perfect democracy there will always be a tendency for groups with very special interests, and which are small and not united for exerting pressure, to find their interests badly protected. Such groups are, for instance, criminals and mentally deranged or feeble-minded persons and their dependents. They are few, and they are not easily organized; and the incidence of the misfortune of becoming one of them is so small—or is, in any case, commonly considered to be so small—that solidarity with them among the outside community is difficult to mobilize. In no Western country is their treatment by society up to the standards of welfare, or even of decency, which are otherwise commonly attained.

The interests of the aging are, on the contrary, usually well protected, because we all know that we must grow old some day. For similar reasons the sick and disabled are not forgotten in the Welfare State. But large families, on the other hand, in spite of the redistributional measures taken, on the whole still remain an ill-favored group. Children have no votes, and parents of large families are statistically only a tiny minority in every electorate. Since young people in Western countries do not usually plan to have many children, and since older people either had small families or, if not, remember that they did not get much support from society, there is little solidarity with large families. The mechanism I have in mind is illustrated very clearly by the fact that the owners of automobiles, even in a country where they are still a minority, are a powerful pressure group which every government has to reckon with most carefully, for the simple reason that many more people hope some day to own an automobile.

In all those issues, where the Welfare State is faltering, progress has to rely on education. The individual must be made to know the social facts more accurately, including his own true interests and the ideals he holds on a deeper level of his sphere of valuations. He will then become more "propaganda safe," to use a technical term that became widespread in America before the outbreak of World War II, but which has now unfortunately lapsed from common usage, presumably because the communications industry does not like its connotations. As his objective knowledge of the national community in which he lives is improved, he will not be misled by the power oligarchy. He will reform taxation and everything else. As he comes to understand his own true aspirations and the conditions of his fellow citizens, he will also feel a greater solidarity with all groups, even those that are small, split, and unhappy, in the national community.

I am quite aware that this prescription is nothing less and nothing more than the age-old liberal faith that "knowledge will make us free." I feel reason for hope in the fact that everywhere the Welfare State has preserved its faith in education and is now devoting more and more efforts—and public funds—to raising educational levels, and in the further fact that the Welfare State in all fields is actually progressing, often against the strongest vested interests of a crafty power oligarchy and the most fierce mobilization of the resources of the communications industry.

Inflationary Pressures

I should like to be a little more specific in illustrating the falterings of the Welfare State in one important respect, by commenting briefly on the tendency of most Western countries to run into inflation. In the present transitional period, this tendency can almost be said to characterize the democratic Welfare State, in spite of the fact that the higher economic levels in the Western countries should make it more possible for them to preserve monetary balance.

To accept an inflationary development without resistance would inevitably have undesirable results for the distribution of real incomes and wealth and for the direction of investment and production. It might be dangerous for the political stability of a country.

To suppress or moderate an inflation, without restoring balance between aggregate demand and supply, necessitates instead a large number of direct acts of state intervention of a type which no group of citizens would like to support for their own sake: rationing, building controls, allocations, price controls, etc. If the whole world is not going in the same direction, or equally fast, it will also be necessary to institute direct foreign exchange and trade controls. What I am here describing is a situation in which most Western countries, from time to time, have found themselves in the post-war period.

The spreading out of such direct state intervention into detailed regimentation results in all sorts of uneconomic misallocation of production and investment. It endangers the standards of morality in business and in the government departments responsible for the controls. The political and economic brains in the governments and political parties, who should be engaged by the major problems of the national economy, become preoccupied with this petty tinkering. Their planning efforts become wasted in a rearguard fight against the price consequences of an inflationary pressure which they have not had the will and strength to prevent. Incidentally, this also tends to orientate the work in economic science away from the broad issues to petty, short-term problems.

Collective Bargaining Between the Producers Alone

There are some general reasons why, in this transitional phase, the democratic Welfare State in the Western countries is in danger of running into inflation. To begin with, every government and every parliament must be tempted to satisfy the citizens—or strategic groups of citizens—a little more than is warranted by the tax burdens it is prepared to impose.

Preventing the sum total of money incomes from rising faster than the national product becomes more difficult as responsibility for public policies is increasingly spread out through provincial and municipal self-government and through all the organizations within the vast infrastructure, which, by collective bargaining, are settling amongst themselves prices, wages, earnings, and profits. These institutions are all operating under the commonly accepted practical assumption that out of the bargainings should come compromise agreements. The urge to reach agreement and avoid conflict must continuously tempt the bargaining parties to attain agreement by being a little more generous to each other than they can really afford at current prices. When prices are managed, the cost of this generosity can usually be transferred to the next partner in the sequence of exchange. This process normally operates most freely in industries dominated by powerful enterprises and strong labor organizations; such, at least, seems to be the U.S. experience. In the advanced Welfare State, however, a power balance between all groups is being attained. Farmers, civil servants, even old-age pensioners, are efficiently organized to defend their interests.

The important thing now is that people are mostly organized for bargaining in their capacity as earners of an income or a profit, not as consumers. As "producers" of one type or another—industrialists and traders in different branches, farmers managing farms of different sizes and specializing in different crops, professionals in different lines, clerical and manual workers engaged in different types of work in different enterprises, etc.—they have all special and specific interests. They fall naturally into separate groups and sub-groups, held together by solidarity of interests against the rest of the community. True, all are also consumers. But their interests as consumers in lower prices and living costs are common, general, and dispersed. For this reason in all Western countries it has proved much more difficult to build up effective consumers' organizations. An additional reason for this is the fact that the women, who control so much of the expenditures for consumption, have shown reluctance to participate in community controls. Only in a few countries have consumers' organizations acquired any bargaining strength at all.

In the present phase of the development of the Welfare State it is a most important fact that the structure of interest organizations, and also the pressures exerted within the parliament and other elected assemblies on the provincial and even municipal level, are strongly biased in favor of the producers' interests in higher income and profits. This is not generally considered as a flaw in democracy. For everybody is not only a consumer but also an earner of income or profit. And in the setting of the Welfare State, the workers' and farmers' organizations are constantly growing stronger by the use of their political power as voters to determine the policies of national, provincial, and municipal assemblies which set the conditions under which they make their bargains. This situation simply means that the institutional setting is such that all people in all walks of life are ever more effectively directing their strivings for higher levels of living into attempts to protect and increase their money incomes. They may grumble about rising prices and costs of living—and use such a trend as a motivation when pressing for higher income—but they have usually no effective means to stop, by concerted action, the rising trend of prices.

In each bargain between the producers' groups, only a fraction of the total national income is determined. They all involve a pair of partners where the one side might very naturally feel that they want the other side to have a bigger share of the national product. As a Minister of Finance in Sweden, Mr. Ernst Wigforss, once had the intellectual courage to explain in the Parliament: if the farmers and workers in that country make up their minds that they want to have, and to give each other, higher incomes, nobody can stop them, as they have all the power. But, of course, they have not the power to increase the real national product so easily.

Not Soluble by Financial and Monetary Measures

It is an illusion to believe that under prevailing conditions —and, more particularly, with the powers invested in all the organizations within the infrastructure, which are mainly producers' organizations in the sense explained above—balance in a national economy can be restored merely by overall monetary and financial controls as in old times. As we know from recent experiences in most Western countries, a trend to rising costs and prices may easily prevail, even while a general contraction, induced by such overall controls, is taking place. Moreover, they cannot be applied effectively enough, and for a sufficient length of time, to enable an upward price trend to be stopped, as the national communities will not permit contraction when it causes large-scale unemployment.

In a democracy of the Western type, this problem of securing monetary stability with full employment can only be solved in a fully satisfactory way by raising the general level of education, intensifying still more the active participation of the people in decisions on all levels, strengthening very much the awareness which all should have of the common interest that the price level should not get out of hand, and creating thereby the basis of understanding and solidarity required for the national planning and coordination of all markets, so that a stable balance can be maintained between aggregate demand and supply without contraction of economic activity. Again I can only fall back on education and more democracy.

We would then not only have stabilized the trend of business development under full employment, but also reduced the necessity, if this balance is lost, for a type of particularly obnoxious direct state intervention. To accomplish this, it would be necessary that, within the institutional infrastructure, strong and effective consumers' organizations should develop which could counterbalance the existing producers' organizations, and neutralize the present dominant bias in collective bargaining towards higher incomes and profits than are compatible with price stability.

The state as such can hardly substitute very effectively for non-existent or abnormally weak consumers' organizations. It cannot have much hope of success if it steps into the collective bargaining between the producers' organizations in order to keep down the rise in wages, prices, incomes, and profits to the pace of the rise in productivity. For one thing, that would imply that the state would compromise its proper role as maker of the rules for the bargaining and as the umpire. Bargaining would be less free. In addition, when consumers' organizations are absent or weak, the state will, as a rule, be acting under the pressure of the existing producers' organizations. Even the state cannot avoid being swayed by the bias in favor of earners of incomes and profits which is inherent in the present institutional system.

In Scandinavia we have had considerable experience of nationwide bargaining between all major groups of income and profit earners. Such multilateral negotiations under state guidance represent certainly a great advance, particularly as there consumers' organizations are not so utterly weak as in other countries and as they are taking active part in the bargaining. But we are far from a solution of the problem of maintaining stable prices with full employment. To accomplish this would assume that the consumers' organizations were much stronger. This is, in my view, the lesson we can learn from this experience. I emphasize that, because a recent trend of thinking, particularly in the United States, seems to expect too much from "state-aided," nationwide and multilateral, bargaining about wages and prices. Such bargaining does not overcome the basic—and inflationary—institutional bias to which I have referred. Only when the citizens become equally effectively organized in their role as consumers as they already are as income and profit earners can a "countervailing" power be realized. Only then can the state free itself from this bias.

8

Economic Planning in the Two Other Orbits

Planning in the Soviet Union

The main and common traits characterizing economic planning in the Western countries can be brought into relief and illuminated by contrasting them with economic planning in the two other orbits of the world. The following brief remarks on planning in the Soviet countries and the underdeveloped countries in the non-Soviet orbit are intended to provide this wider perspective. For the sake of simplicity the former group will be represented by the Soviet Union, which has given the prototype to the planning which is now undertaken in the other countries in that orbit.

Russia half a century ago was a huge, backward, and poor country. There had been some considerable industrial spurts, many of them undertaken by foreign capitalists, but in the main the country was still rural and largely feudal. It was ruled autocratically, had little effective provincial and municipal self-government of a type even approaching a democratic order, and few such voluntary interest organizations as could be of functional importance for reform and development. World War I, the political revolution, the ensuing civil war, and the inroads of foreign armies created turmoil and distress, but not a new order.

It may be interesting to ponder whether in Russia, as earlier in the Western countries, there could at that time have been a liberal revolution, followed by continued industrialization, the growth of self-directing organs for cooperation and bargaining in local and sectional communities, a development towards increasing rationality of popular attitudes, and the gradual growth of democracy, and what the outcome would have been of such a process in the short and the long run. What did happen, in the wake of World War I and several years of serious disturbances and struggle and much vacillation among the Communist leaders themselves, was, in the end, the creation by force of the totalitarian and monolithic state.

Having nationalized all industry and thereafter pressed farming into forced collectivization, the state substituted for that infrastructure of voluntary organizations which had grown up in the Western countries what in effect was all-embracing, centrally-directed state control with ramifications everywhere. Even the cooperative forms, used for agriculture and for many crafts and some trade, became, in effect, primarily media for central state direction, as did the network of trade unions in industry and elsewhere. This whole institutional structure, like the organs for provincial and municipal self-government, which were also built up, was tightly held together by the Communist Party, which again was organized on the monolithic principle and centrally directed.

Through the whole structure of this system of social relations, directions from above were substituted for collective bargaining. The economic planning, which stood out as a most essential feature of the working of the monolithic state, was in its nature programmatic and comprehensive.

Planning in the Underdeveloped Countries

Great poverty is a paramount fact in the underdeveloped countries. Most of them are poorer and less developed than Russia was before the revolution. They are often poorer than the Western countries ever were, even in pre-industrial time. This is particularly true of the most populous among them, which weigh heaviest in any comparison.

For many reasons which I can only mention here—reasons related to the climate most of them must cope with, their social stratification and prevalent valuation schemes, trends in their population development, their greater difficulties in acquiring capital from abroad, their trading position in the world, and the very much greater magnitude of their development problems, due to the fact that they cannot rise like islands in a surrounding of underdeveloped regions—an objective analysis of their situation will for most of them yield the conclusion that they are not likely to develop in a way similar to the historical pattern established by the Western countries. Indeed, it is unlikely that they will develop much, or at all, if the state does not from the outset take a much bigger responsibility for engendering development than was taken by the state during the industrial revolution in the Western countries. There, as I pointed out, industrialization was mainly the outcome of a cumulative process of spontaneous growth nourished by the enterprise of individual profit-seekers, exploiting new techniques to their own advantage.

To some extent, the idea of economic planning which is now spreading in the underdeveloped countries is in the nature of a rational inference from their urge for development and from their knowledge of the adverse circumstances in which they find themselves. The contemporary world is also a very different one, providing a very different set of ideological impulses. Since their industrial revolution a hundred or more years ago, the Western countries have travelled a long way towards economic planning along a path which I have traced in the previous chapters. And the economic planning by the monolithic and totalitarian state in the Soviet countries also provides a pattern which, in one respect, is the more relevant, in that most of those countries are, or recently were, underdeveloped themselves, and as, in general, their planning has produced very conspicuous development results. Quite aside from any ideological influences from the Soviet countries, however, the fact that the underdeveloped countries are bent, as the Western countries were not, upon applying planning in the initial stage of underdevelopment, gives it a very different character which, indeed, shows a similarity to Soviet planning.

By the very logic of the underdeveloped countries' situation, planning becomes programmatic in its approach. It does not, as in the Western countries, force itself upon a national community through a gradual process which finally results in a *fait accompli,* while the community often still remains largely unwilling to accept planning as an idea. In the underdeveloped countries, the idea precedes its realization. As economic development cannot be expected to come by itself, planning becomes a precondition for development, not, as in the Western countries, a later consequence of development and all the other changes which accompanied it. The underdeveloped countries are thus compelled to undertake what in the light of the history of the Western world appears as a shortcut.

All this follows as a consequence of the fact that planning is being applied at an earlier stage of development, and of the further fact that their conditions for development are so much worse that this seems rationally motivated. It is also a part of the logic of the underdeveloped countries' situation that their programmatic planning should be comprehensive and complete, not pragmatic and piecemeal as in the Western countries. In principle and in theoretical approach, planning anticipates public policies. It does not grow out of the necessity to coordinate such policies as have already been initiated.

There is as yet, of course, very little planning in any of the underdeveloped countries. Even India, which has come farthest in planning, has rightly been characterized as a "functioning anarchy." None of these countries is even approaching the level of planning and overall economic state control which is common in all the Western countries. But an idea is also a reality. It is part of the political dynamics in all the underdeveloped countries that this idea is spreading, and that it, differing from both the ideologies and the facts of planning in Western countries, implies a programmatic and comprehensive state direction of the economic development. In this sense, the attempts at planning in the underdeveloped countries, however little has, as yet, come of them, are more akin to the planning accomplished in the Soviet world.

The Legacy from the Western World

Another major political fact is, however, that the underdeveloped countries outside the Soviet orbit want to plan democratically for development. In any case, they are not prepared to accept the totalitarian and monolithic state as a pre-condition for planning.

They have all defined their goals for state planning in terms of the modern democratic Welfare State of the Western countries. This is particularly true of the countries in South- and South-East Asia, which until recently were colonial dependencies of West-European powers. But it is

on the whole true also of underdeveloped countries everywhere else outside the Soviet orbit. The modern Western
ideals of economic progress, full employment, social security, equalization of opportunity, wealth and incomes, and
in the recognition of the responsibility of the state to form
its policies so that these ideals become attained, are often
written into the constitutions when these are new. They
are everywhere propounded in the introduction to planning documents and official reports on major social and
economic problems, and are constantly expressed in decla-
rations by political personalities and intellectual leaders
and, of course, in party programs. They are the official
ideals. Many underdeveloped countries are eager to have
stressed that they are "Welfare States." The fact that the
ideals are so very far from realization seems to provide
a reason to have them preached at every available occasion,
and then usually in more absolute terms than is customary
in the Welfare States of the rich democracies in the Western world.

Though it may sound paradoxical, this similarity of
purpose represents a fundamental difference between the
underdeveloped countries and the Western countries, if
that comparison is made in the way which is the rational
one from a development point of view: *viz.*, as between
the present situation of the former group and the situation
of the latter group at that time when they managed to
lift themselves from underdevelopment. If the underdeveloped countries—supported, incidentally, by the entire world—now conceive of economic development as a
political issue and the responsibility of the state, and if
they define development in terms of a rise in welfare of
the masses of the people, it is, so far as underdeveloped
countries outside the Soviet orbit are concerned, an entirely new thing in history.

There is a similar and equally fundamental difference

in the ideological line followed out in building the political power basis for this "state" which is supposed to accomplish the planning for development towards these goals. The Western countries, at the time of the industrial revolution, had consolidated nation-states, built upon the rule of law, and often including a functioning parliamentary system of representation—in both respects they were, as a rule, much farther advanced than the underdeveloped countries are today. But they were not democracies in the modern sense of the word. Suffrage was generally restricted by income qualifications to a small minority of the people. Only now has full democracy with universal suffrage been attempted successfully without prior attainment of a fairly high level of living and a high degree of equality of opportunity.

The principle of universal suffrage, however, was accepted in almost all underdeveloped countries, and particularly in those which were newly liberated. It was accepted as if it were the only natural thing to do—and as if there were no alternatives. In many of these countries with large illiterate populations, rigid caste and class divisions, and religious or ethnic chasms, democratic rule is prevented from operating, or its realization is delayed. There has recently been a trend in large parts of the underdeveloped world towards military dictatorships of one type or another. In countries where regular elections are held, they are often either rigged or the people are not awakened, informed and organized enough to follow out their interests. Large-scale corruption, nepotism, and petty intrigues for personal power and loot are fairly common and tend to decrease both the efficiency and the prestige of the political and administrative systems. It is a spreading idea that the underdeveloped countries need a "guided" democracy, a "real" and not a "formal" democracy, one that is founded upon consensus and not party struggle, etc.

The meaning of these terms is usually left in considerable obscurity, but their general leaning is towards some form of authoritarianism in greater or lesser degree.

But the principle that the power emanates from the whole of the people and that poor and rich alike should have an equal voice in decisions of public policies is established and entrenched. Moreover, the very apparent shortcomings in the political set-up of the underdeveloped countries where democracy is faltering are generally such as to exclude the Soviet type of efficient totalitarian and monolithic regime—except after a possible communist revolution which would take them out of the orbit which I am here discussing.

Therefore, while the underdeveloped countries are bound to strive for Soviet-like programmatic and comprehensive planning, their political institutions, and the whole organization of their national communities, will set narrow limits to the possibility of adopting such techniques of planning. The underdeveloped countries which are democratic or are actively striving in this direction are not, of course, prepared to have a totalitarian and monolithic regime; neither are those countries where democracy is faltering or even those which have come under military dictatorships; and even if they were willing, they would not be able to exert the fanatical discipline implicit in the Soviet system.

Aside from this fundamental political inhibition, there is also a difference in their economic institutions. Unlike the Soviet countries, they have not embarked on wholesale nationalization of production; nor have they made state enterprise and collectivization the rule. And they have not organized their foreign trade and exchange relations in the pattern of a state monopoly.

It can be said, and it contains an essential element of truth, that what some underdeveloped countries are now actually attempting, and more are approaching, is to use such elements of the Soviet techniques for programmatic and comprehensive state planning for economic development as are compatible with the absence of a totalitarian and monolithic state and with a mainly private ownership and management of production and trade. The offspring of this crossing is a breed of planning which is as different from the planning which has materialized in the Western countries as it is from Soviet planning.

The sole purpose of this parenthetical reference to the underdeveloped countries outside the Soviet orbit is merely to present, in necessarily abstract terms, the reasons why economic planning there is different from that of the countries in the other two orbits, and why the differences are fundamental. They stem from the fact that, unlike the Western countries at a comparable stage, the underdeveloped countries are now attempting to apply planning in advance of development—in order to create the precondition for development—and from the further fact that their political and institutional conditions exclude them from applying the planning methods of the totalitarian and monolithic state in the Soviet orbit. I cannot here enter upon a discussion of the complex of problems connected with economic planning in the underdeveloped countries outside the Soviet orbit. But, both because of its importance in itself and because it illustrates the fundamental differences in economic planning referred to, one particular problem of planning will be briefly considered, the question of decentralization.

The Soviet Way

The Soviet state also labors with its problems of decentralization. It needs decentralization in order not to lose touch with the people, which in no state is a matter of insignificance. It needs it also for reasons of administrative efficiency: in order that developments and their rational redirection according to changing circumstances shall not succumb under the rigidity of the central apparatus. We find therefore that, from the very beginning, what in the Soviet Union corresponds to the public debate in the Western countries has been reverberating in the struggle against bureaucracy and centralism.

But in the totalitarian and monolithic state it is difficult to give substance and reality to a spreading of participation, initiative and influence amongst the people. For natural reasons it becomes much more inhibited, since central control is retained. Take as an example the trade unions. In the Western countries the trade unions are certainly more and more coming to function in a role which in reality is that of public authorities, as they share, amongst themselves and with the employers' unions, responsibility for laying down norms and for establishing long- and short-term settlements that regulate the labor market in which the individual workers and employer move. It is also true that, in this development towards increasing public responsibility, many of the conditions for the unions' operations—even, perhaps, essential elements of their own constitutions—were laid down by state legislation and administration, often at their own prompting.

The difference is immense, however, when they are compared with the trade unions in the Soviet countries. These are subject not only to much more intensive control but also to general direction. They thus become very little more than administrative agencies of a state which is not itself founded upon free elections by the people. In the Western countries, in spite of the ever greater responsibility for public policy, and despite the ensuing increased state control over their activities, the trade unions are still very much free-wheeling institutions, belonging to their members and acting according to their will. As an *ultima ratio* they can go out on strike. Similarly, acting primarily in response to the interest on their own groups, are the cooperatives, industrial and other organizations, private business concerns, and, of course, the provincial and municipal organs for self-government.

In the last instance, it is a question of how much influence is exerted downwards and upwards within the institutional mechanisms beneath the state, and to what extent this state itself is under popular control. And in these respects, there is, as between the Western and the Soviet worlds, a difference in the proportion of those two streams of influence so large that we must speak of a quantitative difference so huge as to become genuinely qualitative.

Even in the latest moves towards decentralization, the Soviet Union has not given up the principles of monolithic uniformity of aim, and central direction of efforts, held firmly in the hands of the leaders of the ruling party and the state. It is not altogether improbable, though, that with the higher levels of living and education, which are gradually becoming realized or coming within sight in the Soviet Union, the system will be loosened up. We might in ten or twenty years' time see a very different Russia. In important respects it will have come closer to the Western world, although the different road it travelled will have lasting effects.

The Soviet Union may be moving towards a less centralized state, with more active participation on the part of the whole people, exerted through the—eventually more independent—organs for provincial and municipal self-government, and the then freer organizations within the institutional infrastructure. This also assumes that personal security and liberty become better protected, and that the state itself becomes more dependent upon the popular will. This dream, which might not come true, has been referred to in this context because, as much as the present monolithic and harshly totalitarian Soviet state, it throws light on the essential characteristics of the modern, democratic, decentralized, organizational state of the Western countries.

In the Underdeveloped Countries

The underdeveloped countries in the non-Soviet orbit are in a different position again, very different both from that of the rich countries of the Western world and from that of the Soviet countries.

Their institutional structure beneath the state level is weak and mostly inimical to development, and reflects the status of underdevelopment and stagnation from which they want to rise. Many underdeveloped countries altogether lack agencies for democratic and cooperative self-government in the provinces and municipalities. People in the towns and villages have often been ruled, and exploited, by appointed officials, taking orders from a central state government of some sort or another—which in the best of circumstances has been under some control by an assembly representing some approximation to democracy —or otherwise by feudal lords of one designation or another, sometimes holding their offices as a hereditary privilege, on the basis of social and economic power in an inegalitarian society. Where some form of democratic representation and cooperative self-government has been in existence in the provinces and municipalities, it has, in a stagnant society, seldom formed a basis for a functioning practice of cooperative efforts by the people to reform and reorganize their society and their own life according to changing conditions and new opportunities, which is the demand raised by the urge for development.

Similarly, the legacy in underdeveloped countries of an

infrastructure of social groupings, outside the formal arrangements under the constitutional order of the state, for
the promotion of common ideals and interests, usually
affords little hope that they could help in economic development without first having been radically reformed and
rejuvenated. They are usually not open in membership
and not democratically ruled, and they are in any case not
animated by a spirit of change and reform. Indeed, many
of the inherited collective formations are in flat contradiction to the goals of development and to the adoption of
democratic methods in pursuing them. They cannot be
reconstructed but must be liquidated, or at least, neutralized. The caste organization in India, like similar social
institutions in other underdeveloped countries, exempli-
fies such an infra-structure, which must be torn down to
make room for the new mobility and dynamism required
for development.

A recent growth in the new industries, and, more generally, in the cities are the beginning, and sometimes more
than the beginning, of industrial and professional organizations and trade unions similar to those in the Western
countries. They are usually still rather weak, and often
not open and democratically ruled. The organizations are
in any case seldom so well balanced that it can be reasonably expected that settlements, corresponding to the public
will, should result from collective bargaining amongst
them. The state has failed to secure a really satisfactory
hold over them by determining the conditions under
which they work, by laying down rules for bargaining,
and by acting as umpire. However, the most important
observation—and this holds good for all underdeveloped
countries outside the Soviet orbit—is that these new
organizations still only involve a very small proportion
of the people in the national communities.

The weakness of self-government and in the organiza-

tional infrastructure is, of course, only one of the indications of the general institutional and attitudinal situation
in underdeveloped countries, which, caused by prolonged
stagnation, at the same time makes it so difficult to break
the stagnation and engender development.

Building up an Infrastructure

I have referred above to the Soviet way of building up an
infrastructure. It implies a totalitarian and monolithic
state, and the rule of a single, strongly disciplined political
party, stretching out its close direction to every village
and every workshop. These underdeveloped countries
have not been prepared to accept the Soviet way of solving
the political and institutional problem. It is to the political
methods and the general social and economic order of the
modern Welfare State in the Western countries that they
would like to give reality in their own countries. What they
are reaching for is the creation, beneath the state level,
of that type of organizational national community with
a wide local and sectional dispersion of participation,
initiative, and influence under a flexible but, in the final
instance, sovereign control by state legislation and administration, which in the Western world has been the
outcome of a long and gradual development under exceptionally favorable circumstances very different from
theirs.

Such underdeveloped countries as have come furthest in
national consolidation and in planning for development
can, therefore, now be seen devoting themselves earnestly
to building up authorities for provincial and local self-
government, using whatever inherited building material
there is available, but mainly following patterns imported
from the Western countries.

They want to regulate the labor market on the basis of

collective bargaining between voluntary and free organizations of workers and employers as in the Western countries. In order to condition the bargaining amongst the organizations, they are introducing arbitrative procedures, modern factory legislation and factory inspection, legislation on working hours, rules for security of employment, and insurance benefits for workers who, for one reason or another, lose their incomes. In these latter respects they are often tempted to go considerably further that what is realistic and effective under the conditions prevailing in their countries.

Attempts are made to set up quasi-independent councils and boards for various public interests, and to delegate responsibility and influence to such bodies. Professional and industrial organizations are promoted, and consulted about state policies. And the business world is exhorted to recognize their social responsibilities better.

For agriculture, which is by far the largest part of their economies, and for crafts and small-scale industry, they are putting their faith in cooperation. Cooperation has, indeed, become a central ideal in these countries, and they are eagerly attempting to learn from the Scandinavian and other Western countries, where the cooperative movement has reached its highest manifestation. They are set upon fostering genuine producers' and consumers' cooperatives in order to raise levels of productivity and, consequently, of savings and consumption, so making even the most stagnant sectors of their economies, which are also by far the largest and most important, progressive. They want to drive out the moneylenders from the villages and the lower- and middle-class blocs in the cities by organizing a new credit system, built upon cooperation and shared responsibility.

These efforts in underdeveloped countries to build up organs for self-government, and for collective cooperation and bargaining, really go to the heart of the problem. They are the chosen means to make a reality of democratic planning for development in hitherto stagnant communities, at very low levels of living, literacy and education. Development implies that stagnation is broken by the people, as they begin to do things in order to improve conditions for themselves. If this is to be accomplished in a democratic way, the people must cooperate and form organs for such cooperation. The alternatives are either that the development efforts will be in vain, or that resort will have to be taken to totalitarian methods. Whether or not the underdeveloped countries outside the Soviet orbit succeed in going the Western way in regard to self-government and voluntary organizations—however different their situation is from that of the Western countries, and however differently their policies must be directed in other and more specific respects—will largely determine not only what sort of economy they will have, but what is to be their national community, and under what type of political system it will operate.

A Fundamental Difference

In a stagnant community, with low levels of living and education, which has inherited a rigid and inegalitarian social and economic structure, the difficulties of building up institutions for self-government, collective bargaining, and cooperation are immense. The fundamentally different problem facing the state in underdeveloped countries is that it will have to plan to build up such institutions. A complex of intentional state policies will have to be framed and carried out in order to initiate them and get them going, while in the Western countries they were not planned, but grew up themselves as a result of technological and psychological changes in the gradual development and then, in their turn, added to all the other forces which were driving the state to intervention, coordination, and planning.

Jawaharlal Nehru time and time again comes back to the theme that the organs for self-government and cooperation, which are now being started everywhere in India, should be run by the people themselves and not by the officials, and he regularly refers to the experiences in England, Scandinavia, and other Western countries. He is, of course, right in maintaining that, once these institutions have been started, they must become the people's own concern, as their organs for local and sectional participation, initiative and influence. Otherwise the whole effort comes to nought, or they remain merely instruments for state administration, which, because of the pretense that they express voluntary forces on the local and sectional level, are less effective and economical than they could otherwise be.

But the fact is that, in a stagnant society, these institutions do not come into existence, except as a result of state policy. The officials have the function of propagating them, starting them, and guiding them. And it will be a most difficult task to do this in such a way that out of planning and instigation from above comes the surge of a movement from below, strong enough to give them an independent life. This process is a totally different one from the historical process behind the present situation in the Western countries, and the problem of getting the process going by state planning and policies is a totally new one, which the Western countries have never faced.

PART TWO

International Implications of National Planning

9

International Disintegration

Fifty Years Ago

I mentioned in the Preface as a major historical fact that those few nations which today form the upper class of world society—outside the Soviet orbit—were also at the top fifty years ago.

The great majority of mankind, placed outside this upper class and, in particular, most of the inhabitants of the regions we now call underdeveloped, in general merely subsisted from year to year and from generation to generation in an existence of fairly uneventful cultural and economic stagnation, studied by anthropologists who were sent out from the Western centers of learning. As economic development was proceeding rapidly in the upper-class group of countries, the international class gap was widening, and it has continued to widen further to this day.

At the beginning of the century, the colonial power system held a firm grip over the globe; the forebodings of the Great Awakening were hardly noticeable. Business interests from the Western countries were acquiring land and managing plantations and mines on commercial lines. These enterprises were often run on the highest level of contemporary technological and managerial efficiency. Today, when, after the breakdown of the colonial system the liberated countries have to plan their economic future independently, they remain important national assets,

139

without which these countries could not possibly survive, let alone develop. Roads, railways, and ports were built, integrating these foreign sections of their economy and a fringe of native business into world commerce.

But almost all of the local demand from these enterprises was for cheap unskilled labor. The practices of strict segregation and discrimination, which the colonizers brought with them as part of their mores, seemed necessary for preserving power and order in the political and economic dependencies. They were, indeed, natural, as the initial differences, not only in color, but in all levels of living, including education, were so immense. The system itself tended to preserve these differences. The enterprises therefore remained enclaves, and the diffused effects to the native economy were weak. Relatively speaking, there was not much growth of indigenous industry and commerce in any of the underdeveloped countries, though there was a little more in some than in others.

From the beginning, the increased demand for labor on the part of the enclave enterprises, the peace and order maintained under the colonial regimes, and their efforts to introduce elementary hygiene and sometimes improvements in the techniques used in agriculture, resulted in a very considerable natural increase of population, which has since accelerated. Average income and consumption, therefore, tended to stagnate at the very low initial levels. The continuing abject poverty of the masses of the indigenous peoples was mostly taken as a natural thing, explained in terms of their lack of ambition and their lower capabilities of intelligence, foresight, discipline, and sustained effort. As the interest of the enclave enterprises were concentrated on having a plentiful supply of cheap common labor, the rapid increase of the populations could not appear as a disadvantage to the colonizers.

Most of the nations in the upper-class group had never

experienced similar poverty. In any case, by the beginning of our century they had all reached a comparatively high level of production and real income per head, and they were all rapidly advancing economically. Their national integration proceeded, implying, among other things, high and rising spatial and social mobility, equalization of opportunities, the growth of cultural homogeneity, and a gradual development towards full political democracy.

Many of us need to be reminded of the relatively high degree of international integration between the several countries in this upper-class group of nations fifty years ago. In fact, before the outbreak of World War I there existed a much more closely-knit world community than today. But only a very small part of the world belonged to it, as it excluded the larger part of mankind.

Within this partial world community one could travel without passport or visa, and one did not need to bother with securing foreign exchange. More important, Europe was largely a common labor market, and emigration to the New World streamed unhampered. A competitive international capital market was also operating, and trade flowed fairly freely, though tariff barriers tended to be rising. Economically, the countries in the old partial world community were thus closely integrated with each other, and movements of labor, capital, commodities, and services played an important role in sustaining economic progress in the individual countries and in preserving international balance amongst them.

Disintegration

One of the major changes in the last half century has been the gradual disintegration of this partial world community of the rich Western countries and their enclaves in the backward regions. The movement of persons, capital, and enterprise, as well as merchandise and services, has been controlled, restricted, and distorted. Exchange rates have become regulated. Currencies have been inconvertible for long periods. Convertibility, when it is restored, is experimental and hazardous and is hedged by reservations, restrictions, and policy interferences, necessary even for its temporary preservation, which make of it a very different thing from what it used to be under the old automatic gold standard system.

By themselves, the technological advances which have taken place during the last fifty years should have increased immensely the opportunities and rational motivation for further international integration. For one thing, transportation, both of people and goods, has become much faster and cheaper in real terms, as have all other communications. Anybody who, at the beginning of the century, had foreseen this development, and had not expected the world wars and other major upheavals following in their wake, would have imagined that by now we would be living in a still more integrated international community.

Instead, there has been a continued trend to international economic disintegration. Around the long-term trend there have been wide fluctuations. The two world wars and the Great Depression in the thirties marked short-term culminations of international economic disintegration. After each culmination there have been reversals in the curve around the trend. Conscious but intermittent efforts have been made to change its direction, and to initiate concerted policies aimed at restoring international integration.

Thus, immediately after World War I, a return to normalcy was commonly expected and, undoubtedly, this expectation itself was then—as expectations always are —a force towards its own realization. In the end, however, this force did not prove strong enough to turn the trend. Thus, the middle twenties became only a short interlude, during which people in the Western countries hoped for the restoration of the old partial world community and also attempted to fashion policies according to this assumption by restoring the gold standard and trying to liberalize international trade. It was followed within a few years by the Great Depression. There was never more than a partial recovery after the Depression, and then came World War II.

Since that war such expectations no longer exist. Though people continuously try to conceal it to themselves by hopeful publicity and propaganda, the fact is that they no longer really believe in a return to normalcy in international relations as they did in the twenties. People are conditioned to expect as normal the occurrence of huge, rapid, unforeseen, and uncontrolled changes abroad and, as a result, international crises. In their fundamental conception of reality, the tendency to international economic disintegration has been accepted as a general condition of internal and external economic policy in all countries.

The Weakening of International Law

One specific aspect, or phase, of the development towards international economic disintegration has been the deterioration of the international legal system as we knew it prior to World War I. Under the influence of international crises and the national policies adopted to cope with them, the body of commonly accepted rules for correct behavior in public and private international relations, which had been patiently and laboriously built over the generations and become part of Western culture, became sickly and dwindled more and more. Now it is uncertain what remains of it, and what power it still possesses.

As the governments sensed the pressure of the continual succession of crises and, in particular, the situation of acute emergency during the two world wars and the Great Depression, they felt less and less that they could afford to be bound in an absolute and firm way by considerations other than the narrowly opportunistic ones of acting in defense of their immediate national interests. It is in the nature of the social institution we call law that every time it is broken it loses some of its strength as a social force. In the beginning, and particularly during and immediately after the wars, it was the rich Western countries—and most often the bigger and more powerful ones among them—that took the most license with established international law.

Now, even more, it is the poor underdeveloped countries that are exploiting the twilight of international law created by these precedents. They are, of course, under particular pressure to do so because of their poverty. They also feel themselves less morally bound by legal arrangements established under conditions when they were dependent and often lacking a free government of their own. The newly liberated nations in Asia, for instance, however legalistically minded they show themselves to be in their relations with each other, and also with the rich countries when the advantage happens to be on their side, do not in their hearts give unquestioned validity to such established rights in their region as belong to Western powers or interests, when these can be related to colonialism.

This factual situation is bound to have important consequences for all relations between rich and poor countries. But in this context my point is merely that the partial disintegration of the international legal situation began much earlier, and that dangerous precedents were set by the great powers in the Western world.

The New International Organizations

It is true that towards the end of each of the two world wars plans were made for organized and concerted international efforts towards economic integration on a world scale. Those plans were more comprehensive and ambitious during and after World War II. International organizations were designed and, in part, set up, with the purpose of bringing into existence a new international monetary system, renewing the international capital market, liberalizing international trade, building international guarantees for stabilizing general business conditions, distributing agricultural surpluses to the under-consuming nations, countervailing fluctuations of commodity prices, and controlling international cartels. As yet we have not come far in the fulfilment of these purposes, but the effort continues. I shall come back to this question in the last chapter of this book.

A great rescue action was staged in the early post-war years, mainly within the old partial world community of the rich countries, when the United States gave large-scale capital aid to the West-European countries so as to get them out of their severe exchange difficulties. So far as restoring economic stability in their national economies was concerned, the Marshall Plan was eminently successful. It is a main explanation of their rapid economic recovery. Indirectly, this generous assistance by one rich country to a number of other rich countries in temporary difficulties had a wholesome effect on economic conditions the whole world over.

West-European Economic Integration?

Marshall Aid went into the further consolidation of the national Welfare States in Western Europe. The intention was, however, that the opportunity would be used for far-reaching integration of the several countries in that sub-region. This was very definitely the aim of the United States in giving the assistance, though the moral force of its urgings in that direction was weakened by the fact that it was not itself prepared to be a party to any international integration. An over-zealous publicity campaign was all the time carried on, playing up the various plans for West-European economic integration, as those plans shifted from year to year. Even the professional economists often felt themselves urged to accommodate their writings to serve this propaganda purpose. However, except for a gradual return from the crude bilateralism and the severe exchange controls into which these countries had been forced after World War II, little came out of these efforts.

The preparations for a Common Market for the six countries in Little Europe, and a wider Western-European Free Trade Area, which represent the most recent turn of these efforts towards West-European integration, are carried on with much more seriousness. The successful implementation of these plans would assume, on the part of the participating countries, both a preparedness to accept huge changes in the localization of industry as between different countries, and a willingness and ability in each of them to preserve a delicately synchronized internal monetary and financial balance. Experiences from recent history make it doubtful that these two assumptions will be fulfilled. The countries whose economies should in this way be made to respond smoothly to the demands for international adjustments within this sub-regional group are all consolidated Welfare States with large-scale national planning. They have bought a considerable increase in internal stability at the price of decreasing their capacity for automatic international adjustment. I shall refer to this in greater detail later.

If nevertheless, as I feel inclined to believe, the effort will not give way to a simple return to the earlier situation, the "integration" that would eventually be achieved might be unlike the promised "free trade." It might instead consist of a complex system of policy measures, regulating and limiting competition between the participating countries by other means than straight tariffs. Quotas, though in less conventional forms, will probably have a new lease of life, often hidden in restrictive covenants between industries or industrial associations: what in a broad way we call international cartels.

From the point of view of the democratic forces in these nations, the danger is that it is easier to internationalize —within the sub-region—the entrepreneurs' and the employers' organizations than those of the workers, and that consumers' organizations are either weak or altogether lacking. But in time it might be possible both to build up a real supra-national political organization with a parliament and government, and to create for the whole group of countries a more complete infrastructure of organizations, where even workers' and consumers' organizations operate within the framework of the larger super-state. We would then have a sub-regional Welfare State for Western Europe, or a part of it, in place of the component national Welfare States.

The road to this goal is, under any conditions, long and arduous. Meanwhile, the agreements between the participating governments and the industries in the several countries will, in the natural course of events, often be reached at the expense of curtailing their economic rela-

tions with countries outside the scheme. This would hold
true even in the more distant future when the vision of
a welfare-super-state could be realized. For this is the mode
of operation of the Welfare State, as I shall show in the
following chapter. Whether in the end the creation of this
bigger unit to replace the many small units would really
be a step towards economic integration in the world at
large is a difficult question to which I am not prepared to
give a definite answer, as it depends upon what happens
more generally in the world economy.

It is in any case important to stress that, by themselves,
these schemes for economic integration of Western Europe
are only regional and, in fact, sub-regional in character,
encompassing not even the whole partial world community
of old, still less the entire world, and that they are being
attempted precisely at the time when all the underdeveloped countries are rapidly coming to life in independent action. From their point of view—which must
also be the point of view of the internationalist—the rich
countries in Western Europe and, naturally, also the
United States of America, should so have managed their
internal and external economic policies that they could by
now have unilaterally abolished barriers to capital movements and trade with the whole world, instead of forming
themselves into a protective "rich men's club." To the
extent that the plans will be acted upon, even if they
should to any considerable extent really integrate Western
Europe or a large part of it, the danger from a wider world
point of view is that they represent a further step towards
compartmentalization of international economic relations.

The Liquidation of Colonialism

Another major change in the period under review is the
liquidation of colonialism. For a long time, the develop-

ment towards international disintegration proceeded almost entirely within the boundaries of the old partial world community of the few rich Western nations and their colonial and quasi-colonial enclaves in the immense backward regions of the surrounding world. World War I has rightly been characterized as mainly a civil war within the partial world community of the rich nations. In this respect World War II started out not very differently.

But, in the end, the latter war undermined almost completely the established political power system in the world, through which a few countries in Western Europe had held the backward regions under their political and economic domination and control. By far the most important result of World War II was to give both the opportunity and the incentive to the beginning of the liberation of the colonial peoples. All international relations are now shuddering under the reverberations of this political avalanche which, as we all know, is bound to continue its advance until all peoples are thrown on their own resources, however badly prepared for independence they may seem to the nations which have ruled them.

The ascendancy of this world revolution is irresistible, and its influence reaches into all corners of the globe. Other poor and backward peoples who, though independent politically, were dominated economically and socially from abroad, begin to raise their aspirations. As the great movement evolves and unfolds, it will have consequences everywhere on ways of life. Its repercussions will fill the history of the rest of the century.

The immediate effect of the emergence on the world scene of all these extremely poor nations as independent states, demanding development as well as independence, was naturally disruptive to what there was of a set pattern of international economic relations. In the first instance, the scope of those relations became enlarged and complicated in encompassing all these new nations which could no longer be so easily controlled as when they were mere appendices to the rich nations' world community of old.

To the economies of the former metropolitan states, the liquidation of colonial bonds, and often the loss of old investments or, in any case, the unhampered use of them, were serious shocks. The new independent states were no longer inhibited from putting into effect economic policies, conceived in the interest of their own national development. In the changed world climate, many other underdeveloped countries, in Latin America and elsewhere, which had been politically independent without making much use of their freedom to initiate national economic policies, now started to do this. The idea of national planning began to spread. All this involved rather sharp changes in the whole international economic system. Some of the old imperial powers, France in particular, got involved in colonial wars which were financially expensive and economically disruptive—the more so as they were entirely futile investments, foredoomed to end in total loss.

This process of the liquidation of economic colonialism has not yet, by a long way, run its full course. From the first, the already advanced stage of international disintegration amongst the old ruling class of the few rich countries naturally tended to magnify the disorganizing effects of the break-up of the colonial empires. It is possible to speculate as to how differently the Great Awakening could have evolved, and how different also might have been its effects upon the relations between the rich and poor countries, had there been no world wars and no Great Depression, and had the rich countries preserved and developed further the fairly high degree of international integration amongst themselves which they had in the beginning of the century.

The Cold War

A third major change, again setting in after World War II, has been, of course, the increasing political power of the Soviet Union and the stupendous increase in territories and populations under communist rule. These sweeping political *bouleversements,* the cold war which developed, the acutely felt risks of further advances of the communist front, of small wars and even of a new world war, which in the atomic age would mean world destruction, have had huge economic consequences.

They have caused all countries, and particularly the rich ones, to devote a very large part of their national income to armaments and, indeed, forced them, to a large extent, to place their national economies on a war footing. They introduced strategic interests as important in all international economic relations, in particular when great powers were involved. They made the restoration of the international capital market, which had collapsed in the early years of the Great Depression, very much more difficult, if not impossible. They broke up the world markets along a political dividing line. Generally speaking, they threw an irrational, perverting, and confusing force into almost all problems of national and international economic policy.

But the trend towards international disintegration of the old partial world community goes much further back. It was well advanced, and rapidly accelerating, long before the colonial empires began to break up, long before Russia was even envisaged as a serious danger, before the cold war and all that is connected with it became a major concern to all countries. We nurture an opportunistic and entirely false conception of reality if we try to believe that these latter historical upheavals should be given all the blame for what went wrong with international relations in the Western world.

Also, the liquidation of colonialism had independent causes. It was not the machinations of Russia, or the communist movement, or the effect of the cold war, even if the October Revolution already produced reverberations in the colonies as well as in the metropolitan countries themselves. Up to now, communism has been, to quote Adlai E. Stevenson, "more the scavenger than the inspiration" of this world revolution. Its further impact may, however, be great.

National Integration versus International Integration

What is perhaps most paradoxical in the recent developments is the fact that, in this historical era of progressive and accelerating international economic disintegration of the partial world community that existed half a century ago, the few rich countries in the Western world, which made up this community, have experienced spectacular economic progress internally, and a speeding-up of their advance towards national economic integration. Within the several nation-states in the group, this fortunate development is continuing with unabated force. It is natural that this tends to turn attention in these lands away from the threatening situation and prospects in the field of international economic relations.

The rich Western countries have by now reached the stage where, in each of them taken individually, further economic progress has become almost automatic. The higher level of economic development attained reflects itself in improved systems of education and training and, more generally, in a broader sharing among people of all regions and classes in the national culture. This growth process towards cultural advance and national unity, together with the increased availability of transportation and communication, has implied, in each of the Western countries, a more effective spread of expansionary momentum from one industry and locality to another. This, in its turn, has again spurred economic progress.

At the same time, economic progress under these conditions has made possible a lessening of internal inequalities. The generally wider elbow-room that follows economic progress, and the lessening of inequalities within the nations, have also laid a firmer basis for political democracy, which has become ever more effectively the form of government in the rich countries. The democratic political machinery has been used to condition the economic system to operate in accordance with the inherited Western ideals of liberty and equality of opportunity for all.

In the rich countries of the Western world, these ideals are operative social forces, and they gain strength all the time by being increasingly realized. No regions, occupational groups, or social classes are allowed to fall far behind what is becoming the general standard in the country as a whole, and that standard is itself continually being raised. Social mobility and individual advance through schooling and training, and through performance on the job, are safeguarded. In particular, an ever greater equality of opportunity is assured to the newly born. This integration of a nation implies fuller utilization of the inherent productive potentialities of the most important natural resource of every country, which is—not least in the richest countries—the people. In the cumulative social process, economic progress, equalization of opportunities, and political democracy are interrelated by circular causation, each one being both cause and effect of the others. With all the failings of the Welfare State in the rich countries, upon which I commented in Chapter 7, this is the trend.

The ordinary citizen, living in these happy countries, has experienced the steady improvement of his own economic fortunes, and sees in the future ever brighter openings for himself and his children in a national community that is continuously getting richer, and is at the same time approaching, by gradual reform, those ideals of social democracy he has been brought up to cherish. It is indeed natural that he does not greatly trouble his mind with thoughts about what happens to international relations, or, indeed, what happens abroad—so long, *nota bene*, as these happenings do not threaten his own welfare and security. When they do—or when he is brought to believe that they do—he is naturally inclined towards a nationalistic outlook: to avoid viewing the international development in a world perspective and from the angle of his ideals of liberty and equality as applied to mankind at large, but instead to narrow his vision so as to make it easier for him to put the blame on the foreigner.

More particularly, the cold war gives him the opportunity to escape responsibility by imputing all the threats to one single origin: the Russians, and what he is inclined to perceive as the international communist conspiracy. In the educational attempts, incumbent upon the social scientist, to make the ordinary citizen's outlook on the world more rational, correct, and genuinely relevant to the complex of problems which he, as a citizen, has to cope with, it is important to stress again and again the fact that the cold war is only one strand in the trend towards international economic disintegration—though admittedly it has broad ramifications.

The inability of the rich countries to find a new and viable international balance amongst their own national economies is certainly not caused by the Russians; nor is their failure to organize better relations with the under-developed countries in the non-Soviet world which are now surging forward to political independence and national economic development. These facts alone provide a reason for dealing with the non-Soviet world, as I have often done, as a separate problem—thus abstracting, in the first instance, from the countries in the Soviet sphere and their policies.

The Role of National Planning in International Disintegration

The above remarks are an attempt at an *aperçu* of recent developments in the world economy at large, and a characterization of the present situation in regard to international economic relations. They are meant to afford a perspective to the following discussion of one specific problem: the international implications of the trend towards economic planning in the rich Western countries.

Planning is national. It is a manifestation of the nation-state, which is everywhere becoming stronger. It is true that, in the Welfare State of the Western countries, both the initiative to, and the execution of, policies is left more and more to the organs of provincial and municipal government and to the voluntary organizations within the infrastructure. Since the total volume of public policies is growing, and their importance in all fields increasing, and since at the same time they are gradually becoming better coordinated by planning, we see in some of the most advanced countries in this group indications of a possible future situation where the state as such can withdraw more and more from detailed direct intervention.

But all this cooperative and bargaining activity in various sections and at various levels of the national community takes place within the set framework of the strong nation-state. It functions under conditions created by huge changes brought about by state policies, according to rules laid down by state authority and with the political and administrative organs of the state as watchful umpires. It could not have developed as it has, had there not been this framework of the strong nation-state, which is all the time becoming stronger as the result of national planning.

In this particular respect the situation of the underdeveloped countries outside the Soviet orbit is not altogether different. What there actually is, in such non-Soviet countries, of planning and coordination in public policy, has of necessity been a state responsibility much more exclusively and directly. As I have shown, a central part of the state's planning efforts in such countries must be directed towards the immensely difficult task of finding the means of decentralizing public policies by building up organs of self-government and voluntary organizations for cooperation and collective bargaining. Meanwhile, the relative weakness of the state itself constantly inhibits all planning on whatever level. In most underdeveloped countries it has prevented the generally accepted idea of national planning for development from materializing in the form of strikingly successful achievements.

A precondition for more effective planning is the consolidation of the nation-state. These countries need to be united and organized to the point where they can have a single-minded and purposive government, whose efforts are not absorbed exclusively in merely trying to hold the nation together and steer it through short-range crises. In so far as more effective planning is accomplished in such a country, it will reflect a more consolidated nation-state. There also, as in the richer countries, planning will at the same time be one of the major instruments of further consolidation and strengthening of the nation-state.

The powers of the state are restricted by national boundaries. In the absence of a world-state and also of effective inter-state cooperation and bargaining, national policies tend of necessity to become nationalistic. It cannot be helped that everywhere national integration is now bought at the cost of international disintegration. Though people are usually not aware of it, this development is causing, from one decade to another, fundamental changes not only in international relations but also in the very structure of the national communities themselves and in the political attitudes prevailing among their peoples. In spite of all the hopeful publicity about international economic integration here and there in the world, the main trend towards economic nationalism is unbroken, and the driving forces behind this trend are the very policies of national planning which, in the individual nations, are so necessary for progress and have had such wholesome results at home.

This second part of our inquiry will be devoted to the trend towards international disintegration and its relation to national planning in the Western countries. In regard to the future, a continual rise of economic nationalism would be the natural course. For the forces which drive the development are interlocked in a circular fashion, each change being both cause and effect of other changes moving in the same direction, with the result that they all cumulate. Thus nationalistic policies, by their effects at home as well as abroad, are themselves continually strengthening the very attitudes amongst the peoples that are supporting and pushing forward further advances along the line of these same policies. These policies thus become the cause of their own perpetuation and strengthening.

The economic policies I am referring to are, of course, not ordinarily motivated in the several countries by their disintegrating effects internationally, but by their integrating and favorable effects at home. It is also a fact, as I shall attempt to show, that the relations between policies and attitudes in the cumulative process towards economic nationalism contain many elements which can be proved by objective analysis to be irrational, even from the point of view of narrow national interests. A seasoned professor should not be expected to underrate the significance of public enlightenment. And it is finally a fact that people have wider interests and can be moved by higher ideals than short-term economic self-interest. I cannot admit that the cause of the internationalist is hopeless. But it needs to be much more closely reasoned.

10

Economic Nationalism in the Western World

The Welfare State is Nationalistic

In abstract terms, the mechanism of the process towards disintegration of the old partial world community can be analyzed in the following way. The direct causes of this movement of the system of international relations have all the time been policy measures, taken by the several states to defend their national economies against the repercussions of the international crises through which the world has been passing in a continual sequence during the last half century. When one crisis passed, the policy measures taken in defense against it tended to be retained. For then a new situation had been created, partly by the policy measures of the several countries, which had to be sustained, in order not to give rise to new disturbances. Moreover, private vested interests had been built up behind such intervention in the normal way. As the national policies had not been coordinated with a view to accomplishing an international balance, these policies, as they evolved, tended to perpetuate, and occasionally to aggravate, the international crises.

The succession of international crises could not, however, have such far-reaching and permanent effects in gradually shaping national policies in an autarkic direction, but for the historically dramatic constellation be-

159

tween this international development and the internal
development in all the rich countries of the Western
world. At the beginning of World War I the social, economic, and political development in these countries had
just about reached the point of departure for the rapid
speeding-up of the growth of the modern Welfare State
which I analyzed in the earlier part of this book. This
was of crucial importance. The presence and the increasing strength, in all Western nations, of internal
forces pressing towards the goals of the Welfare State
strengthened the inclination to take defensive action
against the repercussions of the international crises in
order to preserve stability and welfare at home.

From the opposite point of view, the necessity and,
gradually, the habit in these countries from World War I
onwards of taking large-scale interventionist action to affect
the play of market forces in order to defend the national
community against the effects of international crises
opened up opportunities, without which the Welfare
State would not have developed so soon or so rapidly.
Once more, we see circular causation at work and the
cumulation of forces. Every new emergency in the international sphere gave the occasion for taking a new step
towards perfecting the Welfare State.

As a matter of fact, no logical dividing line can be drawn
between, on the one hand, those policy measures which
were in the nature of protective action against acute
dangers for the national economy arising out of the
sphere of international relations, and, on the other, the
Welfare State policies proper. The fact is that the setting
in which the modern Welfare State has been developing
in the Western world has been one of progressive international disintegration. It is equally undeniable that the
larger part of the complex system of public policies in the

interest of national progress, and of the growth of equality and security for the individual, which today make up the Welfare State, have on balance tended to disturb the international equilibrium. They were nowhere conceived and brought into effect as internationally concerted actions. Effects abroad were not taken into consideration; in any case, in no country and at no time were they given much weight, in the planning and execution of welfare policies.

Indeed, national planning—whether by the state, by public, semi-public, or private organizations, or by individual enterprises—has, for many reasons, almost by necessity an autarkic tendency. For one thing, demand and supply within the boundaries of one country are much easier to forecast, and also to influence in the desired direction, while, from the point of view of national planning, the demand and supply abroad are always more uncertain and far less yielding to national policy direction. In a situation where there is no supra-national authority, and only a minimum of inter-state cooperation and bargaining, almost any policy of intervention in economic automatism becomes autarkic in its consequences.

In particular, the ideals of the Welfare State did not permit internal adjustments in response to changes in the international sphere, if they had to be at the expense of full employment and other essential elements of those ideals. As those ideals increasingly materialized in firm institutions and working practices which could not be easily and rapidly altered, the state was also less able to adjust them, even in situations where these ideals would have permitted it to do so. The national economies have been permanently shaped towards a maximum of internal adjustability—within the framework of fixed rules and procedures adapted to the fulfilment of the ideals of the Welfare State—which makes it increasingly possible to preserve internal progress and stability, but only at the cost of a more pronounced lack of external flexibility. The result is international instability and disintegration.

We will never be able to come to grips with the international problems of today and tomorrow if we do not squarely face the fact that *the democratic Welfare State in the rich countries of the Western world is protectionist and nationalistic.* The peoples in those countries have achieved economic welfare at home—economic progress and a substantial increase in liberty and equality of opportunity for all within their boundaries—at the expense of indulging in nationalistic economic policies. In the circular causation of cumulative social processes, these policies, adopted partly in response to international crises, themselves continually support the trend to international disintegration. As the process of interaction evolves, the entire institutional structure of the state becomes set in a matrix of economic nationalism.

A Moral Ambivalence

If this sketch of the broadest causal relations operating within and between the rich countries of the Western world is correct, it is no fortuitous accident of history that the last half-century has seen a progressive international disintegration, concomitant with a spectacular growth of national integration in all the individual countries. It is, on the whole, the same national policy measures which have had negative effects upon international relations and very positive effects at home in all these countries. Within the boundaries of the individual state, the inherited ideals of liberty, equality of opportunity for all, and common brotherhood have become realized through mighty strides in state legislation and administration, and, within the framework of state regulations, through vigorous organizational activity on behalf of all local and sectional groups of the national community. National integration was advancing rapidly *pari passu* with international disintegration. And on many planes of interdependence, the causation is circular and the process cumulative and bound to proceed further, unless it is redirected in a radical fashion.

Related to this is the ambivalence in the valuation attitudes that good and well-informed persons, in the liberal Western tradition, demonstrate when they become aware of this conflict. On the one hand, they must feel that economic nationalism is wrong, bad, and damaging to the common welfare of all peoples. They feel so when they look at the world as a whole, and when—as they certainly should do, if they are honest and true to their deepest convictions—they then apply to mankind as a whole the ideals of liberty, equality of opportunity, and universal brotherhood which are the moral tenets of our civilization. Clearly, the complete realization of our ideals would create a world without boundaries and without national discrimination, a world where all men are free to move around as they wish and to pursue on equal terms their own happiness. Politically, the implication would be a world state, democratically ruled by the will of all peoples. Somewhere in the religious compartment of our souls we all harbor, in a vague and noncommittal way, this vision of a world in perfect integration, the *Urbs Dei* or *Civitas Mundi*.

On the other hand, in the real world which is so very different from this idealistic image and which tends to become less like it every day, this positive valuation of internationalism *in abstracto* can be of no great consequence for people's political behavior in everyday affairs. The moral ambivalence to which I referred has its origin in the fact that, to a large extent though not exclusively, the operative forces driving development in the direction of increasing economic nationalism have rational motives: strivings in individual countries towards economic progress and security for all citizens, motivated at bottom by the same ideals of liberty, equality of opportunity, and common brotherhood to which I referred as the moral tenets of our civilization, though they operate only within national boundaries. In themselves these strivings are, of course, right, good, and wholesome.

As, however, these strivings in the individual countries, in themselves good and rational, result in international disintegration, we are confronted with a true dilemma. No nation can reasonably be expected to be willing to renounce its efforts to improve conditions at home. To resolve this dilemma the internationalist, therefore, will have to find the means by which national and international ideals can be reconciled in a new and wider "created harmony." He will have to demonstrate how, by international cooperation and bargaining, agreement could be reached on such modifications of national economic policies as would lead to a better integrated world economy, while, *nota bene,* at the same time the policies, so modified, would equally well, or better, realize the goals of national integration in the several countries.

Resistance to the Welfare State

At this point in the argument a brief reference should be made to the resistance which the development of the Welfare State met in all countries. Equalization of opportunities and a broader sharing in the national welfare was an essential part of the goals of the great movement towards the Welfare State. To an extent this had to be accomplished by placing financial burdens on the privileged classes and by restricting their freedom to use their power of wealth as they pleased. For some, the Welfare State implied sacrifices. At least, this was true, apparently, in the short run. But the Welfare State had such a powerful influence in releasing the potential productivity of the people that, in the dynamic process of its gradual realization, an improvement in the working and living conditions of the poor could be carried out in an economically progressive economy, without depressing the conditions of most of those who were initially better off and who, in the first instance, had had to pay for the reforms.

That this could happen, however, was something of a surprise—even to most of the reformers of that period, who usually argued their case in static terms of social justice, for which end they were prepared to demand sacrifices on the part of the well-to-do. The theory of the immense productivity of the reforms is mainly an afterthought, after the anxiety of the upper classes proves groundless. Particularly in the earlier stages of this reform movement it was natural, indeed, that those with vested interests in the old order mobilized political power to protect themselves and tried to resist the launching of the social and economic reforms of the developing Welfare State.

As a matter of fact, reactionary forces all the time carried on a rearguard struggle against the reforms—until now, in the most advanced countries of the Western world the policies and practices of the Welfare State have been so firmly established, and have become so generally accepted, that no political party can oppose them. These countries are gradually reaching the position where the political parties have, on the contrary, to compete with each other before the electorate in proposals for carrying the reform movement still further. This is the stage in the development of the democratic Welfare State which in Sweden has been called the "service state."

We have, then, come very far from the old quasi-liberal

state as it existed half a century ago. The Welfare State is now developing further almost automatically. The social and economic reforms accrue merely as by-products of economic progress, which itself is spurred on by the reforms in a cumulative fashion. No hard fights are now necessary. The reformers become largely dispensable, which undoubtedly renders the national scene less lively and interesting, more occupied with petty bickering than the fight over broad issues, and sometimes animated by bad humor.

But once, not long ago, the reformers had a role to play, a struggle to wage. And, in spite of all their valiant endeavors, this whole development towards the Welfare State would probably not have got under way at that time, and certainly not have gained its irresistible momentum so rapidly, had it not been for the opportunity—to some extent a necessity—for large-scale intervention in the economic life of our countries, afforded by the long series of international crises beginning with World War I.

The Old School of Internationalists

During this whole period, when the Welfare State was still contested, the political forces which attempted to hold out against the popular reform movement had an ally in the old school of internationalist economists, who called for a radical demobilization of the national economic policies in order to restore international economic integration.

These economists insisted upon a return to a system of greater international automatism, where the individual national economies would have to adjust themselves to changes in the world around them, even though this would sometimes be exacting and occasionally cause unemployment and business losses. They had the courage to raise this demand in this very epoch, characterized as it was by recurring violent international crises. They could point out, however, that the magnitude and the obstinate persistence of unbalance in world economic relations were at least partly due to the national policies they sought to reverse. International disintegration was caused, they argued—and with considerable justification—by the reluctance of the governments, and behind them the nations, to let automatic adjustments to changes in the international system take their natural, even if sometimes painful, course.

As it happened, the economists of this school were giving arguments to the reactionaries, who fought the Welfare State because they were against economic equalization. But fundamentally their value basis was a different one: they were internationalists. I do not agree with the practical conclusions of this school, for reasons which I will now expound. But before I proceed to criticize them I want to stress what I know so well from my close personal association with many prominent economists who belonged to this school, that in general they did not take their position because of callousness to the sufferings of the poor, but because they saw no other way of stopping the creeping international disintegration.

They were, in fact, never true allies in their hearts with the political reactionaries. Indifference to the need for redistributional reforms is not in the great classical tradition of economic thinking, in which they, as well as those who share my very different opinions, stand. And I want to add that I agree fully with the old school in their major value premise: the paramount importance of the urgent need to resist the development towards international disintegration, because of the immense dangers inherent in this development. On this basic issue I have no divergent opinion to voice. Indeed, were I not able to see any other way out of the dilemma which I have posed, I would have a split personality, with half my soul in the camp of the old school of internationalists.

A Forlorn Hope

I would not then be able to hide from myself, however, that international integration would be a forlorn hope. The state policies, which economists of the old school wanted to reverse, serve rational purposes and serve them on the whole well—at least so people firmly believe. They are integral parts of the complex of policy measures which have gone into building up, and now hold together, the national Welfare State. The Welfare State is something that our nations are not prepared to give up or even slightly dismantle. The "organizational state" cannot be de-organized, for people would not permit it.

The Welfare State—including all the organs of a lower order—is an increasingly regulatory one. But who is to censure its movements in the interest of internationalism? To believe in the practicability of a return to international automatism becomes sheer utopianism, once the national governments have had the experience of managing the levers of national economic policy without regard for the old taboos, and more than ever when the direction and execution of economic policies have become part of national politics, about which the interest groups are contesting in the individual countries. For, as I demonstrated in Chapter 2, a state of social automatism can exist only as long as those taboos are respected—so long, that is, as certain matters are not objects of policy, still less part of politics. A return to greater automatism in international economic relations would assume that a number of those matters were again fenced off from national policies and national politics. But a social taboo, once broken, can never be re-established.

The economists of the school I am now criticizing have usually not been fools. Most of them did not succeed in remaining unaware of the fact that a return to international automatism would meet overwhelming resistance. In this dilemma most of them have gone a long way towards coming to terms with the political currents and opportunities of their time and consequently in compromising their own thinking. It almost became a vogue among them to forswear allegiance to laissez-faire and old-time Manchester liberalism.

And, by reaching this accommodation, they have not merely implied readiness to accept redistributional reforms, as long as these can be accomplished without interference with production and trade; this by itself is well within the tradition of economic thinking from John Stuart Mill. But it did not lead far, as in reality redistributional measures are mostly connected with just such interference. At the risk of otherwise foredooming their work to irrelevance to what was actually going on in their national communities, the economists of the old school have accepted more, and have regularly swallowed whole structures of nationalistic policy measures. They did it in order to concentrate their fire on criticizing some particular ones.

By compromising their thinking, however, they weakened the rational force of their argument. The dividing line they drew between nationalistic policy measures which should be tolerated and those which should be withstood—differently drawn by different authors and often shifting according to the needs of the moment—was in most cases merely implicit; in any case, it was never made very clear. This is fully explicable, as the attempt was arbitrary from the beginning and lacked logical basis. Under these conditions, of course, they could hardly make out a very plausible case for their right to expect that a restoration of international automatism in any appreciable degree, and consequent integration, would follow the acceptance of their more limited advice.

In the end, they usually scored little practical success. The political history of this epoch is littered with more or less dramatic incidents when those in power, backed by their peoples, acted contrary to the urgent advice of the economists—and seemed to find a special pleasure in so doing.

The New School of Internationalists

The Welfare State implies a closely organized economy. The institutional structure of this national economy is being continually modified, and thereby usually tightened further, under the influence of economic, social, and political forces operating within the national democracies. But as a structure it is supported by the people. It cannot be dismantled, therefore, and in the final analysis this is the reason why the efforts of the old school of internationalists have been so futile.

But the old school of internationalists were right in insisting that international integration can only be achieved by breaking down those barriers between countries which are the effect of national economic policies, replacing them by a more flexible international system. As the nations would never agree to dismantle their national economic policies—for which, in my opinion, they have valid reasons—I draw the practical conclusion that the only means of moving towards the goal of international integration must be to internationalize the existing structure of these policies.

The members of the new school of internationalists have their hearts in the ideals of the Welfare State. Many of us have been among the social engineers who made the blueprints, and who, as experts and sometimes even as practical politicians, actively promoted social and economic reforms aimed at perfecting the Welfare State in our countries. Apart from personal engagement in this great reform movement of our age, we know our peoples well enough to be convinced that, in any case, the movement cannot be stopped and reversed.

But we are not prepared to compromise our internationalist ideals either. If we want to find a way out of the dilemma posed by the tie between national integration and international disintegration, we must face the necessity of redirecting our approach to the problem: we must aim at harmonizing, coordinating, and unifying national economic policy structures internationally. By so modifying national policies that they fit into a scheme of joint effort by the several nation-states to improve their economic conditions, we would clear away much of the effect of the national policies in creating international disintegration, while still preserving their intended wholesome results for the individual nations. According to the definition of planning given for the Western countries, this coordination of national policies amounts to international economic planning.

International Coordination of National Economic Policies

Surely this is the rational solution, and as a scheme it is logically perfectly feasible. The condition is, of course, willingness on the part of the governments and nations to enter into international cooperation and bargaining on a much larger scale than at present.

If that will were present, and government representatives could sit down together in order to shape common economic policies, it would be immediately apparent that some aspects of national policies are not really essential for the welfare of the several countries. They could be scrapped, to our common advantage, if this were done not only in one country but in many at the same time. Some protective measures serve interests which, even if not altogether unimportant in the individual countries, are small compared with the common interest of all nations to be rid of them, provided this could be done simultaneously as a result of a multilateral agreement. The scope for this type of "international economic disarmament" would, of course, be widened if stable international markets could be more firmly guaranteed, and in particular a high and stable world trend of expanding production and employment. For, if general expansion under conditions of greater international stability were achieved so that expansion became unbroken—and if peoples and governments put their faith in its achievement—many national economic policies, aimed at national stability, could be safely done away with.

The efforts towards international harmonization of national economic policies cannot stop, however, at creating conditions where governments would be prepared to abstain from certain policy measures. The major part of the problem concerns policies which national governments cannot willingly give up.

We have to face the fact that the Welfare State is the "organizational state." Neither in the markets for capital and labor, nor for commodities and services, is the play of demand, supply, and price to any substantial extent now "free." It is regulated by state, provincial, and municipal legislation and administration, and by the semi-public and private organizations and big enterprises, which all function within the framework of the state and under its control. In the final analysis, it is these whole complex structures of organized interference in the markets which have to be internationally coordinated and harmonized, if we want to re-integrate the world economy.

Naturally, we cannot demand absolute unification throughout the entire world, of the policies by which markets are now nationally organized. As a matter of fact, they are not unified in the individual states. In the most advanced Welfare State, the trend has been towards a decentralization of community controls, leaving more freedom for the provinces and municipalities, and for the organized local and sectional interest groups, to decide upon how people shall live and work together. But national integration has implied that this has been allowed only within the setting of a common organizational structure for the state as a whole, representing the general rules without which the national community would have disintegrated.

The same principle holds true in international relations, if we want to move towards a more closely integrated world community. In an epoch of continued rapid industrialization, most countries will feel the need for an agricultural policy to protect the living standards of the tillers of the soil. The need to avoid international disintegration as a result of the agricultural policies of individual countries should be faced as a common concern. If there were a basis of international solidarity approaching in strength to the existing national one, it should be possible to reach international agreement on national agricultural policies in the several countries. These policies might be different, but would nevertheless be so harmonized that they did not, as now, lead simply to a competition between the countries to shift their burdens onto each other.

Similarly, all countries have reasons for supporting certain "infant" industries, as part of a national development program. Again, it would be possible to review such national policies from a wider international angle, and to seek a compromise agreement upon lines of national policy which, on balance, would be in the common interest, by permitting maximum economic development in the several countries, while minimizing the ill-effects abroad of protective national policies.

The labor and capital markets are tightly organized in all countries. But it should be possible to attain the essential favorable effects sought by these policies without the almost complete autarky, with negligible, or only severely perverted, movements of labor and capital over the national boundaries, which is the present situation.

There would still be regulations, and probably more of them. But within these regulations, in the new type of international relations founded upon a widening of economic solidarity, there would be very much more freedom of movement for factors of production, as there is now in the individual Welfare State. Moreover, there would be a more rational division of labor and production between the countries, according to the natural advantages of different regions and the aptitudes and ambitions of their peoples.

As was the case in the individual Welfare States when they moved towards closer national integration, so in the world at large this process of international integration would need the impetus of economic progress. Only in a rapidly and steadily expanding world economy would there exist the conditions for mutual generosity. Without this it could not be hoped that the process would attain any real momentum. But international integration, if it were once given a chance to get under way, would itself spur on economic expansion in the same way as national integration has done in the individual Welfare States.

My main point against the old school of internationalists is that international integration has to be argued in positive terms—those of realizing, in the wider world community, the goals of the national Welfare State, which means nothing else than attaining our old ideals of liberty, equality, and brotherhood—and not in the negative terms of wanting to break up the policies by which people everywhere in the Western world have tried to realize those ideals within their national communities.

The Difficulties

The argument has been drawn to its logical conclusion, and aims have thereby been clarified which are very far removed from those realized in international relations today. At this point in the argument, however, the observation is pertinent that, broadly speaking, these aims, as they have been formulated above, are the very directives which, at the end of World War II and in the years immediately afterwards, were given to the international economic organizations as guiding beacons. This was a time of courageous thinking along new lines. For a few years, the new school of internationalists was firmly in the saddle and determined the formulation of policies in the Western world.

To a large extent, these directives were also agreed upon by the governments, set down in the founding documents of these organizations, and confirmed in a multitude of solemn and usually unanimous resolutions. In their practical implementation, though, we have not come very far. Compared with the hopes once held out to the peoples when they were founded, the international economic organizations have been failures. But they still exist, and will continue to exist. Even if our concerted attempts in these organizations are feeble and the results as yet small and insecure, this is their task. What we are grappling with in all of them, however ineffectively at the present time, is exactly to coordinate and harmonize national economic policies: to superimpose international planning over merely national planning.

The difficulties to be overcome are formidable. But the alternative solution, fought for so long and valiantly by the old school of internationalists—simply the large-scale demolition of national economic policies and a return to economic automatism—is completely impracticable and, indeed, politically impossible. In addition, it would demolish accomplishments in our countries of which we are justly proud. The solution propounded by the new school of internationalists is, at least, a sensible goal, however difficult to reach, and one that would satisfy our ideals of both national and international integration.

The plain fact is this: *When once the national Welfare State has come into existence and built its moorings firmly in the hearts of the peoples who in the democracies of the Western world have the political power, there is no alternative to international disintegration except to begin, by international cooperation and mutual accommodation, to build the Welfare World.* This conclusion from our analysis stands not only, and not primarily, as an expression of a political valuation of what would be desirable, but is presented as a statement of a factual situation. Any other conclusion from our analysis would do violence to logic and to what we know about social reality in the Western countries.

11

The Institutional and Psychological Levels

Introversion of Interests

In order to assess fully the difficulties in the way of all attempts at international integration, we must face the deeper causes for nationalistic orientation of economic policies, causes which operate on the institutional and psychological levels.

The very experience of living and participating in the increasingly effective Welfare State of the rich Western countries must tend to turn people's interests inwards. As national integration proceeds, the state becomes more and more that decentralized and non-authoritarian community which I called the "organizational state." Decidedly, this implies a real growth of social democracy, and it is through this development that the Welfare State approaches the ideal which a Swedish statesman, the late Per Albin Hansson, characterized as "the people's home." Without a proportional increase in the incidence of acts of direct state intervention—perhaps soon with an actual decrease in the number of such acts—social relations are increasingly regulated by the people themselves, cooperating and bargaining in the organs for provincial and municipal self-government, as well as within and amongst the voluntary interest organizations and the big enterprises, which are more and more taking over responsibility for what, in

177

fact, is public policy. In a sense, parliament itself, in this
type of welfare democracy, becomes merely one of the
many institutions for cooperation and collective bargaining. And it is the one which creates the framework for all
the others.

In this way the modern Welfare State—and I include
within it all these other institutions for cooperation and
bargaining beneath the state level—fixes prices and earnings, sets standards in all sorts of economic and social relations, regulates seniority rights on the job, and does a
host of other things of clear and immediate importance
for people's individual welfare. It circumscribes and de-
fines people's opportunities to choose their careers and
to advance in them, to get the right remuneration for their
work, to have vacations, and to receive various amenities,
pensions and additional payments. It lays down rules determining how families can get in queue for a particular
school for their children, or to rent a house, or to build
one under prescribed favorable conditions. All the time
these and many other matters are, in the Welfare State,
taken away from the determination of impersonal market
forces.

Instead, they are regulated. They are regulated by the
citizens jointly, in the way I demonstrated. As the Welfare
State, including all the other lower-order institutions for
making public policy, thus becomes increasingly important to the citizens in their everyday strivings, and as, at
the same time, it becomes less and less authoritarian and
determined instead by the citizens themselves, directly as
voters in elections and through their organizations, it
cements its own psychological foundation in people's valuations and expectations.

A growing identification with the nation-state, and with
all the people within its boundaries, is thus a natural result

of the growth of the democratic national Welfare State. At the same time, the policies of the Welfare State can proceed and spread, precisely because of this fortified basis of national solidarity of interests, experienced by the citizens. In a process of circular causation, it becomes both a cause and an effect of the continual perfecting of the Welfare State.

This is the crux of the matter, and also an explanation of why the trend towards economic nationalism becomes so strong in the Welfare State. For a negative corollary to this increase of national solidarity within the ever more effective, and—to the individual citizens—ever more immediately important Welfare State is, without any doubt, a tendency to a decrease in international solidarity and, generally, to the weakening of people's allegiance to international ideals. The national state and all that goes on within its framework becomes the practical reality for everybody, while internationalist strivings are unpractical dreams.

The people in the modern democratic Welfare State of the rich countries of the Western world thus become intrinsically uninterested in international cooperation. This is so not only because, for reasons already mentioned, so many of the economic policies through which the Welfare State is becoming realized are nationalistic in nature. The deeper reason for economic nationalism is that the growth and further development of the Welfare State are apt to build up a human solidarity that stops short at the national boundary.

I would like to see these important problems of the psychology of the national Welfare State, at which I am here merely hinting, made the object of intensive social study: the relation between the development of national welfare democracy and the growth of economic nationalism, and the relation between the strengthening of national solidarity and the weakening of people's allegiance to international ideals.

An Institutional Bias

Even if this introversion of the minds of the people in the Welfare State were emotionally neutral, manifesting itself merely in a great diminution of concern with what goes on abroad and with the needs of the peoples living there, it would represent an irrational element in their attitudes to public affairs. It does not correspond to the true interests of the citizens of any country—"true" in the sense of being correctly perceived and appreciated—to have economic policies framed without consideration for their effects outside the national boundaries. Evidently, it would be to the common good of people in all countries if they could agree to be as considerate of each others' interests as groups of people have learned to become within each individual Welfare State, and if they were prepared to cooperate and bargain equally effectively for international compromise solutions aimed at maximizing the favorable effects at home of national policies, while minimizing the disruptive effects abroad.

There is one particular cause of this irrational institutional and psychological conditioning of people's attitudes, exerted by the national Welfare State, which should be pointed out: the bias in the organizational structure. Within such a state, all special interests, even if only those of small groups, are germinal to organizations, in which they become articulate, and plead and press for their due consideration. That this happens is an essential characteristic of the Welfare State; it is, indeed, its mode of functioning. Through a process of cooperation and bargaining amongst the organized interest groups, there emerges the relative degree of created harmony which is its accomplishment.

But the interest in international cooperation—however real and however big, if correctly assessed and added to a sum total for all the citizens—is not special to any particular group but is general and widely dispersed. It is of less immediate beneficial consequence to any individual citizen or any special group of people in any single country. It cannot give birth to effective organizations pressing and bargaining for it to be considered. Neither can it threaten any of the ultimate sanctions available to the special interest groups within the national community, like strikes and lockouts, boycotts, etc. It easily succumbs, whenever it comes up against any special interest, however petty, defended by an effective organization. Of this, the history of every year's parliament in every country provides abundant examples.

In the internal conflict of interests in the individual Welfare State, there is a parallel to this bias in favor of the special interests and against the general interest. As I pointed out, it has everywhere proved much more difficult to create effective bargaining organizations of consumers, to advance their common interest in lower living costs. The producers, including the employees, all find themselves belonging to clearly distinguished special groups, held together by shared interests, while all are consumers. The consumers' general interest in lower living costs, like the citizens' general interest in international cooperation, is so dispersed, and usually so much less specific and immediate, that, in every Welfare State, it is apt to be sacrificed whenever it comes into conflict with a determined special interest group on the producers' side.

At least in the present transitional stage of the Welfare State, such collective bargaining as takes place is confined mainly to the citizens' activity in earning a living and making a profit, and extends but little to their spending their money on the good things of life. Only in some of the most advanced Welfare States is there even an approach to effective consumers' organizations with real bargaining strength. In all of them, however, parliament and other representative bodies on the provincial and municipal level substitute to some extent for this absence of "countervailing power" on the side of all citizens as consumers. More flagrant cases of exploitation of the consumers by some organized group of producers can thus be stopped. The fact that everybody is also an income earner, and in this capacity likely to participate in a national organization defending his interest in having as high an income as possible, also contributes to making this incomplete and biased system of interest organizations less of a cause of distortion of the public will—though it certainly is not without responsibility for that tendency towards an inflationary trend in Welfare States upon which I commented in Chapter 7.

The relative weakness of the consumers' interest in a Welfare State is not only a parallel, helping us to understand better the weakness of the citizens' general interest in international cooperation. The two interests are, indeed, closely related. As a rule, the special national interests which so often easily overpower the general interest in international cooperation—even when the former are objectively petty and the latter is immense—are the interests of a national group of producers, traders, or workers, while all the citizens lose as consumers. When the interest conflict ranges over national boundaries, the correcting forces are also absent, or at least much weaker than when it is confined within the individual Welfare State. Usually, all the interest organizations are national in scope, as is, of course, the parliament itself.

The Emotional Charge

To this is added the emotional charge. Every special interest can harp on national solidarity against the foreigners as a justification for demanding a degree of protection beyond what is reasonable.

The national introversion of the mind, which I have tried to explain in terms of its conditioning by the practices and the institutional setting of the Welfare State, would be irrational, as I pointed out, even if it were merely an emotionally neutral lack of concern. But it clearly is not neutral in that sense. As it develops, it strikes root in popular feelings which easily become antipathetic to international strivings. Nationalistic policies are then driven further than they otherwise would, or could, have been.

Foreign relations are a field in which people can more freely find an outlet for their suppressed hostility and aggressiveness. And we should have no illusions that those antipathetic forces are negligible, even in the Welfare State of the rich countries in the Western world. They are deeply embedded in the minds of people, schooled and trained as they are, and living as they do under constant experiences of personal bewilderment, conflicts, and tension and the frustration of thwarted ambitions and inhibited desires. In all our societies, crime is fascinating in a way virtue can never be. Novels dealing with adultery have a sale that those picturing a happy marriage could never have.

When the communications industry habitually plays up what is unfortunate and bad, this is, of course, only in response to the demand of the buyers of the news, the general public. That a house is built is rarely much news. That it is burnt is news, and particularly so if it can be suspected to be somebody's fault or to be caused by somebody's intentional ill-will. A scandal or a violent clash in an international organization is widely reported, while quiet, useful work on practical settlements is too technical to arouse any public interest. Very generally, people delight in what goes wrong. The Germans have a word, *Schadenfreude,* which, though it seems to be untranslatable, signifies a psychological phenomenon which is fairly universal in all countries.

People seem to be in constant revolt against their own innermost ideals, and against those individuals who stand up for their ideals. There is a deep symbolic truth about our society in the religious myth of the crucifixion of Christ—in the pettiness of national life, everywhere, it constantly happens. We even notice that when people actually do follow charitable and generous impulses, they feel shy of permitting them to appear so, but pretend, in a sort of perverted puritanism, that they are acting merely in defense of their narrow self-interests. In the negativism which prevails everywhere, this pretense of national egoism is eagerly grasped by people in other nations, and used as a motivation for national egoism on their part. In this setting, it is generally easier to arouse people and get them to join against rather than for something.

These impulses are, of course, operating also in other fields of human endeavor than that of international strivings. They carry a large part of the responsibility for much of the unpleasantness of public life in all countries, and also for the fact that in many countries, as for instance in America, politics is often considered disreputable. To rise up for a cause and for ideals—this implies the sacrifice of putting oneself up as a target for popular abuse, and therefore many potential leaders will be tempted to prefer the anonymity of non-involvement. And, by this process of screening, if it goes too far, politics in a country may itself easily become less worthy of respect, as it will tend to be the playground of the tough-skinned self-seekers. This, then, in its turn, will give confirmation and support to peoples' scepticism. As we saw in Chapter 6, it occasionally even turns against the Welfare State.

But there are counter-forces in internal politics. Interests are involved which are commonly experienced as real and specific. People can identify themselves with organizations, movements and parties formed to defend and further those interests which make for a more positive approach. Also people grow more rational in their opinions, as they become aware of issues and of how they concern their own welfare. In internal politics, they assemble experience and knowledge. The further the national integration of the Welfare State proceeds, and the more politics is focused upon matters of immediate and concrete interest to the individual citizen, the stronger should become the forces of identification and insight which work for realism and rationality.

In matters relating to foreign relations, these positive forces are much weaker, however. Often they are almost absent. This difference is understandable in a world where each national state is rapidly becoming ever more fully integrated, while internationally the trend is towards disintegration. In internal politics, people can succeed in circumscribing the scope of partisanship; they have a basic level of personality where they think and feel in terms of "we." The national Welfare State has immensely enlarged the number of people who are capable of feeling this "belongingness" to the nation. But in the sphere of international relations there are indeed few who have acquired such a basic foothold from which to react in any other way than that of narrow partisanship—right or wrong my country.

Opportunism and Instability

In internal politics, people feel relatively secure, as issues have a clear and concrete significance which is commonly understood. They feel placed before definite, manageable choices which are under the collective control of the citizens in their own country, whom they know and are near. International politics, on the contrary, seems to ordinary citizens a dark destiny, largely outside what they feel to be "our" control: a focus of indeterminate fear. There is, indeed, often an objective element of uncertainty in foreign policy, namely absence of that reasonable predictability concerning the consistency of other nations' future attitudes and behavior, which would be needed for confidence when moving ahead in international cooperation and bargaining. This existing uncertainty can be subjectively amplified to any degree of suspicion and lack of trust, when the world outlook becomes less controlled by reason.

The extreme opportunism and the great instability of public opinion in the field of foreign relations become understandable against this background. Think, for instance, of the amplitude of changes in attitudes of the American public during the last twenty years to the Japanese, the Chinese, the Germans, the Spaniards, the Yugoslavs, the Finns, or the Russians. Also recall the mountains of books and articles which talented persons in America manufactured at every point of this short period in order to give an illusion of reason and permanency to the popular opinions of the day, by rationalizing them in solemn terms of national character and national history through centuries back. Remember the writings on the Germans and the Russians in the years before, during, and after World War II, and those of today. The fact that all this literature is nothing else than a mass of opportunistic rationalizations of shifting attitudes is revealed by the eagerness with which, in consecutive sequence, it was suppressed in public discussion and concealed by its authors. Even the attitudes towards countries like Great Britain, France, or Sweden are highly unstable and respond with great sensitivity, particularly in the negative direction, to what are the opportunistic illusions of the day.

It is an untrue pretense to say, as is sometimes said, that the likes and dislikes are focused on the political systems of other countries and not on the nations themselves, which are supposedly always liked as people. For at every point of time all sorts of political systems are represented both among the liked and the disliked nations. As the cold war develops, people are being conditioned to be even more indiscriminate in this particular respect. When it is felt to be opportune, any political system is tolerated or even acclaimed. Among the nations that have experienced particularly violent ups and downs in public esteem during the last decades there are several whose political system has remained about the same. I need only mention Finland, the Soviet Union, Yugoslavia, and Spain. In public opinion polls the irrationality of these swings in relative sympathy and antipathy is revealed by the interesting fact that people's beliefs concerning the supposedly objective facts of the living conditions and characteristics of foreign nations change in close correlation to the emotions, thus giving the emotions the appearance of having intellectual support.

It would, I believe, be in the service of reason if this instability and opportunism in public attitudes to foreign nations were more carefully studied by the psychologists and the results rubbed in by wide publicity. Knowledge of this should be an obligatory part of the courses in contemporary history. A reminder of their foolishness in the past might calm down people a little and make them less cocksure today. I could even see the usefulness of a silent moment at church services and other public occasions, devoted to common contemplation of earlier opinions in the field of foreign relations. But the possibilities of easily reaching a higher degree of rationality and emotional calm by research and other intellectual exercises should not be exaggerated. There is nothing which the public resents so much as being robbed of its follies.

I am not pointing this out in order to upbraid the general public. This would be a meaningless attempt to a democrat, for what other political authority has he to suggest? I have merely sought to establish an important fact, namely that people's attitudes are immensely more unstable, and far less calm, realistic, and dependable, in international than in internal affairs. The explanation of this is that, while the Welfare States are closely integrated communities where people live in firmly established relations and have objectively known and well appreciate concrete interests so that their ideas are to a considerable degree under realistic and rational control, international relations, on the contrary, are anarchic and consequently allow attitudes to float without rational anchorage in logic and concrete knowledge.

There is danger in this, since foreign policy in the democratic countries of the Western world is just as much dependent on public opinion as national policy, and this is particularly true in America. As a matter of fact, it is more dependent. For, in the integrated Welfare State, much national policy has become harnessed in the working patterns of a widely stratified network of organizations, as well as in legislation and administration. This puts up a considerable institutional inertia against short-term impulses for change. It is thus commonly taken for granted that all interested parties must be heard and allowed to press their view, and that much intensive preparation and planning must precede a health reform, or a change in social security legislation or in housing policy or anything else of similar importance.

To take a foreign policy stand, pregnant with heavy commitments for the future, or otherwise radically to change relations with foreign countries, or even to send troops around distant corners of the world, or to declare war, is actually a much simpler thing to bring about. Such things are apparently done on the spur of the moment. Even when it is known that, in some field of foreign relations, intensive preparatory studies have been made by large research staffs working for the foreign office, they usually do not seem to have had much influence on the decisions taken. The swing of popular opinion is, however, always important to every democratic government.

Hostility and Aggressiveness

We must now again recall that it is not exactly people's most rational, wisest, and most charitable selves which provide the momentum in the dynamics of attitudes in foreign relations. As I have pointed out, such matters are usually left free for exercising one's unattached feelings of hostility and aggressiveness.

Scratch almost anybody, and you find a jingoist. It is a sad truth that the Algerian war has been popular in France, and that the hatred of the Algerians was rising there every month. The Suez attack in 1956 was widely acclaimed by the broad masses of people, not only in France but also in Britain, though in Britain generally not by the intellectuals, whether they were Conservatives or Labour. It was mainly this experience of jingoism among the common people which made the Labour opposition in Parliament so wary when censuring the policy of the Conservative Government to send troops to Jordan two years later.

The people in France and Britain are in the particularly frustrating situation of having to adjust to a progressive process of losing their great power position. Their present psychological and moral difficulties are easily understandable to a Swede, who recalls how his nation had its armies all over the continent, until it was decisively defeated some two and a half centuries ago; only after a long and painful adjustment did Sweden emerge as a happy nation-state. But in the United States, which instead now happens to be in a rising phase of the power cycle, the popularity polls for President Eisenhower, which for several reasons had been declining for a long time, showed a sudden spurt upwards when, in the fall of 1958, he decided to land marines in Lebanon and to assemble the Sixth Fleet near the spot in order to demonstrate the presence of the United States' power in the Eastern Mediterranean—though it should also be recalled that when the situation in the Far East became really threatening, it was the fear of the American people that cautioned the Government. When the Government of Iceland extended its boundary of national sovereignty to 12 miles out into the ocean instead of 3, it was backed by a united nation, as was Britain in protesting against this move and in having the British trawlers, accompanied by frigates from the navy, going inside this new limit to defy Iceland's policy.

To stand up for the interests and rights of one's own country, to get tough with any foreign nation which gets in its way, becomes generally acclaimed as displaying national vigor and virtue. To join with one's compatriots in showing dislike to any foreign nation with which one's own government has a conflict of interests—or an apparent conflict—and in voicing threats and recriminations, actually increases the individual's subjective experience of national "belongingness." Such an attitude is commonly felt to be a unifying force in the nation. It is one of the shortcuts to patriotism. The politician, even the good and responsible one, operating in this milieu, must often feel pressed to exploit this easy device of directing aggression outwards as a means for increasing his power and acquiring a popular backing for his policies. And the same mechanism is operating on the other side of the national boundary.

My examples have been chosen from some of the more dramatic incidents of recent history. But the same forces operate also with regard to the more mundane problems of ordinary financial and commercial policies. That, for instance, American protectionism and immigration policies are related to strong elements of emotional nationalism has been demonstrated and is, in fact, apparent to everybody. It is an equally undeniable fact that those special interests who have reasons of their own to oppose international concerted action in the field of cartels in industry and shipping, or international cooperation for stabilizing commodity prices, or, indeed, the setting up of an international trade organization, have been able to get popular backing by appealing to irrational nationalism.

In international economic relations, the existence of narrow-mindedness and suspiciousness, or the intentional creation of such nationalistic attitudes at home, can, as a matter of fact, often bring definite tactical advantages in the short run. A government negotiating with other governments may strengthen its own bargaining power if it can get the nation solidified behind it by an extra propaganda dose of such nationalism. Even in its slumbering state, the irrationality of the nation at home can be utilized as a tool in international bargaining. This opportunity offers itself in a particularly convenient form for the U.S. Government, which, according to the singular constitutional set-up in the United States, does not necessarily carry the confidence of Congress and can rely on its backing in any specific issue least of all. When it is tactically helpful, the negotiators of the U.S. Government are often tempted to picture Congress and the public opinion in America as more irrational than they actually are. This is the experience of everyone who has ever negotiated with American authorities.

More generally, the temptation to appeal to the irrational impulses in a nation must often be irresistible. Let us assume that a government feels that there are reasons for considerable rearmament or substantial subsidies to prospective allies. A means of getting the citizens to accept the consequent increase of the tax burden is to frighten them a bit more than would be rationally warranted, and to increase their dislike of the foreign adversary even more than he objectively deserves. The temptation to use this device is stronger, the weaker the government is, the more it is under attack by the opposition, and the more the nation is conditioned by its history against making military preparations and forming military alliances in peace time.

An extra disadvantage with all purposive propaganda of this type is, however, that it cannot easily be switched off when that might be desirable. Besides, honest men cannot carry on propaganda directed to the general public, without coming gradually to believe it themselves, at least in part. It is difficult for anyone to assert more than he believes. If he tries, he will end up believing more than he did in the beginning. He has chosen propaganda as a servant, but it becomes his master. This amounts to partial abdication from leadership.

I have been referring here to honestly motivated politics, carried out by responsible politicians. As has often been seen, for the demagogues exploitation of the potentialities of pitching up hostility to other nations is an easy road to fame, popular backing, and power. It can also be utilized to distract people from pressing for further internal reforms. In every country there are, for this reason, vested interests which may feel it to their advantage to support an aggressive foreign policy. Unlike those of a common American stereotype from the period between the two world wars, these interests are many more than those of the manufacturers of arms. And every special interest pleading for protection from foreign competition can gain popular support by masquerading as a national interest, and spreading suspicion and antipathy against foreigners.

International Ideals

Economic policies in democracies of the Western type cannot be realistically analyzed, except in the setting of the forces which operate on the minds of the people. I have therefore touched not only upon the irrational tendency to nationalistic bias of people's attitudes, which is rooted in the institutional setting of the modern Welfare State and which would be present even if it amounted merely to an unemotional lack of concern for the affairs of foreigners, but also upon the negative emotional impulses which are quite generally at work.

But international ideals and the feeling of solidarity with people abroad are also part of social reality. That all human beings are equal, that international relations should be based on friendliness and mutual consideration, and that we should all cooperate to our mutual advantage are thoughts which are intrinsic elements of Western civilization. They are pushed aside considerably by the facts in the situation of every Welfare State, which I have been analyzing in this and the foregoing chapters. But this does not imply that they are entirely powerless. And our hope of turning the tide depends in the last instance on the possibility of strengthening the hold of the international ideals upon common people in all nations.

For a limited group of countries, a shared hostility to an outside group can often be used as a means of reaching greater internal cohesion within their own group. West-European integration and American financial support of it have thus been widely advocated as means of strengthening the front against communism. As I have already pointed out, it is a general human trait that people can more easily be moved to join against, rather than for, something. Similarly, aid to underdeveloped countries has been advocated as a means to stop their going communist and to align them with the Western bloc in the cold war, or at least to keep them neutral.

In order to form and keep together an anti-communist bloc of nations, a continuous need is also felt to maintain the cold war tension on a high level of intensity. The same need is felt on the other side in this world conflict. In meeting these shared needs, an almost perfect cooperation, though of a negative type, had developed between the two power blocs. Each bloc could always rely on the other bloc to provide, by its policies, a spur to determination and unity among its members and a reason why their alliance was necessary: these mutual needs have seldom, in recent years, been frustrated by either side.

As everybody knows, Stalin contributed mightily to the formation and consolidation of the anti-communist alliances, from the West-European organization for economic cooperation to NATO and onwards, and his successors have not in that respect changed the conditions for anti-communist international cooperation in any substantial way. This has to be seen in the light of the conditions within Russia. Every Russian government needs to stand before its own people as the champion of peace. But it can

also make good use of keeping world tension at not too low
a pitch, in order to preserve internal consolidation in its
vast empire. This is a particularly urgent need in the
present dynamic phase of Russia's cultural, political, and
economic development, when levels of living and, in particular, of education are reaching higher levels. The process of "de-Stalinization" is a profound social trend that
cannot be stopped, and few of the leaders would want to
stop it. But they are, of course, all aware of its inherent
dangers for the regime and for the political coherence of
the peoples in the Soviet Union. They need world tension
also in order to hold their satellites in Eastern Europe
securely within the Soviet bloc, and to press forward economic integration within the entire Soviet orbit.

These aims could hardly have been met—certainly not
so effectively—except in a state of cold war. Both for reasons of internal consolidation inside of the Soviet countries and in order to tie them more firmly to each other the
leaders in the Soviet countries must see considerable
advantages in giving maximum publicity to the American
military bases around the Soviet orbit. They reaped a
similar political advantage from the restrictive commercial
policies of America and her more or less willing allies in
Western Europe and elsewhere. Economically, these policies were never of great importance—except by giving an
additional motivation and sense of urgency to the strivings
in the Soviet countries to become self-sufficient in the
production of strategic materials and equipment, which
anyhow was in their obvious interest in the prevailing
world situation. But, as the lists of prohibited exports were
very extensive, these policies left the satellites in a position
where they had to depend on each other and the Soviet
Union almost entirely for imports of importance for their
economic development. The publicity given to this consequence of the Western policies and what Stalin called "the

two world markets" went a long way to create a feeling
among the peoples in the Soviet orbit that they were isolated and that the rest of the world was against them. In
China, the tragic and boundless hatred against the Americans has, of course, been a forceful means of national consolidation under the harsh communist rule, and the same
can be said of China's exclusion from the United Nations,
which has therefore turned out more and more to be in
the communist interest.

In a sequence of circular and cumulative causation,
every offensive or defensive policy measure by one side in
this world conflict justified the other side in proceeding
in the same direction. And what was being done on one
side became a reason to strive for closer ties on the
other side. In regard to the Western world, I would not
deny that the feeling of grave dangers from a common
adversary has at times contributed to more international
consolidation within this group of countries than would
otherwise have been forthcoming. The American Congress
would have been less willing to agree to Marshall Aid for
the countries in Western Europe, had the members of
Congress and the American people not had the feeling that
they were fighting communism. And some underdeveloped
countries have undoubtedly got more financial assistance
for the same reason.

But it is never unimportant how a good thing is motivated. An internationalism founded on the negative feelings of mistrust, fear, and hostility to an out-group is an
opportunistic short-cut, and it preserves too much of the
basic root of nationalism and thus of the irrational spur
to international disintegration. In the long run we must
educate the peoples to be internationally-minded for the
positive reason that mutual consideration is to the common
advantage of all participants. This is the only reliable
foundation.

The common people might be more enlightened than their leaders sometimes assume that they are. When I recently visited my home country, I was surprised to find an under-current of serious concern for the pressing needs of the underdeveloped countries. In their popular movements, particularly those for women and young people, demands have been made that Sweden's financial contributions to these countries should be many times greater than at present. And when recently a settlement of a remaining Finnish war debt was announced, including a partial remission, it was criticized in many quarters as too niggardly on the part of rich Sweden. These developments of public opinion were entirely unsolicited by the political parties and represent very much the reaction of ordinary, well informed people acting in the ramifying network of their organizations. Undoubtedly they are of importance as in the end policies are decided by the people. Now, there is in Sweden, of course, a responsible parliament and a government which is struggling with budget difficulties, as in all other countries, and the rising popular demands for greater generosity will only be met partly and with a considerable time lag. There have been similar developments in certain sections of public opinion in Norway, in Britain and in America and probably in all the rich Western countries.

Under the late Ernest Bevin, the foreign policy of the British Labour Government immediately after the war did not show much respect for international considerations. In the inter-governmental organizations, which were then started, Britain regularly played a decisively negative role—to the extent, in fact, that in these organizations the coming to power of the Conservative Party was at first felt as something of a relief. Now, in opposition—and for this reason more sensitive to public opinion—the Labor Party, however, has come out for a brave policy of supporting and utilizing the inter-governmental organizations for intensified international cooperation. In the field of international aid it has sponsored a scheme of devoting one per cent of the national income, completely without political strings, for financial assistance to underdeveloped countries, and it has been advocating the setting up of a Middle East Development Pool of oil royalties.

These are thoughts which apparently come easier to a party that does not carry the responsibility for carrying on the government from day to day, or to those supporters of a government party who are at a distance from the levers of power. They confirm, however, my opinion that if the governments in the rich countries were prepared to launch out on a large-scale program of financial aid to underdeveloped countries, popular support would not be lacking.

Most other issues of international economic cooperation are usually less appealing, particularly those more directly concerning the ordinary financial and commercial policies, and, in general, those related to the national regulations, settlements and restrictions of the Welfare State. There, its intrinsic nationalism comes to the fore. But, nevertheless, I feel that a determined and sustained educational campaign would not be hopeless.

In the end, the strength of the case for more internationalism, making expansion and progress possible everywhere, is that it is rational and in everybody's interest. Economic nationalism is irrational and more so the farther it proceeds. To let it run its course is costly for everybody. Or, to state it in a positive way, whenever an international compromise agreement can be reached, all parties profit. Every official of an international organization can, from his own experience, quote examples in abundance where it was demonstrated beyond doubt that the overall common gain, flowing from a compromise agreement, if it could have been reached, would have been many times bigger than the sum total of the stakes for which the individual governments held out. Within a large area, fairly independent of the precise terms of the agreement, all parties would have been better off. When, as often, agreement was not reached, this was due to the fact that the negotiating officials—as instructed by their governments, which themselves, in turn, depend upon public opinion in their countries—acted in a narrow and irrationally nationalistic spirit.

The internationalist is right when he insists that there is nothing in the logic of things, or in human nature, to make it impossible to have much more international cooperation. The feasibility of constructive solutions of all conflicts is, indeed, the assumption for public discussion of economic issues within the individual Welfare State. This should be equally true internationally. In the international field, more generosity would be rational, and indeed highly profitable, for all parties.

The demonstrable irrationality, the great costliness to all nations of not having a much higher level of economic cooperation and bargaining, is the basis for what hope we have that we may gradually turn the trend, so that it becomes directed towards closer international integration, emerging from the cumulative effects of reasonable compromise agreements—if, meanwhile, the international crises that we shall pass through can be managed without too much resort to nationalistic policies, and if the people's reaction to the continual series of crises can be prevented from causing too many throwbacks into frustration and fear, mutual hostility, and primitive nationalism.

12

Economic Nationalism in the Underdeveloped Countries

A Wider Perspective

The discussion has been focused on the rich countries of the Western world, whose conditions and policies form the main topic of this book. The special circumstances and the peculiar problems of the underdeveloped countries has been left aside. This falls in line with the usual approach to these countries' international economic relations, in the professional literature as well as in the press and the parliaments. The main concern is their trade and exchange relations with each other.

To some extent, this limitation of interest is also rationally motivated. Though it is true that the peoples living in the rich Western countries are only a small minority of mankind, they have a dominating influence on the world economy. While in terms of population this group of nations only constitutes a little more than one-sixth of the non-Soviet world, their share of total production and income must be somewhere around three-fourths, and of total investment much more, perhaps nine-tenths. World finance, shipping, and commerce are almost entirely dominated by these countries—to an even larger extent, in fact, than the figures show, as a considerable part of what is accounted for as the underdeveloped countries' capital movements and trade consists in the recording of operations by economic enclaves which are closely controlled by business interests in the rich countries, in whose economies the enclaves are integrated more fully than in the economies of the countries where they are located. Even apart from the enclaves, for each one of the individual nations in this group of rich countries, economic dealings with the other countries in the same group are very much larger in volume than those with the whole of the rest of the world.

The way in which the rich countries regulate their relations is naturally bound to be of paramount importance to the underdeveloped countries also. But the rich countries have the power of their wealth. They are free to do what they please with their mutual commercial and financial relations, and also, to a large extent, with their relations with the underdeveloped countries. These other countries are left, on the whole, to accommodate themselves in one way or another to the policies of the rich countries. At least, that is how it looks when one considers only ordinary financial and commercial relations and assumes a *status quo* in the wider political framework for these relations.

There are general reasons why closer economic integration of the rich countries would be in the interest of the underdeveloped countries. It would assume, but at the same time promote, economic stability and expansion. And it could hardly take place without a weakening of economic nationalism in the rich countries. It would imply a strengthening of the machinery for international planning, cooperation and bargaining. Such a development should free the rich nations from some of the inhibitions to seek constructive, large-scale solutions to the problems of their relations with the underdeveloped countries as well. By itself, economic integration amongst the rich countries would imply the reversal, or modification, of many inconsiderate nationalistic policies which are damaging to the underdeveloped countries, too.

This assumes, of course, that, as new channels were opened up between the rich countries and between them and their remaining colonial dependencies, barriers would not be maintained against the poorer countries of the world. If the governments of the underdeveloped countries were not too shy in pressing their interests, this assumption should have some chance of being justified by events. In the general setting of economic stability and expansion in the rich countries, and the inevitable weakening of their economic nationalism, which, in its turn, should accelerate as a result of their closer economic integration, and with the improvement of the work in organizations for intergovernmental cooperation which it also would imply, the reasonable expectation would be a tendency towards an even wider international integration. In fact, it may be that, in the end, the underdeveloped countries would be the chief beneficiaries of a successful re-integration of the old partial world community of the rich countries.

In the final analysis, it is only in this wider perspective of the underdeveloped countries' interests that we can appreciate the importance of a possible approach towards improving the compatibility of the national policies in the Welfare States of the small, rich part of the world. Were the rich countries alone in the world, or could they safely ignore the majority of mankind in the underdeveloped countries—and also the cold war and the peoples and states in the Soviet orbit—the pressure for such an approach would be less needed and in any case less urgent. In the Western world the imperfection of international integration is palpably quite bearable, as people there are well off and becoming better off all the time. The conflicts between the policies of different countries would not be laden with such immense risks of international clashes of interest.

A more intensive treatment of the planning problems of underdeveloped countries lies outside the scope of this book. The following brief references to the international implications of their newly-won independence, and of their national policies under these new conditions, serve only the limited purpose of affording a perspective of the global setting in which the trend towards national economic planning in the rich Western countries now evolves and has to be judged, if the judgment is to be realistic. The main viewpoint is continually that trend and the problems raised by the national policies of the rich countries.

Rational Grounds for More Nationalistic Economic Policies in the Underdeveloped Countries

It is important for the preservation of amiable feelings between the two economic classes of nations in the non-Soviet world—and for the preparation of better relations between them—that the peoples of the Western countries understand and appreciate that the poor and underdeveloped countries, in planning for economic development, have objectively better reasons for nationalistic policies than the rich and progressive Western countries can have.

From the market point of view, being underdeveloped means precisely that, in such a country, industries do not initially have the strength to compete successfully. Otherwise it would not have remained underdeveloped. It means that, without protecting the markets there is not enough of effective demand to absorb its labor force. Labor, therefore, is employed in less productive ways, or is unemployed. Indeed, the purpose of the form of economic planning towards which all the underdeveloped countries are now steering, with the blessing of the entire world, is very much to work out a strategy for providing investment, enterprise, and demand for labor with such a shield against competition from abroad that the national economy will be stimulated to begin development.

Economic activity in the rich countries is on such a very much higher level that markets are not usually small compared with the individual enterprise unit, as they often are in underdeveloped countries. Normally they would not need protection to create markets for national production. If in a particular case the national market is too small for a new venture, this, in a rich country, is a reason for seeking international integration, not national protection. The external economies arising out of any new industrial enterprise, which are a gain for the national economy and a reason for protection—as, being a gain to the industry rather than the firm, they do not enter as profit into the calculations of the individual enterprise—are also much smaller in an already industrialized country. And the rich countries have no wasted labor, but usually operate a full or over-full employment economy on a high level of labor productivity. In the rich countries, finally, the rewards for labor in industry and agriculture do not show that wide gap which is characteristic of an underdeveloped country and which hampers industry, if it is not protected. More generally, the economies of the rich countries do not bear the mark of prolonged stagnation but are, instead, the accomplished, though provisional, result of a long period of previous development, which is rapidly continuing under its own momentum. They are not seriously and dangerously lopsided, as are the economies of the underdeveloped countries.

At this point in the argument, we should recall that an underdeveloped country will, as a rule, need to control its foreign trade, if only for exchange reasons. Pressing towards economic development is bound to strain its foreign exchange situation, as the needs for import of capital goods will increase and higher earnings will have to be offered to workers in order to get them to move as required by the plan. This holds good even should an underdeveloped country have the determination and the ability to put into effect a firmer anti-inflationary policy than most of the rich countries have succeeded in doing, in spite of their easier economic situation, their firmer political institutions, and their superior administration.

An underdeveloped country, bent upon speeding up its economic development, will therefore be compelled to take vigorous measures in regulating its foreign trade, if only for the purpose of restricting less necessary imports in order to save foreign exchange for the imports essential for development. For the same reasons, it will have to push exports, even when this implies subsidies. It would have to follow such a policy, even if it felt no specific reasons for protection. But the underdeveloped country has such reasons, which the rich countries do not have, or have only to a far smaller degree, for utilizing its acts of interference in international trade—primarily made necessary by their foreign exchange difficulties—to protect production.

A clear recognition of the dissimilar circumstances in rich and poor countries, and consequently of the rationality of a "double standard of morality" in judging their foreign economic policies, is a necessary condition for successful attempts to lay down the conditions for wider international cooperation. No integration of the poor countries in a wider international setting makes sense, or indeed can be of a desirable character at all, if it is not accompanied by national development for which the condition is protection.

This, of course, does not imply that the commercial and exchange policies which have been applied by the underdeveloped countries are very enlightened or conducive to good results. On the contrary, in most underdeveloped countries the policies are neither well planned nor efficiently carried into effect. It is this which explains the general tendency in much of the literature to advise the underdeveloped countries to abstain from tampering with their foreign exchange and from protectionism. But this advice cannot very well be heeded as it would amount to giving up hope of economic development. Their economic interests are too obvious. The advice they really need is how to manage their trade and exchange interference more rationally and effectively. The remedy is better planning and more efficient administration, but not abstention from planning and interference in their foreign relations.

The Political Need for Nationalism

There are thus good reasons why underdeveloped countries should give their foreign economic policies a pronounced nationalistic direction. Taking account of these reasons and following out the logical inferences from them by practical policy measures would not necessarily involve any emotions at all. My next point, however, concerns the emotions: a strong streak of nationalistic feelings is an essential element in the political life of underdeveloped countries. It is rational for the political leaders there to foster such emotions.

In those poor countries which, until recently, were colonies, or political dependencies under other appellations, the spread of nationalistic feelings was a pre-condition for waging the fight for liberation from foreign domination. This is now, of course, as true for the peoples who are still under colonial or semi-colonial bondage. The nationalistic emotions, needed to arouse the peoples against the foreign rulers, cannot simply be turned off when their independence is won.

Moreover, nationalistic emotions among the peoples in the underdeveloped countries have still an instrumental role to play. Many of these countries are struggling for national unity against all sorts of centrifugal forces. That first condition for the formation and execution of national policies—a consolidated nation-state with effective con-trol everywhere by a government, an administration, and a system of unchallenged law courts—does not exist.

Even when that first objective is in sight, efforts must be continually directed towards national integration. Eco-nomic development is not possible under other conditions. The new nations must be moulded into effective collective entities which can decide upon, and enforce, those far-reaching policy measures which will release their peoples from cultural and economic backwardness. The primary task facing the political leaders of the underdeveloped countries is to attempt to lift the masses out of apathy and frustration; to give them a vision of economic develop-ment; to inspire them to enterprise and cooperation; and to instil among them the discipline needed to strive effectively, to work diligently, and to make sacrifices to improve their conditions. This can only be done by inspiring them to unity of nationhood.

The initial situation in all these countries is one where most of the people are culturally isolated in local and provincial communities, and often split within these com-munities by social, religious, and ethnic chasms, and usually by extraordinarily wide economic inequalities.

This stale and rigid social structure, which is not conducive to cooperation for economic development, is the consequence of long stagnation. Now it is a major obstacle to progress.

It must be broken. The amorphous, dispersed, and divided masses of people in villages and city slums, illiterate, poverty-stricken, and living under the spell of traditional *mores,* must be transformed into national communities where they can experience that cohesion and common purpose which is needed as a basis for democratic planning. The sluices for social and economic mobility must be opened; opportunities must be equalized; the spread of expansionary momentum from one industry and locality to others must be made more effective; the level of general education must be raised; and a widely disseminated sense of participation in the ambitions of a common culture must be created. To start this a nationalistic impetus is needed.

Nationalism in the underdeveloped countries as it is now rising is thus not—as it mostly is in the developed countries—associated with reactionary political attitudes, but with the movement towards modernization and reform. It is increasingly a force for equalization of opportunities and for democratization of social and economic conditions. That this is so constitutes an immensely important political difference, the significance of which is only slowly dawning in the Western world. The instigation of nationalistic feelings among backward peoples is a precondition for social and economic progress. If progress is the goal, to foster these emotions becomes a rational means for accomplishing it.

In none of the rich Western countries today can nationalistic feelings have that justification. The nearest parallel I can think of was the need to arouse the feelings for their new nation of immigrants to the United States in the era of mass immigration. But today there is no country in the Western world which has good reasons for stimulating nationalism, even amongst a particular section of its nationals. National integration is already everywhere accomplished to a very high degree, and is proceeding further under its own momentum. In all the rich nations, the development of the Welfare State is now turning people's minds inwards to an irrational extent. Generally, nationalism in the Western countries is now an irrational force, driving them to more disruptive policies internationally than are in their own long-term interests.

Nationalism Beyond Reason

In other words, in underdeveloped countries, struggling for social unity and economic progress, a heavy dose of nationalism is a necessary stimulant; and it serves them well to take it. But it is a dangerous drug. The real situation in most of these countries, and the latent tendency in all of them, is that nationalism, when once awakened, has immense propensities to boundless growth. It may reach an intensity which has no rational justification. It can then easily be deflected from being only a positive urge to internal solidarity and cohesion and devotion to national unity and integration, becoming instead a negative resentment against foreigners in general and of foreigners belonging to certain nations in particular.

It is, indeed, only natural that nationalism tends to mount and then to turn sour: into displaced aggression. All the institutional and emotional mechanisms, which I analyzed in the two preceding chapters in regard to their effects in the rich Western countries, are, of course, effective in the underdeveloped countries as well. And there are many specific elements in their situation, in addition to those recorded as operating in the Western countries, which, in underdeveloped nations, must tend to leave an even freer field for such a growth and direction of nationalistic emotions, and, indeed, to spur them on.

All these countries are becoming aware of their extreme poverty and backwardness. This is one side of the Great Awakening which is gradually taking place. The other side of it is that hopes of progress have been awakened which in most of these countries are still largely frustrated. Their relations with the rich countries have been marred by dependence and inequality. They have been oppressed and discriminated against in their own lands. In order to win national independence, many of them have had to fight against a colonial power from the other side of the ocean. They have experienced the greed of the foreign rulers, and the exploitation of splits and tendencies to opportunism amongst their own nationals. This in any case will often be their historical view, even when it is not an entirely correct one.

They will cultivate the belief, not entirely against reason, that the misery and backwardness of their nations is not their own fault but that the international system should be blamed for it, at least in part, as it has permitted such a blatant inequality of opportunity between nations to arise. Such understandable grievances against the upper-class nations and, in particular, the old colonial powers, can serve as rationalizations of a nationalism, turning it into animosities directed outward, which become boundless and not controlled by a rational analysis of the events that have passed, and still less of the new nations' real interest in the present and the future. The much lower level of education in underdeveloped countries makes restraints by logic and objective knowledge on such feelings, when they go beyond reason, less effective.

Internally, many of these countries are steeped in ethnical, cultural, and religious fanaticism, and this contributes an emotional load that can easily be diverted into a swell of nationalism. In many countries, the liberation from foreign rule has implied a rise in that type of emotional strain between groups who feel themselves to be different. With all the forces for disintegration powerfully present, a rather intense nationalism may seem motivated, as may a partial redirection of existing aggressive attitudes against the outside world. Not to transgress the limit of rationality must then require a precarious balance. When, as in Burma and Indonesia, there are actually regions where movements are seeking separation from the new states, which have acquired their boundaries and are now trying to establish a national identification, it may seem opportune, and is always tempting, to turn the heat of nationalism not only against the rebelling groups but also against the outside world, if for no other reasons than to compromise the rebels.

Even when an underdeveloped country is fortunate enough to have little or no internal split in allegiance, it has to wage the fight against the result of poverty and stagnation, present in the form of wide social disparities between people in different localities and regions and different occupations and classes, and in the rigidities of various sorts in the social and economic structure of the nation. The political leaders will feel the practical need to foster nationalistic feelings in order to weld the nation into an effective political unit and to start the process of national integration, which is necessarily involved as a major element in any successful drive towards economic development. The limiting lines of national allegiance must, for this purpose, be drawn and emphasized. Particularly with the background of colonialism and dependency, this can hardly be accomplished without fostering at the same time feelings of distance from, and grievances against the rich and powerful countries, the relations to which have so radically changed, and are changing still.

The crucial fact is that, in the general situation of a poor, underdeveloped country, where people are beginning to sense the ambition of winning independence and progress, to foment negatively-tinged nationalistic feelings is the obvious way to seek a response from the masses of the people as well as from the educated elite. It therefore becomes the most effective means—sometimes the only means—of acquiring and keeping political power, which is the first duty of every politician, prior to any attempt he may make to accomplish something of value for his people or the world at large. The political life of an underdeveloped country is then easily turned into a competition between individuals and groups in appealing to, and thereby constantly stimulating, nationalistic sentiments among the people. The politicians, who hold power, usually have an additional motive to appeal to nationalism, and to slant it in the negative direction, in their need to divert the attention of the masses of the people when things are not going as well with economic development at home as they may have promised. Aggressive nationalism affords an outlet for frustration.

The politicians can thereby easily bring themselves to a position where they are virtually compelled to take policy steps against foreign interests which are not motivated by the country's true development interests, but only by the intense nationalistic feelings amongst the people, which must be satisfied if they are to retain power. In this process, and because of these very policies and the discussion around them, the nationalistic feelings, which compelled the politicians to take those steps, are spurred to new intensity.

All things considered, it would be reasonable to expect

that today the flames of nationalism in the poor countries, turned into outwardly directed aggressive resentments, would burn hotter than they do. Part of the explanation for why they do not is certainly that large sectors of their populations are still engulfed in the divisions, isolation, and apathy of poverty and backwardness. Another part of the explanation is the fact that the intellectual, moral, and political leadership in many of these countries—very definitely, for instance, in India—belongs to individuals who are steeped in our Western civilization. They themselves feel the immense danger in the situation.

Up to now, they have been in a position where they could afford to abstain from spurring nationalism too much, particularly in its negative manifestations. In both respects things might well change. Indeed, we should expect them to change, as the Great Awakening reaches farther down to the masses of people, and as the old leaders depart from the scene.

Interest Clashes

Until a few years ago, most of the poor countries were, either as colonies or otherwise, so politically and economically dependent on one or more rich countries that, on the whole, they were prevented from demonstrating any economic nationalism in foreign relations on their own behalf. Such "nationalistic" policy measures as were taken in their name were, for the most part, aimed at protecting the interests of the metropolitan powers that ruled them. National liberation means that a state's power can now be used in the interests of its own people.

Even without the urging of such consecutive waves of explosive, irrational, and aggressive nationalism as I have referred to, the economic policies of an underdeveloped country must, particularly in the earlier stages, take on a nationalistic tinge. Undoubtedly, an underdeveloped country has good reasons, which developed countries do not have, for nationalistic economic policies. These reasons are based on the fact that they have inherited an economy that is severely unbalanced and frustrated by inhibitions to economic development. It is then also unavoidable that these policies must, more particularly, be mainly directed against those amongst the rich countries with whom traditionally they have enjoyed the closest economic relations. For these relations represented colonial and semi-colonial dependence, which has to be ended as a fulfilment of their national liberation. And this, of course, goes against the interests of the countries which had enjoyed privileges that must now be taken away from them.

A great number of long-established international economic relations have to be broken in this process, or changed in a radical fashion. In many cases, an underdeveloped country will want to nationalize foreign-owned installations for exploitation of its natural resources. We will probably see many more instances of such forced changes of ownership and management control in the near future. In such transactions, entirely outside the rules of a market economy, the granting of compensation can hardly be entirely freed from arbitrariness—even if the will to fairness were strong amongst the nations which are now asserting themselves, which, of course, cannot always be expected to be the case. Those nations will often feel that the investments have been repaid, and more than repaid, during the long years of politically protected exploitation.

The reasons for a particular step in this process of economic liberation may be strong or weak, sound or unsound. The financial settlements offered may be objectively more or less fair to the old owners. In any case, they will often create resentment in the countries on which they are pressed. And in all the rich countries, this process, as it evolves, will almost by necessity lessen the confidence of Western entrepreneurs and governments in business investments and in business relations generally in under-developed countries. In turn, such reactions in the rich countries will tend to hamper economic development in the underdeveloped countries and to breed frustration. This is, however, apt to push nationalistic emotions among their peoples still further, and will also tend to turn those emotions in the negative and aggressive direction, which can again have effects on their economic policies. And so, by circular causation, within the countries as well as through their relations with each other, nationalistic emotions may cumulatively tend to rise in intensity. The political distance between the rich and the poor nations, and the differences in outlook on their own and on each other's needs and problems, may then grow wider and wider.

International Instability

We should not be surprised to find poor countries some-times pushing their nationalistic policy measures to a point where, at least immediately, the main purpose may seem to be to cause disadvantage to foreign economic interests rather than to enhance their own welfare. Their political independence affords them the opportunity of using that element of real power which consists in making themselves a nuisance of some sort or another, or threaten-ing to do so.

Indeed, as we have all to live on the surface of the same globe and are in many ways necessarily dependent on each other, the dissatisfied members of the world com-munity, as they rise to national power after a long era of political and economic dependence, apathy, local isolation,

and social chasms, have available blackmailing powers of
considerable efficiency. And they will gradually learn how
to use these for the promotion of what they conceive to
be their own interests and rights. In many cases the people
in an underdeveloped country feel—or will come to feel
under the influence of the emotional strains of irrational
nationalism—that they have been so maltreated by the
world as a whole, or by a particular rich country, that they
may consider themselves just and fair in using all political
means at their disposal. Emotional nationalism can provide a substitute for rational motivation for feeling self-
righteous.

The underdeveloped countries are now politically independent, or are rapidly reaching independence, but they
are all exceedingly weak militarily, financially, and com-
mercially, when acting within the established political,
legal, and institutional framework. This combination of
political independence and great weakness on the part of
so many countries with such large populations is a
dominant element of instability in the world today. In the
rich countries, commentators on the political processes
within the United Nations express their dismay and fear
of the increasing difficulty of hindering the poor underdeveloped countries from forming the majority—or even
the two-thirds majority prescribed for decisions on important issues. Of itself, this anxiety is over-ambitious on
the part of the United Nations, and founded upon an
altogether exaggerated idea about the significance of voting
in the world organization in its present stage of development. But it reflects, although in an undemocratically
biased way, a real cause of worry concerning the society of
nations as represented in the United Nations.

The real reason for anxiety, however, is, on the contrary,
that there are so many independent nations, with such
very large populations, living in a framework of established

relations that gives them little power. For the feeling of being powerless is a temptation to reckless nationalism, and to the indiscriminate use of all the means a poor country feels it has at its disposal to assert its interests. Responsibility for the common interests of a community, and preparedness to obey its rules, is a state of mind which follows the genuine creation of such a community, and full participation in deciding upon such rules. Otherwise it is the adaption of the weaker members to a stable situation of authoritarian concentration of power, as the world experienced it in colonial times. The stability of colonialism is gone, however, without yet having been replaced by any new system of international stability.

A Parallel

The world situation is in many ways similar to the fluid and uncertain internal conditions in the rich countries of the Western world during that early stage when political democracy was only "in the air" as an ideal and a hope, and when trade unionism was on the march, although workers had not yet established their right to seek collective bargaining on equal terms and their right to strike in order to back up their demands. The workers who then occasionally rose in the face of overwhelming power could not be expected always to be too considerate in their selection of weapons. The more they felt themselves to be an "out-group"—without a vote, without much support even from individuals in the upper classes, and without the feeling that they were able to induce fundamental changes by orthodox means in the national community which belonged to the "others"—the more they acted merely on the impulses of frustration and sometimes desperation, and the less considerately could they be expected to behave in their struggle.

It is also fully understandable how, at that juncture of the social development in the Western countries, many—at first almost all—in the upper classes expected anarchy and ruin if the poor masses were given the vote: it would put the national community at the mercy of the uneducated and irresponsible have-nots. The full democratization of our nations could not, however, be stopped. It gradually led to a new balance of power and to social stability and security, accompanied by unprecedented economic progress. The irresponsible became responsible as they were vested with legitimate power. Even the workers' strikes became regularized, and in the most advanced Welfare States the resort to this *ultima ratio* is becoming a rare occurrence, because it is hardly ever needed. I doubt if there will ever again be a major labor conflict in Sweden.

We are very far from even a semblance of the democratic Welfare World. If anything is certain, however, it is that a new situation of international stability cannot be brought about by reversing the liquidation of colonialism. The underdeveloped countries are, and will remain, politically independent, and those who are not will soon have their freedom. It is possible to speculate as to whether it would have been possible a generation ago to steer a wiser course, if people in the rich countries had then been fully aware of the prevailing wind. It might have been feasible to plan things so that the big change would have been less abrupt and less exacting for all parties. But such speculations do not help much today.

To use threats of military sanctions in order to force the poor nations to respect the interests of the rich countries and to obey rights and arrangements laid down before they had any say is, in the longer run, an equally hopeless policy, analogous to attempts in the Western countries to destroy the workers' unions by police raids. In the atomic

age, moreover, it is becoming a mode of behavior that is
rapidly losing all its appeal. People in the rich countries
are growing ever more conscious of the danger of unleash-
ing a third and final world war, and are wary about small
wars too. In addition, as France has recently experienced,
petty guerrillas, if they are supported by passive resistance
and cooperation among the masses of a people, can stand
out against great armies equipped with the most modern
lethal weapons.

Nor can the poor nations very well be bribed to be
permanently of "good behavior" by petty hand-outs. Even
when the aid is considerable, conditions of that type, at-
tached to economic aid, cannot be pressed very far or for
very long. This has been proved to the world, including
the poor nations themselves which are to be conditioned
in this way, by the many examples of countries which,
while demonstrably behaving "badly," must nevertheless
be given aid. Even rather moderate requests, yes, even
the unfounded suspicion of the presence of political
strings, can apparently undermine the popular backing
of the government in an underdeveloped country, where
national conscience is rising.

To maintain in power a friendly and, from the rich
countries' point of view, "well-behaved" authoritarian
government by military and other aid is equally obviously
a frail and risky policy. Again, to operate a system of
individual bribes given to politicians and groups in order
to keep a nation on the "right" track, or to do so indirectly by tolerating an actual situation of large-scale
corruption and graft through which such aid is dispersed
and appropriated by crafty politicians, officials, and other
persons in the ruling circles, is, in the longer run, an even
more surely self-defeating policy. This would, if it were
applied systematically on a scale large enough to make it
temporarily effective, not only undermine the government

in the underdeveloped country, but also arouse disgust and criticism at home when the facts have become more widely known.

Naturally, the rich countries can discriminate in their financial and commercial policy between "good" and "bad" countries, individually and collectively, but as experience shows, only up to a point. More generally, they can retaliate by taking more negative positions than they would otherwise be prepared to do against all poor countries as regards several matters. They can refuse to enter into effective international cooperation in order to strengthen the economic and bargaining position of the underdeveloped countries. But, by showing negative attitudes towards international cooperation, and by remaining luke-warm to their development problems, the rich nations are in danger of merely feeding frustration in the poor countries, thus causing the tide of aggressive nationalism amongst their peoples to rise even higher.

The plain fact is that the rich countries do not have strong sanctions to enforce their will, once the authoritarian international system of political and economic colonialism is gone. Only insofar as real advances could be made towards a democratic Welfare World—implying a growth of international solidarity on the part of both the rich and the poor nations and, on this basis, a rising trend towards international cooperation to equalize opportunities on a world scale—can it reasonably be expected that, in the long run, the political leaders of the poor countries will feel that they can afford to abstain from breaking rules and using their powers to blackmail the rich. On the other hand, it is equally apparent that nothing can more effectively consolidate the rich nations in negative attitudes towards the poor nations' desperate needs and ambitions than a few flagrant cases of blackmailing. Again, we are up against a vicious mechanism of circular causation with cumulative effects.

Marx in a World Setting

It is difficult to avoid here making a reference to Marx. Marx had little to say which directly concerns the present world problems. In fact, Marx and his more immediate followers did not envisage very clearly the post-colonial problems with which we are wrestling, and this should not surprise us, as he wrote so long ago and so many things have happened since. What, in the tradition of Marxian analysis, was later written—for instance, about the importance of colonies as an outlet for the alleged surplus of capitalist production—does not seem very relevant to present conditions.

Marx himself mainly focused his analysis on the internal development of capitalism in one country, and mostly drew on his study of England in the stage of early industrialization. He forecasted a widening gap between the few rich and the multitude of poor, and in the end a violent clash, when the growing and embittered proletariat grasped power by the use of force. Marx was proved wrong by what actually happened in the Western world. As the poor organized themselves, they acquired power without revolution and the rich yielded gradually. With power followed participation, loyalty, and responsibility. And the result was again social stability, won on new terms in the form of the national Welfare State of the rich Western countries.

On the international scene, a drama is now staged, which could end in a Marxian catastrophe on a vastly larger scale than Marx ever envisaged. There is a tremendous income gap between rich and poor nations, and the poor nations represent the masses. The gap is widening. The poor nations are becoming class-conscious. But it is possible that, once more, concessions by the privileged, as the under-privileged grow stronger, may create a new harmony.

Undoubtedly, the Welfare World is very much more difficult to bring about than the national Welfare State. The latter developed within already well established national communities, while the world community is almost nothing more than a brave hope. The more correct comparison would be, if we could imagine it, that the privileged classes in any one of the Western countries had been living in a fortified island by themselves, defended by a strong army and police, remote from the mainland where the poor lived and had spoken a different tongue and had had a different color and culture; and that the island and the mainland had not been held together by a single state, with a long history, firmly established on the basis of the rule of law, and habitually exerting power to legislate, administer, and tax. The national Welfare State would then undoubtedly have met immensely greater difficulties in coming into being. Marx's forecast might have come true.

More fundamentally, the deterministic and therefore essentially fatalistic theory of the economic causation of international conflicts—which is implicit in so many present-day speculations about international relations, by people right outside the Marxian tradition of materialistic historical determinism—assumes that the conflicts will be allowed to remain unresolved, i.e. that no great efforts will be made to achieve constructive international settlements. In its essence, *it is a theory of how war comes and not of how peace can be preserved,* in the same way as Marxism was a theory of the inevitable revolution and not of the building-up of the Welfare State by peaceful

gradual reforms. Here we see, indeed, the inherent ma-
terialism of this view, as it discounts the power of the
reasoning ability and the ideals of men in their practical
strivings. This defeatist assumption may be tempting in
view of the present state of faltering international solidarity. But, logically, there is no foundation whatsoever
for assuming a fatal outcome to be necessary. It can never
be repeated too often that history is man-made, and therefore not a blind destiny but our responsibility.

Harmony of economic interests certainly does not ensue
as a result of the unhampered operation of market forces,
as was assumed in the old philosophies of natural law and
utilitarianism, which still are the mode of thinking of
traditional economics, as also of the Marxian heresy, as
I pointed out in the Introduction. But harmony can be
"created." In the rich countries of the Western world the
class struggle has been tamed and harnessed in mighty
institutional structures on the basis of an ever fuller
realization of the ideal of free and equal opportunity for
all. There is nothing in the logic of things, or in human
nature, to prevent us from attaining a "created harmony"
in the international field as well—though admittedly it is
a much more difficult task. Its accomplishment is a fully
realistic alternative to letting the international class struggle mount towards the "inevitable" revolt as predicted,
implicitly or explicitly, in the deterministic conception of
the economic causation of international conflicts and wars.

The Cold War

This world conflict of interests—born out of the existing
immense inequality between the rich and the poor nations
in the world, and now gradually becoming released as the
latter nations win their political independence without,
however, sharing in wealth and power any more equally

than before—would exist, even if there were no Soviet Union and no bloc of countries politically lined up with that country. And even then it would be difficult to resolve. But the formidable strength of the communist bloc and the cold war naturally make the outlook more sinister.

To exploit in their own interests the dissatisfaction among the underprivileged countries outside their bloc must be a natural political strategy for the communist powers. This should not surprise anyone who accepts the cold war as a fact. If a similar opportunity were available, it would not, of course, be missed by those Western countries who are in alliance against them.

Apart from any strategic interest in the conduct of the cold war, however, the communists have also a solid basis for siding with the poor nations in those important elements of their ideology, which through Marx and others they have inherited from the main stream of liberal Western thought, stretching back, as I hinted at in the Introduction, to John Locke and still earlier exponents of Western egalitarian idealism. In relation to the underdeveloped countries they have the fewer inhibitions in making themselves the spokesmen for these old Western values, in that they themselves are emerging from the status of have-nots and are engaged in building up their own strength, without outside help and actually in violent opposition to the rich Western countries. Their heritage of such old Western values should not be forgotten, if we want to appreciate realistically the palpable fact that the communists exert a considerable moral influence in the underdeveloped countries—an influence which is not only, and not even mainly, a consequence of their rising economic, political and military strength.

They have stolen our fire. It is on this level of moral ideas that the major struggle for the souls of these countries, of which the Western nations now are becoming so intensely aware, is being waged and will ultimately be decided. And we deceive ourselves if we believe that we can create a vision that can successfully compete with political communism merely by offering liberty in some form, while shying away from the other main component ideal in the Western heritage: equality. The social revolution in international relations is rising, and will have to be accepted if all our hopes are not to succumb under its heavy tide. It is in this perspective that Justice William Douglas' advice becomes understandable: that the right place of the Western nations would be at the head of the world revolution.

13

Towards a New World Stability

Conditions

The international class conflict could be permitted to grow to catastrophic dimensions, and could then end in calamity for our civilization. Or it may be resolved by a series of gradual accommodations, approaching the establishment of a new situation of stability in the world.

No attempt will be made in this book to forecast the future development of this conflict of interests between the two classes of nations in the non-Soviet world: the powerful rich and the powerless poor, who are so many, and who are now becoming their own masters. The reason for this disclaimer of foresight is not only the conviction that prognostications on the really large and fateful issues are valueless—they have always proved grossly inaccurate in the past, and we have learned to expect the unexpected —but also the moral conviction that prognostications are in their very nature illogical and, indeed, preposterous. The future is continually our own choice. There is no blind destiny ruling history.

We are not entirely free, though. There are facts and given causal relations. In general terms, we know a good deal about what conditions would have to be established before a new world stability could be reached.

Negatively, we know that stability cannot be accomplished by a resort to force and pressure. A return to dependence of a colonial type is excluded. The poor nations will only be satisfied by an ever fuller independence.

We also know that mere political independence, without equal opportunity, economic progress, and the right to share wealth and power, will not be enough. In the end there is, in these world-wide problems, no practical alternative to international disintegration other than to initiate the development towards the democratic Welfare World, and this is the reason why these wider considerations have a bearing on the problems of economic planning in the rich countries of the Western world.

We thus know that, if a new stability is to exist in the world, the rich nations will have to be prepared to modify their economic policies in the interest of a broader sharing of opportunities. For this there is undoubtedly an ideological preparedness in the Western world. The Great Awakening is, of course, from their point of view, nothing else than the rapid spread over the globe of the old ideals of liberty, equality, and brotherhood, which are the cherished tenets of Western civilization, and which have increasingly become realized in the last two generations within the national Welfare States of the individual countries of the Western world. Very much will depend upon the rapidity and forcefulness of a positive response in the rich countries to a wider sharing of opportunities.

Finally, however, we know that the main driving force behind such a fortunate development, if it could be realized, must be the exertions of the poor nations themselves. No upper class has ever stepped down voluntarily to equality with the lower class, and as a simple consequence of a moral conviction given up their privileges and opened entrance to their monopolies. To be induced to do so, the rich and the privileged must sense that demands are raised and forcefully pressed, and that power becomes assembled behind them. At that stage, moral ideals in the upper class are given their chance to play a supporting role.

For this reason, the stronger the poor nations become, the more the attainment of a new situation of world stability is made possible. The stronger they become, the more will they be in a position to abstain from the policy measures which build up resentment against them. As always, loyalty to the community will grow as they acquire strength, assurance and a sense of belonging. This is a reason why success in their efforts towards national planning for development is such a paramount world interest.

Their Mutual Isolation

To gain strength, the poor nations also desperately need to join forces, to pool their resources, and to coordinate their policies in a planned fashion. Their similar histories and present situations should afford a basis for this. Most of them are colored and have bitter memories of segregation and discrimination practiced against them by people of European stock. In the protests which can unite them, the word "racialism" will regularly be found together with "colonialism." Above all they are poor, mostly illiterate and backward, and they are being made conscious of it. The important thing is that they are not satisfied with liberty, but demand equality of opportunity and common brotherhood as well. They describe themselves as "underdeveloped," with the clear implication that they should have economic development and a fuller share of the good things in life.

One of the most important functions of the international organizations has been to assemble representatives of the poor countries in forums where they can experience their solidarity of interests and give voice to their shared grievances. On the political plane they are already finding common ground even in specific issues, for instance in their joint support for the liberation movements in the still remaining colonial dependencies. But in economic matters they have hardly established any joint policy, other than to demand more aid and to harp in general terms on the necessity of broad reforms in the structure of international capital movements, shipping, and trade. Without more intensive economic relations among themselves, in particular more trade and division of labor within the several regions, the attempts towards forming a common front in general economic issues are bound to be largely empty demonstrations.

Their weak mutual economic ties, the lack of practical cooperation even in the regions and, indeed, the underdeveloped state of their ordinary mutual trade relations stand in dramatic contrast to the similarity of their interests and their aspirations. In the main this isolation is a result of long ages of economic stagnation, and more particularly of colonialism and other forms of foreign domination. Traditionally, the underdeveloped countries have confined their economic relations—and, indeed, their political and cultural relations too—almost exclusively to one or a few of the rich countries which used to dominate them and which had an interest in monopolizing such relations. The whole transport system had, in fact, been adapted to the old colonial and quasi-colonial matrix of forced bi-lateralism, dominated by the interests in the rich countries. Roads and railroads were built within each one of the underdeveloped countries and shipping facilities were provided for the commercial relations across the oceans. But even today—except for the new airlines which are expensive—regular transport facilities between neighboring countries, necessary for intensified commercial relations, are not available in most regions, or are inefficient and unduly expensive.

The colonial powers had also permitted, and often pro-
voked by their policies, developments which, now the foreign domination has relaxed or disappeared, have left awkward unsolved problems, tensions and resentments between neighboring nations. Consider, for instance, the
artificial boundaries created in West Asia, when the Otto-
man Empire was cut up and divided between Britain and
France after World War I; the Indian moneylenders and
landlords in Burma; the imported Tamil laborers on the
plantations in Ceylon; and, of course, the hostility between
India and Pakistan in the wake of partition. After World
War II, the cold war has, in some regions, caused estrange-
ment amongst neighboring countries.

The situation of mutual isolation which the governments of underdeveloped countries are inheriting is not
one that can easily and rapidly be changed. To build new
commercial links is under all conditions a laborious task,
and particularly so in the underdeveloped regions. Greatly
improved facilities for transport between neighboring
countries would also require heavy investments, which
would have to compete for scarce capital resources with
all other development needs.

To this must be added the fact that the old established
commercial relations cannot be lightheartedly severed. It
is, indeed, strongly in the interest of the underdeveloped
countries not to break them. They certainly need to preserve their trading relations with the rich countries that
previously dominated them politically and economically.
They need to widen these relations to all other rich countries, by freeing themselves from the relative monopolies
held by the business interests in the metropolitan countries. It is mainly from the rich countries in the Western
world—together with the Soviet Union and the Eastern
European countries—that they can buy capital equipment
for economic development. But they also need to comple-

ment these relations by breaking up the artificial barriers amongst themselves in the regions and in the whole world. They need to trade with each other and to cooperate in their common interest. This would also strengthen their bargaining power in dealing with the rich countries.

A Problem of Planning

Towards this goal of multilateralizing their trade, and in particular of building up trade relations amongst themselves, the underdeveloped countries have not made any real progress. The national communities which came into being as political and economic colonialism disintegrated, had, as their first task, to consolidate the new nation-states. In many of these countries there is still much to be accomplished in order to reach this first goal of effectively governed national communities. The idea of planning for development, as it spread to these countries, was spelled out in terms of narrow national planning. The exchange difficulties had the same impact of turning economic policies in the direction of autarkic self-sufficiency.

As in the Welfare State of the rich countries, and, for various reasons, even more than there, a tendency towards nationalism is implied in all planning. Political power within national boundaries is its basis, and it becomes directed towards putting the national resources to more effective use for national development. Foreign relations, including relations with neighboring countries, are the independent and uncertain variables in planning. As in the rich countries, insofar as planning for development became a serious matter in an underdeveloped country and a real concern felt by its people, it tended to turn their interests inwards.

Keeping all these things in mind, it should not be surprising that the efforts at economic planning in underdeveloped countries have been narrowly nationalistic and, in particular, have nowhere involved any serious attempts at overcoming the abnormal and unnatural commercial isolation from other underdeveloped countries, even in the immediate vicinity. On balance, it may even be a fact that this isolation, inherited from colonial times, has in many cases become intensified. Nothing else could perhaps have been expected under the circumstances. It would not have been rational, practical, or even possible.

Nevertheless, I am convinced that closer commercial relations amongst underdeveloped countries in general, and those in some region in particular, will in the future come to stand out as an eminently practical and important problem. I am then assuming that the underdeveloped countries in general will be reasonably successful in engendering substantial economic development. This is a very important assumption for my argument and it might not be valid, but in that case world development as a whole is bound to take a more sinister turn. I will now briefly enumerate the reasons why, under the assumption made, I expect the problem of trade and regional economic cooperation among underdeveloped countries to rise in importance.

The Future

That the levels of transport facilities and trade among underdeveloped countries are abnormally low implies that to raise these levels would be to their mutual advantage. The widespread idea, which is a spiritual heritage from the colonial era, that these countries are not complementary in their economic structures is exaggerated. Even with their present economic structures unchanged, I believe that more trade in many products would be advantageous. In many parts of the world it would be practical, for instance, to work out regional instead of national plans for agriculture and food. Some are deficit countries, but some are surplus countries, and the latter might be willing and able to increase their production and exports of food, if they were assured a regular and stable market.

The advantage of closer economic cooperation will stand out as much greater, however, if the underdeveloped countries advance in their economic development. All these countries are bent on industrialization. To build up a complete structure of industry in each country is not easily practicable and in any case not very economical. And it becomes less easy and less economical every day, as modern technology on the whole gives increasing advantages to large industrial establishments. These countries can all proceed faster in their industrial development if they can reach, through trade, a division of labor and a certain specialization amongst themselves. This holds with particular force for the smaller countries, but it is also true for the larger ones. Even India, with a population of over 400 millions, is still—and will remain for many five-year plans ahead—a rather small country economically, with an export market not very much bigger than that of one of the smaller countries in northwestern Europe, none of which would think of the possibility of expanding further on the basis of that type of national industrial self-sufficiency which is too often posited as the ideal for national planning in underdeveloped countries.

As was shown, the underdeveloped countries have strong reasons for protecting their infant industries which the rich countries do not have. As their home markets are small and their resources of capital for investment scarce, as is also their supply of enterprise and managerial and technical skills, it would be in their common interest if they could arrange their industrial protection regionally and not simply nationally. These countries have much

more valid economic reasons for a "common market" than
the rich countries of Western Europe, which, like the
United States, could, and in my opinion should, have so
managed their affairs that they would now be in a position
to open their boundaries to the whole world for the flow
of capital and commodities, instead of closing up amongst
themselves in blocs. Such a "common market" would imply joint planning.

Another reason why in fifteen or twenty years' time the
idea of regional instead of simply national planning and
protection will enter the practical politics of underdeveloped countries lies in the increasing difficulties many of
these countries may meet in raising their exports to correspond to their future import needs. Those of the underdeveloped countries which have large deposits of oil or minerals may have the right to look with confidence on their
future export prospects, but hardly the others. On substantially higher levels of production, income and consumption, they will need bigger imports, however much they
succeed in substituting home produce for imported goods.
They will then have to enter the world market as exporters
of manufactured industrial goods. If this happens on a large
scale—which corresponds to the assumption that underdeveloped countries will generally have a reasonable measure
of success in their strivings towards development—it will
probably meet resistance in the rich countries. Wages in
the poor countries will continue to be relatively low, and
their exports will be looked upon as "dumping."

It would naturally be in the interest of international
economic integration if the rich countries became positively
interested in providing the underdeveloped countries with
export outlets. They would then be systematically scrap-
ping their protection for such industrial goods as the
underdeveloped countries become prepared to export. The
argument would have a particular force in regard to labor-

intensive industries, because the rich countries should have better uses for their scarce labor. A determined move in this direction is a part of the adjustment of commercial policy in the Western countries, which these countries should now be prepared to undertake if they rightly appreciate the world situation and their own long-term interests. Theoretically, it would be a fully logical line of action. Practically, the temporary disturbances would not at Western levels of production and income be too difficult to meet, especially compared with, for instance, the conversions every country is prepared to undergo, and indeed to plan, in the case of a war or a major recession.

It is possible—perhaps likely—that in the end such a movement towards a change in industrial structure in the rich countries will, as a market adjustment, happen unintentionally, in the hard way and with a time lag. Perhaps we have seen the beginning of such an adjustment in the textile industry, but we there also see the resistance it provokes. With the nationalistic direction of interests in the Welfare State, and particularly with the decentralization of influence to bargaining organizations on many levels, there will normally be strong attempts to withstand such an adjustment. I recall that the Welfare State has habitually won internal stability and flexibility at the price of a lower degree of international adjustability. Meanwhile the underdeveloped countries, if they really emerged as producers and exporters of industrial products on a large scale, would find themselves fiercely fighting for markets against powerful vested interests for protection in all the rich countries, supported by labor as well as business. I will return later to the problem of the commercial policies of the Western countries.

There is a possibility that the countries in the Soviet world, which have centrally controlled economic systems and can direct their trade more or less at will, would, in this situation, be prepared to preserve certain outlets for industrial exports from the underdeveloped countries. Of such a preparedness we have, as yet, no indications whatever. For underdeveloped countries that wanted to avoid becoming too dependent on the trade monopolies of the Soviet countries, the exploitation of such an outlet—if it were made available—could hardly do more than mitigate their general export difficulties somewhat.

In this situation the very fact of the underdeveloped countries' success in economic development and industrialization, if it should materialize, would greatly increase their mutual usefulness as export markets. This implies and assumes, as all trade does, division of labor and industrial specialization. In its turn, it would then make further progress in these countries' economic development easier and more possible.

The Interest of the Rich Countries

There is thus an intimate link between two lines of policy: planning for economic development within the individual underdeveloped countries and establishing closer commercial relations amongst themselves. Each is a favorable condition for the other. The present unnatural isolation among underdeveloped countries is, as I pointed out, a result of stagnation and colonialism and an indication of their underdeveloped status. Both policies, if they were successful, would strengthen the underdeveloped countries and give them, in their dealings with both the rich countries of the Western world and the Soviet countries, a bargaining power corresponding somewhat more closely to the size of their populations.

If my thesis, that a substantial increase in the bargaining power of the poor countries is necessary to attaining a new situation of world stability, is acceded to, the two policy lines would very much be in the interest of the rich countries, which as *beati possidenti* have the major stake in the establishment of that stability. So far as economic development is concerned, this conclusion is accepted in general terms in the Western world, and the only doubt concerns whether this interest is large enough to warrant any substantial sacrifices of short-term commercial and other interests. As regards the intensification of the underdeveloped countries' mutual commercial relations, and in particular their joining together behind common protective walls to exploit, in a planned way, the possibilities of industrial specialization, this is a policy line which will, in most Western countries, meet the resistance of the unreflecting.

I have referred to the fact that the underdeveloped countries themselves have as yet been mostly narrowly nationalistic in their economic planning, and in their economic policies generally. But it has been very evident that, whenever some of them, in the international organizations and more particularly in the regional commissions, have taken steps towards bringing up a question of closer regional cooperation in some concrete matter of commerce, shipping or development, the Western countries have habitually taken an adverse view and retreated only under very strong pressure. In regard to technical assistance, most of the underdeveloped countries have again been eager to preserve the most narrow national basis for the planning and administration of this activity. But it has been noticeable that in general the Western countries have felt the same interest quite strongly, and particularly wanted to avoid regional planning of such aid, as have, incidentally, the Soviet countries.

The short-term interests of the rich countries in discouraging the ganging up of the poor countries in a region or the world for concerted action is, of course, obvious. In the longer range, however, our hope of world stability is dependent upon the underdeveloped countries' using all the means at their disposal to increase their strength and power.

Not Only Aid

Leaving aside this question of mutual cooperation amongst the underdeveloped countries themselves, there is now a growing consensus of opinion in the rich countries that they should be prepared to initiate economic policies in order to enable underdeveloped countries to develop economically, and to do so rapidly.

Usually the discussions about these policies have been focused almost exclusively on capital aid and technical assistance given free. This is particularly the case in the country which provides the biggest share of assistance, the United States. But capital grants and technical assistance given free of charge can never be anything but a rather minor part of the total complex of economic policies which the United States and all the other rich countries should adopt, if they really wish to help the poor countries in their struggle for economic development. This would remain true even were such aid expanded to the much larger volume that is called for on rational grounds, and even were that aid organized in a rationally justifiable, multilateral, and truly international framework.

This complex of economic policies, which the rich countries should adopt in addition to providing aid, comprises a redirection of their whole manner of doing business—or of not doing business—with each other and, in particular, with the underdeveloped countries. These countries are at the rich countries' mercy because they are poor. For their welfare and their success in engendering economic development, they depend heavily on the rich countries' policies in regard to trade and the movement over their boundaries of people, capital, enterprise, and techniques.

If the rich nations made a determined move to shape their general economic policies more in the interests of the underdeveloped ones, this would be of a vastly greater consequence to the economic development of those countries than any aid which they could ever hope to get. If instead the rich countries persist in carrying on their ordinary business with the underdeveloped world on the principle of narrow economic nationalism and adjustments to the wishes of short-sighted vested interests at home, even generous aid becomes nothing more than a palliative.

One explanation of this emphasis on aid is undoubtedly charitable feelings. There is in America a basic sentiment of generosity toward those who are less fortunate—a sympathy for, and solidarity with, the underdog. This has its roots in America's singular material and spiritual history. I believe that important elements of American behavior in external and internal relations would be misunderstood if this trait were not recognized. The concern for the down-and-out is, unfortunately, not so strong among the other nations in that one-sixth of the non-Soviet world which is well off and economically progressive. A measure of the practical consequence of this is the fact that, directly and indirectly, the United States is probably paying close to ninety per cent of the capital grant aid and technical assistance in various forms which are actually given at present to the poorer majority of mankind. But this same generous America often turns out to be niggardly and selfish in its ordinary commercial and financial policies and practices, as in various degrees do all the other rich countries.

These attitudes and behavior patterns are reflected in the public discussion in America of the country's international responsibilities. Good and public-minded Americans in the great liberal tradition, whether they happen to vote the Republican or Democratic ticket, are continuously pleading for more generous American aid to the underdeveloped countries, and for aid without political strings. These Americans persistently put forward the perfectly valid argument that the basic justification for aid is simply that the peoples of underdeveloped countries become healthier, happier, and economically more progressive, and that they thus will have a better chance to become freer and stronger as independent nations. Yet, in contrast to the energy and courage displayed in holding up to the nation its duty to give more aid to underdeveloped countries, and to give it more wisely, stands the shy half-heartedness—even among the nation's intellectual leaders —in facing the need to break down the heavy barriers of nationalistic policy measures which dominate America's foreign economic relations. The situation is not very different in the other rich countries, except that they are less willing to give aid, though they might now be becoming more willing.

To understand this disparity of attitudes, we have again to focus our attention on the fact that the Western countries are all democratic Welfare States. They are rich, and even considerably larger amounts of aid would not substantially lower their own living levels. The idea of assuring the needy an allowance in cash has an immediate appeal, and it fits into the type of thinking which is basic to their own national social security schemes. But even more important is the fact that aid in cash does not upset the complex system of public policies, which form the substance of the national Welfare State, and does not adversely affect any special interest group. Basically, the greater willingness to give cash aid than to change commercial and other policies is another international implication of the Welfare State in the rich countries.

Trade

What would be requested of the rich countries in the field of trade would first be to recognize the rationality of the "double-standard morality" in commercial policies, which I referred to in the last chapter.

In a better integrated world the rich countries should, in the common interest, largely abstain from putting up barriers to foreign trade and, in particular, should open their markets to the underdeveloped countries. I have already given the reasons why, as industrial development gets under way in underdeveloped countries, outlets should be given them for industrial exports as well. At the same time, it should be admitted that the underdeveloped countries cannot themselves follow this principle without compromising, perhaps seriously, their ambitions for planning economic development. The rich countries, and in particular the United States, have often acted upon the opposite "double-standard morality," insisting upon following a protectionist policy on their own behalf, while preaching the virtues of free trade to the underdeveloped world.

Their commercial policies are to an astonishing extent dominated not only by such special group interests as can be understood to have a considerable weight—like, for instance, those of the textile industry and its workers in Great Britain and elsewhere, to which I have referred—but also by interests which are clearly petty. That the oil industry can move the State Department in Washington around is remarkable, but not surprising. But that, in an underdeveloped country in South East Asia, the American organization for technical assistance does not dare to help the country develop its fishing industry, because it would upset a few American exporters of canned fish, is perhaps shocking to the uninitiated.

Moreover, in all the commercial dealings with under-developed countries, business interests in the rich countries, supported by their governments, are now habitually using their superior bargaining power to press the poor countries to import commodities which they could produce themselves by putting their un-utilized manpower and other resources to work, or which they rightly consider that they cannot afford to import, at least not in the quantities and with the freedom that are urged upon them. Under-developed countries are everywhere pressed to import what they could do without as condition for leaving them a market for their exports for which the demand is often none too brisk. Their need for credits when they are out to buy industrial equipment is often utilized to impose upon them prices and other conditions that are unfair and burdensome. A greater consideration for underdeveloped countries in all such matters would help to bring about a very substantial improvement in their economic situation.

Special Trade Problems

Within the general framework of these principles, a number of specific policy goals were proclaimed in the years during the war and immediately afterwards, when economic thinking and planning for concerted international action were so much more constructive, courageous, and free than at present. Several of these policy goals were singled out and given prominent places on the agenda of the international economic organizations which were then created.

For various reasons, the world market prices of primary products, which at present constitute the bulk of the exports of underdeveloped countries, show violent fluctuations from month to month and from year to year. The consequent changes in their export incomes quite regularly amount to sums many times bigger than all foreign aid put together. Measures to stabilize these prices would, therefore, be powerful means to improve the economic conditions in underdeveloped countries. On balance, such measures would also be in the interest of the richer countries—both for internal reasons and because of their commercial interests in keeping the import demands of the underdeveloped countries at a steady and high level. They represent, therefore, an "aid" which need not cost the rich countries anything. In spite of this, there has been little progress toward concerted international action in the field of commodity price stabilization.

There are several reasons for this discouraging outcome. The purely technical and financial difficulties implied in international price stabilization, though real enough, have not been the main inhibition. More important has been the lack of zeal and ability on the part of the underdeveloped countries to push their interest themselves—a weak and inefficient government and administrational apparatus is unfortunately often a main characteristic of an underdeveloped country. The most important hindrance has, however, been the growing unwillingness on the part of the rich countries to take serious measures in this field.

One factor determining their attitude has been the fear that they might be inveigled into supporting schemes with fixed prices permanently above true "equilibrium" levels. But, in addition, there are in all of the rich countries special interests in preserving the speculative character of commodity markets. Those special interest groups may be small in themselves, but, with the overwhelming majority of people indifferent, they generally swing the decisions. For the international and common interests have no organized pressure groups in the protective Welfare State of the rich countries, while there are always nationalistic emotions which can be played upon by special interests bent upon preventing positive action in the larger interest.

No illustration of the economic nationalism and the lack of internationalism can be more striking than the following: It is in the rich countries accepted as almost a self-evident duty to take effective measures to give the small minority of farmers higher prices than would be received in the market while, at the same time, the same nations have cold-heartedly refused to consider attempts even to stabilize commodity prices in the international markets—without raising them—in the interest of the great masses of people in the underdeveloped countries. And these attitudes are taken even though an international stabilization of prices of primary products would, on balance, have been to the advantage of the rich countries as well.

A second policy goal was international control of industrial and shipping cartels. This would be of considerable importance to the underdeveloped countries and would, at the same time, not require any real sacrifices on the part of the rich countries, but, on balance, would be rather to their advantage. Nevertheless, here, too, proposals for action are being quietly buried, and for very much the same reasons. Measures against restrictive business practices are taken in most of the richer countries individually, but in the international markets cartels have so far been given free play. At least in Western Europe, it would be regarded as strange and almost subversive to suggest that the foreigner should be protected from having to pay whatever he can be forced to pay.

Credits

Economic development in an underdeveloped country necessarily implies the formation of capital on a relatively large scale. By far the larger part of this new capital must be produced by savings in the country itself. The success and speed of the country's development policy will, however, depend on the possibility of acquiring a part, even if only a small part, of its capital needs from abroad, to help pay for the higher imports of capital goods and other consequences of the development policy on the balance of payments. Similarly, the underdeveloped countries will have to pay for most of the industrial techniques and know-how they need. Only a minor portion can be acquired gratis under national and international technical assistance schemes. This is particularly true in the industrial field.

The international capital market broke down in September 1931, and has as yet not been re-established in anything like its former scope and shape. But even before the collapse of the capital market, indeed even in the days before World War I, comparatively little capital went to those parts of the world which we now characterize as the underdeveloped countries, and which were then called the backward regions. And this, of course, is related, both as cause and effect, to the fact that, then as now, there was not much economic development in those areas. Nevertheless, colonial governments, and private corporations operating under their protection, as well as governments and corporations in those other backward countries which enjoyed a more or less precarious political independence, could then sell securities on stock exchanges in the Western countries in order to finance the building of railroads, ports, electric power stations, and other public utilities. It is the breakdown of the international private long-term capital market which has forced the governments in the richer countries into the international finance business.

Governments, however, are rather badly equipped to function as international financiers, and their activity in this field is not exactly an encouraging experience. I would not say that politics was ever excluded from international financing, even in those days when it was conducted through depersonalizing market processes. But politics enters through the front door when the giving of a loan becomes a decision to be taken directly by an agency of a government, responsible to a representative assembly of the people. And our analysis in Chapter 11 of the formation of public opinion in the field of foreign relations in the nationalistic and protective Welfare States of the rich countries makes it understandable that the species of politics which is involved in national financing cannot be expected to be very enlightened. Against this background it is a rather remarkable fact that the International Bank for Reconstruction and Development, which with only slight exaggeration has been called an American government agency, has done such a competent job, and also that the other government agencies for foreign credits, again mainly agencies of the American government, have not handled their task worse than they have. Equally remarkable is it that they have succeeded in squeezing out such relatively large sums for underdeveloped countries. But taken as a whole, the aggregate financing activity of the governments and the International Bank does not amount to more than a minor part of what could have been expected from the private capital market, had it continued to exist and had it played a role for industrializing those countries similar to that which it once played in the now developed countries.

There has been direct investment, but most of it has gone into the tightly controlled enclaves where oil and minerals are extracted. In spite of all exhortations, private industry in the rich countries has shown little interest in going out to build up an industrial base in the underdeveloped countries. Government policies in those countries have sometimes been used to reduce the chances of substantial profits from such investments. In many countries there is a prejudice against foreign ownership of industrial establishments, particularly in the basic industries. In all of them there is a widespread feeling that direct investment is too costly a way of inducing capital inflow. And the need they feel most is for capital at fixed interest, so as to permit all sorts of large-scale social and overall investment. For such undertakings their governments or other public authorities have to take the entrepreneurial responsibility, since they are not such as to induce direct investment either at home or abroad—at least not on conditions which are acceptable to the governments in the underdeveloped countries.

And so the underdeveloped countries do not get more than very little of the capital they need for economic development. Among the general causes for this situation, the political tension in the world and the fear of war loom very large. By its direct and indirect effects, this political factor probably accounts for most of the difficulties of re-establishing an international market in which buyers could be found for bonds and shares issued by governments and business enterprises in the underdeveloped countries. In the economically advanced countries—natural sources of capital supply—conditions of a fairly steady boom and full employment have reigned since the war, making investment opportunities at home appealingly profitable and secure.

The difficulties in the way of again building up an international capital market are immense. Nevertheless, I feel that we must try to do it, if we do not want to see the collapse of all our hopes of a developing progressive welfare democracy in the world. Government lending and the activity—on an expanding scale—of the International Bank will certainly be important in any further restoration of the international capital market. These organs should play a special role in introducing the counter-cyclical force in the capital market which was so widely requested in the early post-war discussions. But the task is too vast for these organizations. Many more, and different, channels are needed.

Routes and guarantees must be found for getting private capital to move more freely again across natural boundaries. We should, if possible, try to make it natural again for ordinary people with funds to keep some of them in securities issued by the underdeveloped countries. Even if the most important capital need of these countries is long-term lending to their governments, other public authorities and business corporations, there is also, I feel, scope for increased direct or entrepreneurial private investments. Suggestions have been made for a new method of cooperation in the economic development of underdeveloped countries, in which business firms in the rich countries would provide part of the capital, to be invested for a limited time only, and under government guarantees for the transference of both profit and amortization. The foreign firms should also, for the initial period covered by this credit arrangement, provide management and be responsible for the introduction of techniques and managerial know-how.

Whatever methods are selected to enable capital to move not only between the rich countries but also from the rich countries to the poor ones—instead of in the opposite direction, as would be the prevailing tendency in many countries, were it not checked by controls—they will require changes in the underdeveloped countries' attitudes toward foreign capital. In my opinion, many underdeveloped countries hold their interest rates too low to attract capital, and too low from the point of view of the real scarcity of capital related to their plans for development.

But positive inducements in the rich countries will also be needed. Inside the individual national Welfare States in the Western world, the need for inducements, in the form of subsidies or guarantees of various types, to steer capital towards the underdeveloped regions within their own countries has been recognized and accepted for many decades. Without such intentionally applied interferences in the play of market forces, the banking system and several other institutional segments of the capital market would have operated—even more than was actually the case—as an apparatus for siphoning off to the richer regions the savings in the poorer ones. And, undoubtedly, a main conclusion of a serious study of how to build up again the international capital market will be the desirability and, indeed, the necessity of providing similar inducements for private capital to move from the rich to the poor countries. The costs to the rich countries of such inducements would be less than those of financing grants-in-aid.

It is, perhaps, natural to feel that, at present, the international tension, the acute risk of wars and revolutions in various parts of the world, and the nationalistic and discriminatory policies in underdeveloped countries exclude any serious and large-scale efforts on the part of the rich countries to provide the poor countries with more capital for economic development. But certainly to let these countries starve for capital seems, at the same time, the surest way of increasing the risk of wars and revolutions and of spurring their nationalism.

No Easy Solution

I have carried to its logical conclusions my discussion of the changes in ordinary trade and financial policies that are needed for the rapid progress of international integration, encompassing the underdeveloped countries as well. It is, of course, by no means practically possible, as yet, to render these conclusions politically acceptable. The earlier analysis of the institutional and psychological mechanism operating in the democratic Welfare State of the Western countries makes this understandable.

The Welfare State is narrowly and irrationally nationalistic. The very fact that its public policies have such deep and widespread roots in a decentralized structure of interest organizations makes it particularly difficult to reorientate all these policies in a unified manner. This is particularly the case when, as in the present case, the motives for such reorientation do not emanate from immediately felt urges within the national communities but from the recognition, after intellectual analysis of wider world relations, of a common and general interest. I would be less than candid if I pretended to have an easy solution to this problem of practical politics.

In passing, we should note that the totalitarian and monolithic Soviet state has a definite advantage in this respect. With a complete state monopoly over foreign trade and financial relations, and with a central direction of the entire economy, such a state can take wider matters into consideration, and can easily readjust its commercial policies in the way it wants. It can, with regard to a particular underdeveloped country or to them all, take a coordinated view of imports and exports, which the government of a Western Welfare democracy can do only with great difficulties, because the importers and exporters are usually diverse groups acting without consideration for wider interest, not only in the markets themselves, but also through their organizations when they influence the commercial policies of the state. Again, the Soviet state can easily make room within its centrally planned economy for sudden and substantial additions to imports from an underdeveloped country, and it can, in the same way, arrange payment for exports and other commercial conditions to fit into the wider view of their relations to that country.

This is commonly considered to be a particularly sinister aspect of Soviet foreign grant aid; in the cold war, this may well be true, both generally and in particular cases. But, more fundamentally, it represents the type of coordinated adjustment of foreign economic policies which is in any case needed to serve entirely rational economic interests. The carrying out of the conclusions reached above in regard to the Western countries' commercial and financial policies would, indeed, necessitate such a coordinated adjustment.

The Western countries are, of course, not prepared to submit themselves for this purpose to a totalitarian and monolithic rule. Nor are they prepared to nationalize their foreign trade. Their practical problem, if they want to rationalize and coordinate their policies in this field, is how to accomplish this within the structure of the protective and nationalistic Welfare State, which is apt to give its widely dispersed special interests such formidable power in blocking policies which would be rational in the common interest. As the Western countries do not want to give up either democracy itself or its deeper foundation in the spread of participation, initiative and influence through the vast infra-structure of interest organizations, there is no other solution than the long and arduous one of educating the people to see and clearly understand their true interests, even the general ones which are common to them all, and to the world.

Aid

When I stress the primary importance of a readjustment of the Western countries' ordinary economic policies, and in general of their way of doing business with the underdeveloped countries, this does not imply, of course, that aid would be unnecessary or unimportant. Indeed, the permanent establishment of a considerably higher level of aid to underdeveloped countries, in cash and technical assistance, is urgently called for. It would produce, among other things, a more solid basis for a wholesome development of those ordinary economic relations which are so

much more important. A sudden large income equalization
on a world scale is both an impossible and, I am inclined
to believe, an unimportant objective. But certainly, as part
of a much wider complex of economic policies, there is a
need, for economic as well as social reasons, for policy
measures which imply a limited income redistribution.

My main criticism of the present state of affairs in the
field of grant aid and technical assistance is that the
United States has been left to pay almost the whole bill for
such help. It is not difficult to explain why this has happened. The pattern was set many years ago. At the end of
World War II the United States, unlike its allies, found
itself not only undamaged by military action but much
better off economically than at the beginning of the war.
In this situation it was natural that the United States, almost single-handedly, undertook the responsibility for
rendering the financial assistance that was needed for reconstruction and recovery.

By far the larger part of this aid went to the countries of
Western Europe, which—apart from the Southern European countries—must be included in any international
comparison with North America and Australasia as part
of the small minority of countries which are economically
well off. This pattern, of one rich nation rendering non-
commercial aid to the other rich nations, was fortified by
the Marshall Plan and the European Recovery Program,
for which external finance was provided by the United
States. This is not the place to discuss all the wholesome
effects for Europe, and for the entire world, of this large-
scale capital aid from America to Western Europe. In the
present context, however, one of its detrimental moral
effects must be pointed out: that the people and the politicians, both in the United States itself and in Western Europe, became conditioned to accept it as normal and right
that the United States should take upon itself practically

the whole of the financial burden of providing international aid in any part of the world where it was required, with only token contributions coming from other economically advanced nations.

Naturally, it has to be remembered that the United States' production and income is a very big part of the total production and income of all the rich countries taken together, and its share of the burden in any fair scheme for international aid would be a large one, even if not so large as that which the United States has carried so far. A very important moral element of every scheme for redistributing income, national as well as international, should be that the burden be shared in a just and equitable manner. It is not fair, and will never be felt to be fair, that a man who lives in Stockholm, Geneva, or Brussels should not share the burden of aid to underdeveloped countries equally with a man in the same income bracket living in Columbus, Ohio, in Detroit, Michigan, or in Denver, Colorado.

Most of the things which are imperfect and wrong in our present aid schemes spring from this lack of justice in their financing. In America, the situation is naturally felt to be unfair, even though little is said about it. This is undoubtedly a main reason why it has not proved politically feasible to raise further the level of assistance to underdeveloped countries, as well as why the suggested appropriations for aid are constantly in danger of being whittled away in Congress.

It also helps to explain why some of those who, in America, are urging higher appropriations become tempted to argue their case in terms of political or even military strategy, and, more generally, why it becomes so difficult to keep the appropriations free from political conditions. This leads naturally also to the labelling of an increasing part of legitimate economic aid as military.

When international aid becomes unilateral, and politics

thus enters into its distribution, moral standards are apt to crumble. Economic standards, too, will be more difficult to uphold. A selection according to political interests is often bound to imply the diversion of aid to the less necessitous countries, or to those least capable of using it effectively for economic advancement. In the receiving countries, unilateral aid may have equally unfortunate effects. The political conditions of the aid are resented by their peoples. Indeed, political strings and the existence of ulterior motives will be suspected, even when they are not present.

The direction and control of the use of aid will also, in many cases, be less efficient. An underdeveloped country may be willing—even happy—to take from an international agency advice which it is not ready or, because of popular resentment, not able to accept under prodding by a single country, least of all when that country is very rich, powerful, and careless in its public utterances.

These are, of course, important reasons why aid is best channelled through an international agency. But it would be almost preposterous to suggest that more than a minor —indeed, almost a symbolic—part of the total flow of aid should be so handled, as long as one country pays almost all of the costs. A fairer distribution of the financial burden is, therefore, a condition for transferring any substantial part of aid and technical assistance to underdeveloped countries into an institutional framework which is multilateral and truly international.

The Direction of Aid

I have felt for a long time that aid to underdeveloped countries should be placed in a definite and more rational order of priorities. This type of international cooperation, where there is not a *quid pro quo* in the ordinary way of business relations, should in my opinion be concentrated on a few fields where such aid would be particularly natural, and felt to be so, both in the countries that are giving aid and in those that are receiving it.

Firstly, those underdeveloped nations who are short of food should be given what they need for attaining adequate nutritional standards. The rich countries should make up their mind that they do not want to make money out of selling food to starving peoples. In many countries, a major limitation of economic development is the valid fear that, when the unemployed and underemployed are set to work, they will consume more food than is available. It should be recognized that when, at the same time, other countries are laboring with the problems of food surpluses, this limitation of development is not only cruel but unnecessary and, indeed, absurd. This is, however, no reason why only those rich countries which have food surpluses should carry the burden of the costs of such aid. In any reasonable scheme of international cooperation, the costs for such a scheme should be shared by all the rich nations.

What is more, aid should never be looked upon as a permanent solution to the problems of poverty. Aid should always be a help to self-help. For that reason a definite time limit should be set to the provision of food without pay, and a condition should be made that the aid-receiving country do everything it can to raise yields in agriculture. Otherwise there is always the danger that the food aid would only buttress its complacency. Secondly, therefore, the rich countries should also decide to give, free of charge, everything that it would be practical and economic to import from abroad in terms of tools and equipment, technical assistance, and training in order to assist underdeveloped countries to raise their agricultural production of food for consumption. Insofar as surpluses of fertilizers were available, those could be part of the aid. Otherwise, aid should instead be given to set up fertilizer factories in underdeveloped countries where conditions for fertilizer production are favorable.

In a rational scheme of international cooperation, this problem of providing enough food for rapid economic development should be viewed not as a narrowly national problem, but as regional and, indeed, world-wide. Some underdeveloped countries are, and should increasingly become, food exporters, while others could concentrate more on non-food crops and manufactured industrial goods for export. The interests of the former countries should be guarded. They are not, of course, in a position to give away food as the rich countries are. They should in many cases even be aided economically to produce more food for commercial export. If their exports went to other underdeveloped countries as part of the food aid they received, the rich countries' contribution would consist in paying the former countries for their food export to the latter.

Thirdly, the rich countries should, in addition to meeting the fundamental request for more food to eat, agree to give everything that can be provided from abroad in the way of equipment, advice, personnel training, etc., for the most rapid advance the underdeveloped countries can manage to engender in sanitation, health, education at all levels, and research, including surveys of their natural resources.

There should be one general condition for aid in these three directions: that the recipient should use the aid in an economic and efficient manner. If, as I am proposing, the rich countries declared themselves willing to provide all the additional food that some underdeveloped countries need, and all financial help which they can effectively administer for raising productivity in their agriculture, and improving levels of sanitation, health, education, training, and research, the costs would not imply any substantial lowering of economic levels in the rich Western countries.

The great desirability of giving aid generously for these specific purposes would be more readily understood by the general public in the rich Western countries. If aid was given to feed hungry people, to make it more possible for them to grow more food themselves, and to raise the poor nations' levels of health and education, fewer people in the rich countries would be inclined to raise political conditions or to discriminate in giving aid. It would be less tempting to conceal aid in the twilight of "soft loans." In the underdeveloped countries themselves, there would be less suspicion of ulterior motives. Aid would be understood and accepted as the purely humanitarian effort it is, or rather should be.

If there were more funds available for aid to underdeveloped countries than are needed for these three forms, I would give the fourth priority to paying for equipment and other productive necessities from abroad, in order to speed up the formation of various types of overall capital such as irrigation and power facilities, ports, roads, store houses, etc. Such large-scale investment is necessary in order to give the basis for development, both in industry and agriculture. It is of a particular strategic importance in economic development, as it is labor-intensive and can thus make use of the productive resources of which an underdeveloped country has surplus, labor. If food ceased to be the cruel bottleneck it is at present in many countries, and if undertaking these investments in overall capital would not compete for foreign exchange, underdeveloped countries would find it advantageous to give them a higher priority rating. A large part of the loans from the International Bank have this purpose, but it would be rational to use grant aid in order to make it possible for many underdeveloped countries to intensify their efforts in this direction.

If these forms of economic aid were made available in

considerably larger quantities, industrial development, which rightly is such a paramount objective in all under-developed countries, could then be left with more hope to their own efforts, upon which it will anyhow have to depend. I have already referred to the fact that, at present, the lack of food, and the fear of increasing the scarcity of food in an inflationary process are often limitations to all development, and in particular to rapid industrializa-tion. That limitation would then have been removed. In all underdeveloped countries, raising the levels of health, education, training, and research would decrease the im-pact of other brakes on industrialization. The widening of the basis of available social capital would have the same effect. Moreover, other favorable conditions for industrial development in underdeveloped countries would have been created if the rich countries were prepared to under-take the changes in their ordinary commercial and financial policies and business relations which I have referred to above, and which would be so much in the interests of international integration. In the final instance, those re-forms in regard to trade and capital movements are, of course, more important than any grant aid for develop-ment could ever be.

It is difficult to see how these changes could be brought about, except under concerted and sustained pressure exerted by the poor countries, making the maxi-mum possible use of the existing inter-governmental or-ganizations. A rational organization of aid and technical as-sistance, and in particular the inauguration of a priority sys-tem of the type sketched above, is only possible, of course, if aid is being planned internationally by inter-govern-mental agencies, instead of being handed out unilaterally by individual governments. And only an internationaliza-tion of aid can provide the political and psychological basis for so raising its level that aid becomes a really important means of policy for the economic development of under-developed countries.

The Nationalization Issue

This chapter is a review of the problems which require, in the interests of achieving a new world stability, a re-orientation on the part of the rich nations. As such, it would not be complete if I did not at least touch upon the issue of nationalization of "Western assets," mentioned in the previous chapter. It is a fact that, in almost all underdeveloped countries, there is a strong dislike of foreign control of large-scale enterprises, particularly those exploiting their natural resources of primary products. This dislike of major foreign enclaves is so strong and general that, in all probability, we shall soon see a good deal more nationalization of foreign holdings in these countries.

The poor countries' dislike of foreign holdings is, indeed, natural. What should cause surprise is that it meets with such fierce opposition, and such obtuse lack of understanding, in the Western world. These negative attitudes are not confined to shareholders and other interested parties; they are strong also among workers, farmers, and all sorts of ordinary people. But in this respect people in the underdeveloped countries are really not different from those in the Western world. They are only aiming at establishing their national economic independence, which the Western countries possess and have always possessed—or at least for such a long time that it is now taken for granted.

Let us chose for comparison a rich little country like Sweden. Foreign enterprises are certainly welcomed more cordially there than almost anywhere else, if they want to establish themselves in the country and take up production in competition with the nationals. Double taxation treaties have been arranged to accommodate such foreign guest entrepreneurs. They can bring with them into the country any number of officers, engineers, and workers they think they would require. And as Sweden is a country where foreign trade is exceptionally free from tariffs and other barriers, they will have no difficulty in importing whatever they want in the way of raw materials, semi-manufactured goods, and machines.

But we should realize that this open-door policy is based on the tacit assumption that Swedish competition is strong enough to see to it that it will not be advantageous for the foreigners to use the open doorway very much. If foreign enterprises in Sweden should multiply and, in particular, if they started to lay their hands on the land, the rivers, and the ores, there would be the most intense resistance on the part of the Swedes. And then, very quickly, laws would be put into effective use which, as a matter of fact, had been written into the statute book by conservative parliaments long ago and have been left standing by future generations, making government permission necessary for any foreigner who wants to own real estate in Sweden or acquire shares in ordinary Swedish corporations.

I may add that if existing legislation would not suffice to prevent foreigners from grabbing the land, or even from becoming too influential in an important field of industry, the Swedes would not hesitate to make new laws, as radical as they would find necessary. They would most certainly not shrink from nationalizing foreign property, if there were no other remedy. The only reason why this whole thought is so strange and hypothetical in Sweden is, of course, that for some centuries the national community has not been attractive to foreign enterprise and not so weak in local talents and financial resources as to make it advantageous and feasible for foreign interests to intrude in a massive way upon the country.

And this then permits the common man or woman in

this small and rich country—which has not been at war since Napoleon's time, which has never been invaded or held under foreign occupation, and which happened to sell her last colony more than a century ago—to have little real understanding and sympathy for the strivings for economic independence in the poor countries. These people who, for all their petty bickerings, have arranged things so well and so democratically for themselves, and who on the whole are such good citizens, such pleasant and accommodating neighbors, such cooperative comrades in the workshop, such well-adjusted marriage partners, and such reasonable and loving parents, are apt to be thoughtless, heartless, and unintentionally arrogant when reacting to happenings outside their experience in everyday life. There they are fettered by ignorance, easy-going opportunism, and an unreflective loyalty towards the other rich nations, which are most like themselves.

When they read in their newspapers—where international news are furnished almost exclusively from agencies of the big powers in the Western world, which have vested interests to defend—how in some faraway backward country native agitators want to nationalize plantations or mines or other well managed business establishments, they raise their eyebrows. They glide easily into lines of thought which were the rationalizations of colonialism and which are still lingering though for opportunistic reasons not so openly announced as in earlier times. What contributions have those natives made to these enterprises, except by their cheap labor—plus the accident that the resources have been planted by God in that soil, upon the surface of which they carry on their miserly life as their ancestors did before them, without, of course, having created these resources or even having had the guts to begin to exploit them before the white people came? These agitators, even if they are prime ministers or presidents, must have been inspired by the international communist conspiracy against democracy and the free world. So far as international relations are concerned, even the workers and farmers in the rich countries are upper class in their attitudes to really poor people abroad. And the intellectuals are often even more fixed in opportunistic ignorance and in solidarity with the Western world, which unfortunately in this connection means the old colonial powers.

During the Suez crisis a few years ago, I made a reflection which seemed to be rather original in the rich countries, and which was certainly so in my native Scandinavia with its important shipping interests. Assume, I thought, that such a thing as the Suez Canal were crossing the territory of the United States, Britain, France, Norway, or any other Western country. Does anybody really believe that any one of these nations would have long permitted it to be controlled, managed, and fiscally exploited by a foreign corporation, which, until almost the end, even put up resistance against employing nationals in responsible positions? And would they feel even as restrained as the Egyptians did by an international convention, concluded several generations ago at a time when the country was not only dependent but actually occupied by foreign troops?

And would any Western country find itself satisfied by having other big enclaves for exploitation of its natural resources in the hands of anonymous foreign corporations, which often are so big even in their home country that they can be seen to influence that country's foreign and, in particular, economic policies?

The Beam in Our Eye

These questions need to be raised. Already by raising them it becomes clear that, as a matter of fact, the Western world has not yet become prepared to accept the underdeveloped nations as equals, having the right to look on their own national life in the same way as Western nations look on theirs.

As always in relations, where there is not a genuinely established basis of equality, those who have the upper hand are not consciously aware of their discriminatory way of thinking. There is a beam in our eye. I believe that the common man in the Western world, the worker and the farmer as well as the richest shareholder in one of the enclave corporations, is most seriously and honestly convinced that the underdeveloped nations and their leaders —and even such an exquisitely cultured man like Jawaharlal Nehru or a pious man like U Nu—are doing him grave injustice, when they accuse him of lingering inclinations towards an imperialist and colonial way of thinking.

But of course, as a matter of plain facts, the underdeveloped nations and their leaders are correct. And the sooner the Western nations could eradicate from their minds this very clear and obvious bias, the better they would be able to serve their own interests in the underdeveloped countries, which are admittedly considerable.

The Disentanglement of Economic Colonialism

The practical problems are of a most complicated and difficult nature: how to disentangle all these very large foreign property relations inherited from long ages of colonialism and economic dependency; how to build up new economic relations between the rich Western world and the underdeveloped countries on the basis of the latter countries' independent nationhood; and how to do this with the minimum loss of mutual good will and the maximum protection, and even promotion, of economic values and interests on both sides in production and trade.

This is a challenge to free and constructive thinking and to statesmanship to be met both in the rich and the poor countries. The poor nations will be well advised not to take by onesided action and force what, by biding their time, they might acquire by quiet pressure and negotiation. For the rich nations, it is an equally urgent interest that they purge from their minds the untenable notion, which is a legacy from colonialism, that people in the poor countries should continue to be prepared not to think, desire, dislike, and act in the same way as they themselves do as a matter of course.

Whether it will happen peacefully and be handled with wisdom to the mutual advantage of rich and poor countries —which theoretically would be quite possible—or will mainly proceed through violent clashes and crises to the destruction of values and goodwill, the gradual and probably rapid disentanglement of the colonial economic enclave structures in the underdeveloped countries is an irresistible historical process, which will follow its course to the end. Basically it will be a movement along the Western way: towards national communities more akin than they are now to those of the Western countries. Only if seriously mishandled on the Western side—which, as very recent history shows, cannot be excluded—could it move the underdeveloped countries towards alliance with the Soviet bloc and thereby indirectly also influence their manner of planning in that direction. That is, however, a problem from which I abstract in the present inquiry.

14

The Growth of Inter-Governmental Economic Organizations

National Economic Planning Leads to the Need for International Planning

International integration cannot today be restored simply by tearing down barriers to emigration, trade, and movements of capital and enterprise. It has to be organized. The national economies no longer adjust themselves to changes in the international sphere in such a way that stability, flexibility, and a maximum common advantage for all countries ensue automatically.

This was, indeed, never the case, even if it was argued in the old equilibrium theory of free trade. It is less true than ever, now that the governments and the peoples have become conscious of their will, and their power, to resist such automatic adjustments in their own national interest. The goal of greater international integration and, indeed, the prevention of such gross international maladjustments, damaging in the end to all nations, as follow from random change and uncoordinated national policies have now to be negotiated and solved in a process of inter-governmental cooperation and bargaining.

I stated, therefore—as an inference from analysis, and not simply as a valuation—the thesis that once the Welfare State has come into existence in the rich Western countries, and once the underdeveloped countries are becoming independent and are launching upon individual national economic policies in the interests of their national development, there is, as a matter of fact, no alternative to continued international economic disintegration, except to strive for a Welfare World. The trend towards national planning leads by a process of causation to the creation of a need for international coordination and planning. The emergence of the extreme and fundamentally different type of national economic planning in the Soviet countries, under a totalitarian and monolithic state, only strengthens this conclusion with regard to the rest of the world—and, indeed, as a long-range hope and endeavor with regard also to the whole world.

The institutional forms which offer themselves for international coordination and planning are the intergovernmental organizations. And so, at the end of our study of the trend towards planning in the Western countries and the international implications of this trend, I now want to clarify my view of the role of these organizations in the process under study.

The Surge of Organized Inter-Governmental Cooperation

In view of what I have said, we should perhaps not be surprised that in this era of international disintegration there have also occurred the first real attempts in history to establish worldwide inter-governmental organizations, with the ambitious task of providing diplomatic instruments, which can be used by governments to join together in concerted action for constructing a better integrated world economy by harmonizing their national economies. Indeed, these attempts were twice launched at the very culmination of the sequences of international crises through which the world has passed during the last half-century; at the end of World War I, and, on a still grander scale and with even more determination, at the end of World War II.

The constitutional forms of our present system of inter-governmental organizations were fixed in the last years of World War II. Some of the organizations were built on the remnants of older organizations which had been set up after World War I; others were entirely new. In these years of high hope, it was, in fact, more or less an accident of history what organizations were, or were not, created. If, for instance, the housing experts had kept themselves to the fore, they would undoubtedly have got a specialized agency for housing, as there is now one for agriculture and nutrition or as forestry got its place reserved in that agency. A worldwide authority for economic development of underdeveloped countries, which has been proposed, though as yet without practical results, would, if the proposal had been made then and pressed for, met much less resistance. And if the International Trade Organization turned out to be still-born, this was the result of the ambition of the planners to codify in abstract terms a whole doctrine—of free trade with all sorts of reservations —instead of using the favorable opportunity to set up a mechanism for negotiation of practical trade issues. For, while the planners wrestled over the niceties of this doctrine, time went by, and the few years when it was easy to start inter-governmental organizations passed. At this juncture, disillusionment reigns supreme. Any initiative in this direction is met with suspicion or plain apathy.

This lively activity in building up inter-governmental organizations for economic cooperation was born out of initiatives and planning by those rich Western countries which were allied in the great cause against fascism. It was primarily an answer by the governments of these countries

to the sufferings and anxieties amongst their peoples during
the war. The promises of closer international cooperation were a part—and a most needed part—of the efforts
to keep up morale amongst the soldiers and the people back
home, and was also meant to broaden the forces of
rebellion in the enemy countries. People had to believe
that, when once the war had been won, the world would
be radically re-made into a happier, more harmonious and
stable place, where broadly planned progress and security
would result from joint efforts by all peoples in their
common interests.

To foster these hopes was thus in the opportunistic
interest of the governments. Indeed, planning and propaganda for inter-governmental organizations for the post-
war period were a not unimportant component of the
psychological warfare of the Great Alliance against the
fascist powers. The most grandiose illusions about future
international cooperation were widespread. The thinkers
and the planners were given their field day, and were often
invested with political authority. The people at home and
at the war front were promised not only full employment,
social security, economic development, and a rapidly
rising level of living when the war was over, but also, as
a basis for all that, an organized peace and close international cooperation.

And this was much more than empty propaganda. The
people who spoke and the people who listened sincerely
meant and believed that this would be accomplished. And,
as usual, the propaganda had its greatest effects on those
who made it and on those among their listeners who most
wanted to believe it. A rereading of what was published at
that time is now a disquieting and trying experience, but
most useful for keeping our minds and consciences in a
healthy state.

We are reminded that responsible leaders of the Western

nations trusted the effectiveness of the inter-governmental economic organizations which were then set up. Practical policies were blueprinted to stabilize the world economy, and in particular to speed economic progress in under-developed countries. It was perceived that, in the new conditions, international integration could not be pursued by attempting to restore in a higher degree the economic automatism of an earlier era, but had to be the result of planned and coordinated efforts similar to those by means of which the Welfare State had been taking shape in the rich countries. The dismantling of privileges and mo-nopolies, the agreement upon common rules and the ap-plication, to international relations also, of the principle of sharing risks and burdens were therefore widely ac-cepted as the proper means to the end. As general ideals, these policies were written into the founding documents of the organizations. To an even larger extent, and more precisely, they were formulated in thousands of books, articles and speeches which formed the ideological basis to what was then undertaken.

Not only the dreamers, but many quite sober economists, political scientists, lawyers, and practical politicians ac-tually expected even more than this. Not a few envisaged, as a study of what was then written clearly reveals, that these organizations would develop into a real world com-munity, founded on the will of the peoples and on the enforcement of law and common decisions arrived at by due procedures, as laid down in gradually perfected supra-national constitutions. In this functioning world com-munity, the nations would come to feel the solidarity of their welfare interests, and their loyalty would grow towards the common purpose of giving an ever fuller realization to the ideals of peace and progress, liberty, equality, and universal brotherhood. When the opening words of the Charter of the United Nations invoked as initiators to the great enterprise: "We, the Peoples," this was not merely a pompous overstatement, but expressed a sincere hope and devotion, widely held in the years of great calamity.

A Relative Failure

All wars, however, bring intensified nationalism in their wake. When the fighting has ended, the war alliances, as a rule, break up. National administrations, too, have an ingrained tradition of negativism in all matters of inter-governmental cooperation, and we have been studying the institutional and psychological mechanism behind this. And so the international organizations became something very different in reality from what was expected. The illusions, which had been such an opportune solace in the years of great strain, turned into bitter disillusionment.

Leaving aside the glorious vision of the rapid emergence of a functioning world community—which to most people now has faded away as an even more distant prospect— and considering only the immediate practical tasks for the inter-governmental organizations in the economic field, as they had been agreed upon when they were set up, one cannot but conclude that they have been relative failures. Only to a much smaller extent than was anticipated and planned have they been permitted by the governments to become organs for real international settlements of prac-tical issues through cooperation and bargaining. Much of the effort in the inter-governmental economic organiza-tions is lost in empty, hostile controversy and the building-up of tactical defense positions of *non possumus*. Other-wise, there is often merely a perfunctory going through of the motions without arriving anywhere. This is set down bluntly, because in these grave matters nothing else than the utmost candor is healthy.

The Economic and Social Council and the General Assembly of the United Nations have thus been primarily discussion forums and platforms for nationalistic propaganda. They have made hardly any substantial progress in terms of action in the direction of the main purposes, accorded them by the Charter, of both initiating and coordinating international action on a broad scale in the economic and social field. In recent years the Council in particular has sunk to a level of unimportance which must appear almost scandalous in view of these declared purposes.

The regional Economic Commissions have been more down-to-earth and have made modest beginnings towards regional cooperation and bargaining in a great number of practical and technical problems. But their attempts to approach major economic issues have mostly been frustrated.

The Food and Agriculture Organization has the mandate to tackle the problems, not only of more productive methods in agriculture and greater prosperity among farmers, but also of higher nutritional levels through international action for the disposal of surpluses. However, suggestions and discussions concerning these wider issues have not so far been transformed into practical solutions. They have even been suspect as utopian idealism.

The International Labor Organization was already outmoded a generation ago, but did not use the purgatorial opportunity of the war years, or the new start after the war, to become the comprehensive and more broadly based inter-governmental organization for social policies which is needed. Its basic approach to the social problems in their economic setting, which is to view it as *die Arbeiterfrage* —embodied in its program and practices, and in its tripartite structure, representing employers and workers, and only these interest groups, besides the governments—

really reflects the situations as they were conceived, and the problems as they were formulated, in Bismarck's Germany and Lloyd George's Britain, but not the actual situations and problems as they were taking shape in the advanced democratic Welfare States in the Western countries even before the war. This, and the economic stagnation in the other countries, doomed the organization even in that period to virtual irrelevance in terms of concerted inter-governmental action for synchronizing national economic policies towards reaching specific social goals; this has been even more pronounced in the post-war period. The partial influence that the organization has succeeded in winning over labor legislation and other matters in underdeveloped countries—which has increasingly become the main focus of its activity, particularly as it was afforded less and less real influence within the Western countries—has not always been conducive to their economic development. Too often, it merely strengthens the tendencies, anyhow at work in these countries, for social policies not to reach down to the lowest income groups, and for the strivings for general social security to become directed towards guaranteeing privileges for minority middle-class groups which industrial workers there still constitute, and will continue to constitute.

The International Monetary Fund was created to provide a system of regular channels for international payments and an organ for purposive international cooperation in determining exchange rates, which should no longer be left for unilateral decision by the authorities of individual states. Outside the field of studies, consultations and advice, the functions of the Fund have been restricted largely to distribution of emergency credits, which naturally is not unimportant. But it has as yet not started to function in its main assigned fields of action.

The International Bank for Reconstruction and Development has probably come nearest to realizing the original intentions of its founders, though its operations and those of its appended organs have been on a relatively small scale. It has not even begun to substitute in a major way for the now defunct international capital market of old, or rather, for the capital market we would need, if the underdeveloped countries were to develop industrially as the Western countries did.

The proposal to set up an international agency for distributing capital aid, the Special United Nations Fund for Economic Development, was blocked by the great Western powers, led by the United States. Even now when, in a minor key, it is coming into existence, the sums which will be placed at its disposal will be so small that its activity can hardly have anything more than a symbolic importance.

Until now, the plans for setting up an international trade organization have been blocked; meanwhile GATT has carried on a limited activity, mainly to check the raising of tariffs.

No practical agreements on an important scale have been reached to counteract the fluctuations in the international prices of primary products which, particularly in the poor underdeveloped countries, have such damaging effects.

Moreover, the program for the international control of industrial cartels has been quietly buried. The existence of an international agency for shipping was for a long time prevented, in spite of the fact that it was framed so as to disturb the vested interests as little as possible. Other inter-governmental organs have been forcefully kept by the Western countries from interesting themselves in the harshly monopolistic freight market even as an object of study, in the same way as they have been prevented from touching on other international monopolies, like those operating in the oil market or in the production and sale of pharmaceuticals.

The Credit Side

On the credit side, many of the inter-governmental organizations can point to real accomplishments, in the collecting and dissemination of statistics and other descriptive material in many fields, and in producing studies of great importance to the learned profession, to private industry and commerce in all countries, and to the individual governments themselves. As a result, we know very much more about what happens in the world and what the problems are.

The inter-governmental organizations also function as important media for consultation and for diplomatic contacts between governments, and sometimes—as in the regional Commissions of the United Nations—between industries and industrial organizations in the several countries. Many vexing problems have been solved by such consultation. Some organizations actually succeed in arranging regular cooperation between governments or industries in technical matters of all sorts. The organizations have most decidedly perfected and widened what in old times was called the concert of nations.

Most of the inter-governmental organizations have for many years been active in technical assistance to underdeveloped countries. In many of them, this has become the major activity. Technical assistance was a most important post-war innovation and certainly represents a real accomplishment which should not be underestimated.

But neither should it be overestimated. Even if we add to what is done by the inter-governmental organizations the very much larger technical assistance which is carried

on outside the United Nations by individual governments
—mainly through the Point Four Program of the United
States and through the Colombo Plan—it is still exceedingly small in scope. This is true whether it is
measured in terms of the budgets of the contributing
countries or of the real needs of the receiving countries.

They Do Exist

The most important thing about the inter-governmental
organizations is the fact that they do exist, and that they
will continue to exist. Once they have come into existence,
they will not be liquidated in peace time. The governments may hinder them from performing important functions. But they will never dare to take the responsibility
of dissolving them. In that sense, the inter-governmental
organizations are among the most stable of human institutions.

Even when an organization is weakened, it shows an
amazing resistance to dissolution, which contrasts strongly
with the frequent instability of public opinion in all countries in regard to international questions generally and the
work of inter-governmental organizations in particular.
The League of Nations continued to exist, and to carry on
work during the whole war—work which, incidentally, in
the field of economic research and planning, was not without merit and importance. When it was later formally
dissolved, it was only because the United Nations and a
whole score of new organizations were created in its stead,
in order to carry on its work on a grander scale.

The International Labor Organization likewise survived
the war, and was set moving again with a much bigger
budget—in spite of the fact that it conservatively stuck to
an outmoded structure and approach which has made its
activities increasingly inconsequential.

The Bank for International Settlements in Basle was fiercely attacked for collaboration with the fascist governments during World War II. It was many times burned in effigy, and at Bretton Woods it was solemnly declared dead and was buried by means of a formal resolution. Journalists danced on its grave. But today it lives stronger than ever, and has been the chosen instrument for putting into effect the European Payments Union, which was one of the more concrete and solid accomplishments of West-European economic cooperation.

The social scientist, seeking to explain this remarkable general experience, can point to many causal factors contributing to the sustaining strength of inter-governmental organizations. One is the vested interests of members of the secretariats in preserving their jobs and their livelihood. Responsible officials, however, also feel the urge of their fundamental allegiance to the common cause of international cooperation and desire to keep on trying against all odds.

But, by itself, this secretarial drive for the self-preservation of the organization would not carry much weight. In addition there are vested interests generously planted in all the member countries. Around every organization there are a great number of persons everywhere, often hundreds or even thousands, to whom the organization represents a means of serving an internationalist ideal. In their case, too, it carries an element of status at home. And, for some, it further provides a regular and respectable reason for travel. For a steady-going organization like the International Labor Organization, specializing in rather lengthy meetings, the tripartite constitutional arrangement, comprising governments, employers, and employees, may have its greatest political importance in spreading its basis of active participation and of vested interests more widely in the several countries, even outside the state administrations.

The Force of the Ideal

It would be unrealistic not to recognize these spurious factors and this is the reason why I have mentioned them. Yet they can only be contributory. The main explanation of the fact that the inter-governmental organizations generally survive, even through the most disappointing periods, is undoubtedly that people, at bottom, behind the façade of nationalistic attitudes, do believe in, and do desire, international cooperation. This is their general and long-run faith, however negative their attitudes may be on particular issues of the day. As a social force the ideal of international cooperation is just as real as the nationalistic emotions, the suspicions and the animosities which so dominate the positions taken on concrete issues, and which keep down the effectiveness of the organizations. As I have pointed out repeatedly, this ideal is backed by sound reasoning.

It is like people's religion, like their adherence to the democratic ideals of equality for all and of the inalienable right of human beings to life, liberty, and the pursuit of happiness. Everyday shortcomings in attitudes and behavior in all our countries do not obliterate these ideals, nor do they exhaust them of significance for how we actually feel, think, and act. Indeed, all our social institutions would crumble and anarchy would reign in the family, the neighborhood community and the national state, if those institutions were not constantly supported by very general norms of the type which are usually given their full expression only in a particularly solemn, religious or quasi-religious setting.

In everyday life, these norms are constantly infringed upon by opportunistic transgressions, but they are un-questioned in principle and they do exert their long-range influence. So-called "hard-boiled research," which fails to perceive the force of ideals in our lives, becomes plainly unrealistic. It will never catch the "meaning" of human institutions. It will not be able to explain the perseverance of these institutions under adverse conditions, or their propensity to grow in strength and perfection under favorable ones. The difference is only that the interna-tional ideal, as yet, is so very much weaker as a social force, and that the international community is so much less fortified as an institution, than ideals and institutions in a state.

Often the impact of the international ideal seems to be a negative one. I have already pointed to the masochistic and perverse character of many of the attacks on it. People are constantly revolting against their own ideals, and because of this, idealism is not conducive only to what is good. They can become angry with the United Nations as an institution, or at UNESCO, or any other, or all, of the inter-governmental organizations. But these organizations are, after all, only the formal matrices of the efforts of all the governments to cooperate amongst themselves and thus, to a thinking person, not a very proper object for resentment, any more than is the state of which he is a citizen.

More fundamentally, however, and in the long run, the ideal has a positive influence. Against all human weak-nesses, it tends to determine the trend. In the turmoil of opportunistic short-range attitudes, the general desire for international understanding and cooperation also exists, and it also has its share of influence in the compromise behavior of human life. The ideal supports the continuation of the inter-governmental organizations, once they are in existence. This explains the very obvious hesitation in every nation to destroy any one of these organizations, even when it is not very effective.

Indirect evidence that, at bottom, people everywhere have a reserve of international understanding and international idealism is provided by the fact that when ordinary persons, in our inter-governmental secretariats, often drawn from the civil services of widely different lands, have the chance to live in a situation where it becomes their natural role to serve the common good, they transfer to this common allegiance with little or no effort. As a matter of fact, whenever something, however small, is accomplished in international cooperation—an agreement on a uniform classification of coal, on simplified customs procedures for goods transported across frontiers, a commodity agreement, an agreement on non-discrimination in tariff rates—these accomplishments also give the participating national delegates feelings of belonging, and of satisfaction in serving the larger community, which are not dissimilar from those experienced by international civil servants. Every practical achievement, however humble, has, like every failure, a cumulative effect. For it works upon the attitudes to international cooperation which, at the same time, represent its conditions.

The psychological impediments to be overcome in making international cooperation more effective are all concerned with how to get governments, and behind them parliaments and ultimately peoples, to experience allegiance to the common cause, and to do this when, in fact, international cooperation is still so weak. For while, on the one hand, the main means of fostering this larger allegiance amongst people are their actual experiences of cooperation, cooperation cannot develop except on the basis of allegiance. This is the eternal problem of man and his institutions. The development of institutions presumes human attitudes fitting them, but such attitudes develop only in response to living in the institutions themselves.

This is the basic psychological difficulty in international cooperation. Like many other social problems, the overcoming of this difficulty truly amounts to something very much like trying to lift oneself by one's shoestrings. Nevertheless, many times in history a vicious spiral downwards has been arrested and turned into a cumulative process upwards. Our one asset is the basic internationalism, on a high level of our sphere of valuations, which I have pointed to, and which is supported by the demonstrable fact that international cooperation is rational and in our common, i.e. everybody's, interest.

The Illusion of False Optimism

It is an illusion to believe that the force of this international ideal can be strengthened by falsifying the record. To inject unfounded optimism is like fighting crime or family disorder by publicity which incorrectly plays down their actual frequency. The belief that to speak the plain truth is under all conditions wholesome, while illusions and false-to-fact propaganda are always damaging in the end, is the acquired conditioning of a scientist. But in this particular case I have found this belief supported by practical experience. Unfounded optimism tends to backfire when the course of events corrects opportunistically propagated, but false, beliefs.

The internationalist does his cause a disservice by concealing from himself or the public the fact that the intergovernmental economic organizations have so far been relative failures, at least as regards major accomplishments. He is unwise if he leaves it as a monopoly of the sceptic, the cynic, and the reactionary nationalist—who is against the strivings in the inter-governmental organizations and does not want them to succeed—to criticize them for what they do not achieve.

Much pious propaganda by the publicity departments of the inter-governmental organizations themselves and by idealistic individuals and groups in all countries, supporting the ideal by disproportionate praise of a great diversity of minor accomplishments in a variety of fields, but keeping silent about all that the organizations should do but are not doing, is misdirected. As the governments who dominate the organizations are not willing to let the publicity departments spread the really important and very much needed information, which concerns how much more international cooperation there ought to be in the world and why it is not undertaken, it can be seriously doubted whether these organizations should have any publicity agencies at all.

In any case, the internationalists in all countries should not allow themselves to become fixed in a defensive position against the sceptics, the cynics, and the nationalists. Instead, they should take it upon themselves to criticize, in a realistic and constructive manner, the functioning of the inter-governmental organizations—i.e. the activity and the inactivity of the governments who make up the organizations, and which are responsible for what they accomplish or do not accomplish. It is the internationalists who have the right to be dissatisfied.

Why Has This Happened?

To carry out this constructive criticism of the inter-governmental organizations and to get into focus the efforts to spur a development towards international cooperation, we need to ask: Why has this happened? Why have the widely held hopes of fifteen years ago been, so far, so largely frustrated?

Towards the end of the war, I happened to belong to those few who, in broad terms, foresaw this development. I urged greater realism in the analysis of the probable international political situation after the war—and not only in regard to the relations with the Soviet Union, where most people at that time harbored so much wishful thinking in their expectations of harmony—and greater restraint when planning the general programs for the new inter-governmental organizations, and in raising expectations about what they could accomplish in a short time.

I did not advise against creating them, though, or against attempting to get them to function, in fostering international cooperation, as effectively as was feasible under the given political conditions. Today, after having been a participant in, and an observer of, this work for ten years, I am more convinced than ever that we are on the right track and that the efforts must be pursued. And I am not without hope. If a major war is avoided, I believe that the trend will be for the inter-governmental economic organizations to grow in importance. They represent the future form of diplomacy between nations. In another fifteen years' time, I believe that we shall be able to present a very different sort of balance sheet.

Not the Responsibility of the Communists

For the time being the inter-governmental economic organizations are, however, relative failures, when measured by the expectations widely held when they started. We cannot escape responsibility—as we are often inclined to do—by putting the blame on the Russians and the political world conflict which we refer to as the cold war.

The Soviet Union and most of the other countries in the Soviet bloc did not take any active part in the preparations for the International Trade Organization; nevertheless, it did not come into being. Their non-cooperative attitude should not have prevented the rest of the world from starting the organization and getting it going. The countries in the Soviet bloc do not account for more than a minor part of the total world trade, and their share in the total trade of all the non-Soviet countries is still smaller.

The irony in the situation was underlined some years ago, when the Soviet Government announced that it had reconsidered the whole matter and had come to the conclusion that they had been wrong: that more than bilateral trade agreements—which had been their earlier aim—was needed; that the ITO charter was an excellent instrument, and that they were now prepared to join the organization. In the United States—which originally had taken the main lead in pushing forward the work on the charter for the International Trade Organization but had later torpedoed it when it was ready and practically agreed —this was the *coup de grâce,* not for the ITO which was then already dead, but for any realistic hope that the United States would in the end accept the humbler makeshift which had meanwhile been worked out and been proposed under the auspices of GATT.

Likewise, if the International Monetary Fund did not become the intended powerful inter-governmental monetary authority, providing regular channels for international payments and regulating the exchange rates by multilateral procedures, the cause for this cannot have been that the countries in the Soviet orbit did not in the end cooperate in setting up the Fund. This should not have prevented all the other countries, which together are so much more important in world commerce, and more particularly in their own commerce, from organizing their financial relations in a satisfactory way.

Not only the inter-governmental organizations mentioned, but all organizations in the United Nations' group had, in fact, to start their work as "non-Eastern" organizations, since the governments of the Soviet orbit did not, until fairly recently, show any interest in actively participating in them. But that did not help them to become more effective.

The Fault of the Western Powers

Neither can the relative failure of the inter-governmental economic organizations to live up to the goals established and to the expectations prevailing when they were set up be ascribed simply to the very unbalanced world situation in the post-war period. In fact, they were all proposed and set up for the precise purpose of meeting this future situation, and for producing a detailed plan to restore, and thereafter to preserve, world economic balance under the radically changed conditions in the wake of the war.

There is no escape from the conclusion that the basic cause of the failure of the inter-governmental organizations to function as efficient organs for genuine economic planning, bargaining, and cooperation to anything like the extent that was anticipated lies, quite simply, in the fact that the governments of the individual national states, and behind them their peoples, were not prepared to let it happen. More specifically, they were not prepared to accept the limitations of their freedom in the sphere of national economic planning and the consideration for each other's interests, which are implied in cooperation.

The responsibility for this failure has to be placed on the rich Western countries which are by far the most influential in the international concert. The underdeveloped countries have made continuous attempts to urge the international organizations into action. Most of those attempts have been badly prepared and coordinated, it is true. The main explanation, however, of the futility of their advances is that, in face of resistance from the rich and powerful Western countries, they carried no weight.

National Integration and International Disintegration

Not only in the Western countries, but also in all other countries, economic planning, and, indeed, even the dispersed form of national policy which, in the several underdeveloped countries, raises the need for national coordination and planning, has been a force inimical to international cooperation in the present phase of world history. It is a most disquieting fact that the strengthening of the ties within the individual nations and the increasing scope of national economic planning have tended to push towards international disintegration. If we should believe that international disintegration is a necessary consequence of national integration, we would be doomed to despair. For national integration is a deep-rooted historical trend which cannot be reversed; nor do we want to reverse it.

The idea behind the creation of the inter-governmental economic organizations was, however, that economic balance in the world, and at the same time national stability and progress in all countries, should be secured by inter-governmental planning and concerted action, directed towards a coordination of national policies in the common interest. It is this internationalization of national economic policies which has largely been prevented. The organizations have not been utilized for this agreed purpose, except to a minor extent.

At a still more basic level the cause of the relative failure of the international economic organizations has

been the nationalistic sentiments in the individual countries and the lack of real human solidarity with peoples
outside the national boundaries, which has been the topic
of analysis in the preceding chapters of Part Two of this
book.

The Mechanism of Nationalism

We should now recall that all problems of concrete and
practical international cooperation are exceedingly intri-
cate and very difficult from a technical point of view. My
own personal experiences in ten years of multilateral inter-
governmental negotiations convince me that it is unwise
to underestimate these technical difficulties and the very
laborious and time-consuming staff work that is required
to reach results. But the difficulties could be overcome—
if the will to reach a compromise were present.

It is also my experience, however, that most of the time
this will is lacking, even when there is a clear convergence
of all the separate national interests to reach agreement.
While in every country there are organizations, political
parties, and pressure groups to defend special interests,
there are nowhere powerful organizations to defend a
country's part in the general interest of international cooperation. The special interest groups are left free to harp
on the nationalistic emotions that can always be evoked.
As a result, the legislatures, governments, and administrations usually tend to act in a much more narrowly nationalistic fashion than would correspond to the attitudes
of the enlightened sections of the general public. And
so the negotiators in the international councils become
conditioned to fight fiercely for the national penny, while
losing the commonly desirable pound.

This is the mechanism of narrow nationalism, hamper-
ing the nations from reaching the compromise agreements

which would be in the interest of all. I have often reflected over the lack of enlightened generosity that characterizes inter-governmental bargaining and differs so widely from the way in which big business makes its deals: in a spirit of much more *largesse,* mutual faith, and confidence, with a sense of the true proportions and a real preparedness to make small concessions to secure big profits. Another comparison, equally disadvantageous to inter-governmental negotiations, is with organized collective bargaining in the labor market in some of the highly integrated Welfare States, where labor conflicts have become very rare occurrences.

For this there is only one remedy: a more enlightened citizenry. What must be recognized as—up to now—a relative failure of practically all attempts at organized international economic cooperation should be thought over carefully, not with a view to discouraging sustained efforts, but rather to guiding them more wisely.

The efforts can be founded upon the international idealism of all people, which I believe is a reality, though it is so often pushed aside by narrow national considerations and negative impulses.

Upon this basis the efforts have to be directed towards providing the widest and most sustained dissemination of knowledge: of the gains that would accrue to all peoples from every step, however modest, towards international cooperation; of the very real dangers inherent in the present trend; and, not least important, of our own responsibility, particularly in the rich Western countries, for this trend.